Catering Handbook

Catering Handbook

Edith and Hal Weiss

 VAN NOSTRAND REINHOLD
New York

Library of Congress Catalog Card Number 70-151297
ISBN 0-442-00728-0

Printed in the United States of America

Van Nostrand Reinhold
115 Fifth Avenue
New York, New York 10003

Chapman and Hall
2-6 Boundary Row
London, SE1 8HN, England

Thomas Nelson Australia
102 Dodds Street
South Melbourne 3205, Victoria, Australia

Nelson Canada
1120 Birchmount Road
Scarborough, Ontario M1K 5G4, Canada

16   15   14   13   12   11   10   9   8   7   6   5   4   3   2

Preface

When we began our own catering enterprise, Plain and Fancy Caterers, we were surprised to find that there were no books available that completely covered all phases of catering. Through our own practical experience, after much hard work, long hours, and many trials and tribulations, we succeeded in operating a catering business that was both enjoyable and profitable.

Our trial and error method of development, however successful we became, demonstrated clearly to us the need for a comprehensive book that would serve as a guide and aid to anyone interested in operating a catering business. Our experience and combined 30 years in food service gave us confidence that we could produce such a text. The *Catering Handbook* is the result of our mutual endeavors. We believe that the book is an invaluable source of information covering all aspects of catering and the numerous problems that may be encountered by the starting caterer.

There are basically three types of catering covered in the book: banquet hall, off-premise, and mobile unit. We discuss in detail the needs, advantages, and disadvantages of operation for each type of business.

Chapter 1 is an introduction to the food service field, defining the various types of catering. Chapter 2 covers the purchase and maintenance of trucks and heavy and light equipment, with suggestions on how to do so economically, a problem faced by many starting caterers. The most efficient kitchen layouts for the three types of catering are described in Chap. 3, as well as sanitation and accident prevention, both in the kitchen and the dining room. An outline of the basic staff requirements for all types of catering is given in Chap. 4. The responsibilities of each staff member are fully discussed in this chapter, as well as the types of uniforms customarily worn.

Chapter 5 covers the how-to's in attempting to start one's own business, whichever type it may be, and Chap. 6 discusses advertising and public relations, both indispensable items in promoting any business. Chapter 7 considers such concerns as insurance, licensing, bookkeeping, food purchase, and inventory.

Chapters 8 through 10 detail the arrangement of an affair, from cost estimating, to menu preparation, food purchasing, room arrangement, table setting, and such fringe services as music, photographers, etc. Chapters 11 and 12 cover in full the bar, including serving champagne, and the occasion cakes. Many recipes and methods of preparation are given for centerpieces, including melon and fruit baskets in Chap. 13, and food decoration is discussed in Chap. 14, with many illustrations showing the finished results.

Chapter 15 lists sample menus for different occasions, ranging from a small luncheon to a buffet and sample foreign menus, which will brighten any caterer's appeal. Good food and tasty dishes are essential in running a successful catering business, and Chap. 16 is a compilation of some of our own recipes, covering profitable and appealing dishes. These have been used by us with success for many years, and we assure you that you will, too.

The appendices include a glossary, where to get additional information on specific items, a listing of schools in the United States and Canada that teach various aspects of catering, and additional reference books. The people we have credited in this book were of extreme help to us and will be of service to anyone desiring specific information.

We hope that you will have many successful functions in which the *Catering Handbook* will play in important role.

EDITH AND HAL WEISS

Contents

CHAPTER I

Introduction to Catering

1-1 INTRODUCTION

The catering industry's basic purpose is to supply what is needed for the planning and execution of functions on given dates and at specific locations, where food is of prime importance. The catering industry also prepares the foods that are brought to places of work, to homes, and to self-service parties.

The increased demand for catering services outside the home is brought about by the general high level of business, the large number of working families, and the limited facilities in small houses and apartments. Since few households are equipped to serve many more than the immediate family, large-scale entertaining must be done outside the home, either in restaurants, banquet halls, or public meeting rooms.

Even if space and facilities permit entertaining at home, outside professional help is usually needed, since live-in domestic help is a thing of the past. The host and hostess who wish to have good food graciously served and still be able to spend time with their guests will call on the professional caterer.

Many public meeting halls that have well-equipped kitchen but no permanent or regular kitchen staff are designed with the caterer in mind. Persons renting the facilities of the club may use any caterer approved by the club management.

Industrial plants and various other institutional operations that are not large enough to support any permanent restaurant or snack bar will need the services of the professional mobile unit caterer.

Good food is a major consideration at fund-raising affairs. Other community activities, such as fairs, local flower shows, and art exhibits, are also occasions where professional help in required in planning for the refreshments to be served.

Whether the need is to serve a small formal dinner in a private home, or refreshments at a political rally for hundreds, or to prepare box lunches

1

for 75 youngsters for the 60 days of summer camp—the call goes out for the professional caterer, who offers a uniformed trained staff to serve practically any need.

Any caterer should be able to supply the food and services needed for the following occasions:

Breakfast	Dinner
Brunch	After-theatre buffet
Morning coffee break	Midnight supper
Lunch	Birthday party (for all ages)
Pregame snack	Anniversary
Picnic or barbecue	Office party
Tea	Open house
Shower	Cocktail reception
Wedding	

This is only a partial list. Each of the general classifications may be expanded almost indefinitely. Breakfast, for example, can mean anything from a company executive breakast at 9:00 a.m. with 25 attending, to a wedding breakfast at 11:30 a.m. held at a banquet hall with 250 guests.

1–2 BASIC TYPES OF CATERING SERVICE

The caterer may be defined as one who provides a supply of food with the equipment and staff required to serve the food. The menu, number of guests, time and type of service desired, and location are decided upon in advance by the host. In a banquet hall, the price includes rental of the room. If off premises, there may be an additional charge for service. Regardless of the number of guests, this is a private affair not open to the general public. The host pays for the entire affair.

For our purposes, catering services fall into three major categories, defined as follows.

1. *Banquet Hall:* The caterer has a banquet hall and possibly several other public rooms with a kitchen and commissary attached. He can offer complete service and staff. Banquet hall and rooms are open only when an affair is in progress. The customer comes to the banquet hall caterer.

2. *Off Premises or Location:* The caterer has a kitchen or commissary but no banquet hall, rooms, or facilities for serving. He may cater in private homes, public meeting halls, churches, or temples or do straight delivery of prepared foods. The caterer goes to the customer.

3. *Mobile Unit:* A mobile unit is a specially designed panel truck for route service specializing in snack-type foods and fast service. Food for the mobile unit is prepared in a central kitchen or commissary, then placed in the trucks for sale at various stops. No cooking is done in the mobile unit. The caterer goes to the customer at place of work or play.

The banquet hall and off-premise caterer should be flexible enough to work in any one of many places, including

1. his own kitchen and banquet hall,
2. his kitchen but with service off premises,
3. club or meeting-room facilities,
4. business offices and civic centers,
5. beaches and picnic grounds.

Other terms with which every caterer should be familiar are the following.

1. *Restaurant:* Defined as a public eating house, it is situated at one location, is open stated hours, and has a variety of items on the menu. Specialty resturants may have very few items on the menu; however, a choice is always given. The patron makes his choice and pays accordingly. Generally no reservations are necessary. The patron may enter the restaurant any time during its open hours and expect to be served. Many restaurants now offer private rooms for private catered parties. The customer comes to the restaurant.

2. *Inplant:* Usually a permanent facility located in an industrial plant or school, it operates exactly as a small restaurant with the exception that it is open only to employees or students where it is located. It has stated hours and may be subsidized by the management. The customer goes to the facility. Many inplant feeding facilities are "let" on competitive basis with all types of interested caterers bidding.

1–3 HOW EACH SERVICE OPERATES

A. Catered Banquet Hall

The large hotel with a ballroom and kitchen facilities is the oldest of the public catering services as they are known today. The banquet hall offers the same catering facilities but is not in the hotel business. Since the actual catering services offered by the independent banquet hall and the hotel banquet hall or ballroom are almost identical, they shall both be considered as banquet hall catering here.

The banquet hall is a very large room with a stage or raised platform at one end. In addition to this stage, the banquet hall should have

1. tables and chairs to seat the maximum number of guests permitted in the room;
2. dishes, flatware, and glasses to serve all guests;
3. linen (see *To Buy or Rent* in Sec. 2–3C) ;
4. chafing dishes and buffet service items;
5. public address system;
6. facilities for showing films and slides for business meetings;
7. easy access to street or lobby and parking lot;
8. large well-lighted dressing rooms for brides, fashion shows, etc.;
9. coat check rooms;
10. easy access to storerooms for tables, chairs, and platforms;

11. direct connection to the kitchen;
12. kitchen equipped to feed maximum number of guests;
13. adequate lighting and spotlight arrangements;
14. electrician and carpenter on call.

In addition to the large ballroom, the banquet hall caterer should have smaller rooms available for smaller or more informal groups. These rooms might be decorated in any of the following ways.

1. *Round Table or King Arthur Room:* Decorated in dark wood colors with shields and copies of ancient armor, the Round Table or King Arthur's room is ideal for businessmen's lunches, meetings, and conferences. The room might feature one very large round table and several smaller ones as needed. A popular sales feature is to limit this room to men only for lunch, although it might be opened to couples for the dinner hour.

2. *Flower Room:* The Flower Room's decor is of light floral decoration, where the flowers are changed with the season. It is most attractive for women's groups for bridal showers, luncheons, card parties, etc.

3. *Local Hero Room:* The Local Hero Room is decorated with old newspaper clippings attractively framed, trophies and awards, or copies of awards won by any local hero.

4. *Foreign Rooms:* The appeal of faraway places is very strong. The decoration of such a room is dictated by its name, e.g., "Venetian Room," "A Corner of Paris," "London Lounge." All rooms should have easy access to the kitchen, lobby, and parking lots, and be serviced in the same manner as the main ballroom.

B. Off-Premise (Location) Caterer

The caterer with no banquet hall accounts for much of the catering business. He has a kitchen, commissary, and staff but no rooms for serving. No food is consumed on the premises. All serving is done in a variety of locations, and the menus offered must be extremely flexible to fit the wide variety of facilities he will find at the different locations. (Banquet hall caterers may also do off-premise catering, but often do not wish to tie up their equipment and staff for these affairs, except in the case of very large affairs such as conventions.)

The off-premise caterer offers highly personalized service, since the caterer always goes to the customer. The location of the affair may not always be in the customer's home, but in various clubs, temples, and churches, as well as public meeting halls and business offices.

Off-premise caterers also account for a large volume of "delivery only" and "take-out" business.

To discuss the details of the service, the client may come to the commissary–office, or the caterer may go to the client's home or office. Theoretically, the menu should be exactly what the client desires. However, since limited facilities will necessarily limit the menu, the caterer should see the kitchen and familiarize himself with the arrangements of the area where he will work before planning the menu. Where no kitchen facilities are available, as at office parties, the caterer must supply a portable stove, heating units, and chafing dishes. Under these conditions, the menu should be kept very simple.

C. Mobile Unit Caterer

The arrival of heavy industry to the suburbs has brought with it the need for the mobile unit caterer. Even when there is a restaurant in the vicinity, a huge industrial plant might cover vast tracts of land, and mealtimes will not allow time for traveling great distances. The snack or break periods often allow just enough time for a cup of coffee and the snack, with no travel time at all. The obvious solution to this problem is to have the snack and coffee come to the worker; hence the need for the mobile unit caterer.

Similar situations arise at small train stations and bus terminals where traffic is not sufficient to support a permanent snack bar or other food dispensing unit. At nonpermanent operations, such as fairs, exhibits, conventions, and construction projects, the people on the job in these locations away from urban restaurant facilities need the mobile unit caterer.

Fleet Operator: Whether the mobile unit is independently owned or part of a fleet, the basic service it offers is the same: to bring light food directly to the worker at his job. When a fleet owner is in charge, he may operate in one of several ways.

1. He may own all the trucks outright and employ drivers, who are actually delivery men or women, on salary, covering stated and specific routes that he outlines. The fleet owner has complete control over the menu and the amount of food and supplies placed on the truck, although he will be guided by the driver's daily order sheet. Drivers turn over all receipts at the end of each day.

2. The fleet owner may lease his trucks on an annual basis, with the understanding that drivers purchase all food and supplies from him. The driver pays for what he takes, and arrangements are made for the return of unsold items. The fleet owner might suggest routes, but it is the lessee's responsibility to find his own stops, plan his own stops, and plan his own routes and delivery schedules. Profits from the day's sales belong to the driver.

3. The fleet owner may rent his trucks on a daily basis, with the price of the rental including food and equipment. The independent driver who has made a contract to cover a one-day special at one of his regular stops can rent the additional truck to increase the volume of his business, until such time as he may be able to lease or purchase the additional truck.

4. An excellent source of additional income for the fleet owner is the sale of sandwiches and paper goods to the independent driver, who may have one or two trucks but no facility to produce his own sandwiches, nor storage space for paper goods purchased in quantity.

D. Restaurant

Basic restaurant operations will not be covered here except where they concern catered parties. (The restaurant caterer is usually considered a banquet hall caterer, although there are times when he will prepare food to be supplied for off-premise functions such as house parties.)

The restaurant offering rooms for catered affairs assumes that the patron will make his choice of foods from the menu currently in use at the restaurant. Because this meal is part of the restaurant's standard menu, it often costs less than the same meal prepared elsewhere. Specialty restaurants, such as Chinese, Italian, etc., have a built-in appeal for the host who wants that particular kind of food.

In a small operation, the restaurant manager or owner might double as the catering manager. However, if the catering volume is large, a special catering manager and staff would be needed.

The restaurant owner who is looking for the catered affair to increase his business in off hours must consider many things.

1. Is there room for catered parties? Perhaps additional space can be made by cleaning out unused storerooms and decorating them simply but attractively or by partitioning off part of a large dining room.

2. If a catered affair is scheduled during normally busy hours, will reguar and new "drop-in" customers be cheated of good food and service because the regular staff is busy with the catered affair?

3. Can the kitchen handle the additional load (even with the addition of new equipment)?

4. Are there newer methods of food production that might be put into practice in the kitchen to increase the output?

5. Would the anticipated additional business warrant the additional expense of redecoration, kitchen equipment, staff, etc.? Because a restaurant is in the food business does not automatically mean that it is in the catering business. When a regular restaurant has the facilities and is making a bid for catered affairs, all its advertising should indicate that facilities for catering are available, and inquiries should be invited.

CHAPTER 2

Equipment

2-1 PURCHASE AND MAINTENANCE OF
HEAVY EQUIPMENT

Heavy kitchen equipment is expensive and is intended to last for a long time. The caterer anticipating the purchase of heavy items—ranges, ovens, refrigerators, freezers, slicers, or grinders—should consider very carefully what his requirements are. Any reputable restaurant supply house will gladly assign a salesman to assist in determining what is needed in planning the kitchen operation. The caterer should also consider the opinion of the chef or other professional persons who will be using that equipment. Present needs and possible future requirements should be kept in mind.

For the beginner with a limited budget there is much good heavy and light equipment that can be bought secondhand from the same supply house that handles new equipment.

A. Ranges and Ovens

The starting caterer might consider buying only one range–oven combination [Fig. 2–1(A)]. However, he must also plan on space for additional items of equipment, as all caterers, large or small, eventually need more ranges and ovens. Stack ovens [Fig. 2–1(B) and (C)] are useful in that they may be added to the cooking area one at a time as business increases without the loss of valuable floor space.

Many of the newer ranges and ovens are being manufactured with adjustable legs which allow for cleaning under and around the oven with a minimum of effort. The positioning of these ovens can be a great factor in reducing fatigue caused by unnecessary and excessive stooping, bending, and walking.

Whether the range–oven is bought new or used, care should be taken in its use and maintenance. All ranges and ovens should be cleaned thoroughly as often as possible while being used. One day a week should be set aside

7

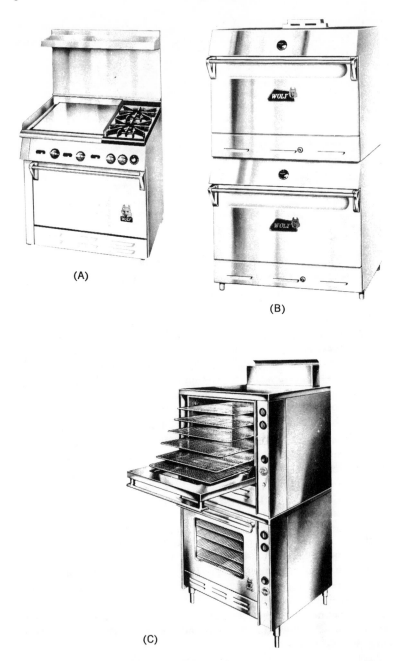

(A)

(B)

(C)

Fig. 2–1. (A) Range with regular and "fry-top," or griddle, and oven. Inside oven dimensions are 29 in. wide × 22 in. deep × 13 in. high. Adjustable legs also available. (B) Heavy-duty double-decker bake and roast oven. (C) One unit and double-decker air-flow oven. (Courtesy of Wolf Range Corp.)

for general kitchen (and equipment) cleanup so that a regular routine is established. The ranges and ovens will operate to a greater degree of efficiency and last much longer if properly cared for.

In all cases the manufacturers' instructions should be followed exactly regarding installation and adjustment of temperature controls.

B. Refrigerators, Freezers, and Walk-In Boxes

Certain foods must always be refrigerated. These include:

1. all dairy items: milk, cheeses, butter, cream, etc.;
2. sandwiches made in advance, waiting to be delivered;
3. molds and salads, with and without gelatin;
4. salad vegetables;
5. meat—raw or cooked;
6. poultry—raw or cooked;
7. fish—raw or cooked.

Some foods may be stored in the freezer, others in a cool dry place before preparation. Prepared foods, waiting to be moved to a job or to be served, *must be stored in a refrigerator.*

As soon as a caterer is set in a location, whether banquet hall or another type of operation, space should be allocated for the walk-in refrigerator. It might be necessary to wait until business warrants the purchase of such a large piece of equipment, but it should be considered early. While the business is small and growing, the sectional ice-boxes backed up with a home-type refrigerator can be used successfully.

The type of operation will determine the ultimate need for refrigeration and freezer equipment. It is good practice to work with existing or secondhand equipment to learn exactly how the business will go. Once the business is established, the purchase of larger equipment can be made as it is needed. The restaurant supply houses usually have selections of good used refrigerators, freezers, uprights, chests, and cabinet models from which to choose.

A careful scheduling of all food deliveries as close as possible to the actual preparation time will eliminate extra handling and can save on refrigeration space.

C. Slicer

This is a vital piece of equipment and should be purchased at the very outset. (See Fig. 2–2.) The savings from machine-sliced meat as opposed to hand-sliced meat is measurable and considerable. A good slicer should have the following features:

1. large blade,
2. heavy body to prevent sliding when being used,
3. easy-to-read control handle,
4. safety *off* and *on* switch.

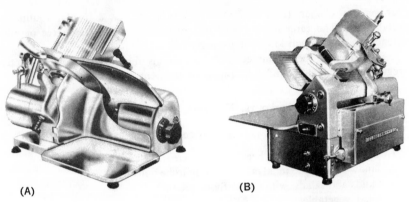

(A)   (B)

Fig. 2–2. (A) Semi-automatic compact slicer and (B) variable-speed automatic slicer. Semi-automatic slicer is hand-driven while automatic slicer would be used where great quantities of food must be sliced. Food chute is driven back and forth automatically with speed adjustable as required by the texture of food to be sliced. (Courtesy of Globe Slicing Machine Co.)

In addition, the slicer should be easy to clean and should be cleaned after every use. It is an expensive piece of equipment. With care it will last a long time and pay for itself many times over. Safety guards should be on at all times and the machine should be covered when not in use.

D. Grinder

The grinder (Fig. 2–3) is the work horse of kitchen equipment and thus it should be considered a heavy-duty machine. However, more than one caterer has begun his operation with a house-type grinder. By using it with care, it can given many years of excellent service.

All grinders are equipped with fine, medium, and coarse cutting plates. Unless there is a very definite reason for dicing food by hand, everything to be diced, chopped, mashed, or ground can be put through the grinder for uniformity and speed.

Fig. 2–3. Grinder or chopper has patented dual-cutting knife that precuts, mixes, and chops in one operation. (Courtesy of Globe Slicing Machine Co.)

E. Pots and Pans

The menu to be offered, the specialty items, and the type of service will all help in determining the type, size, and number of pots and pans that are needed. There are no rules governing this. Each catering service will have to determine what is needed and what can be used efficiently in its own kitchen.

Much of the purchasing of these items should be done as the need arises. In purchasing all types of kitchen equipment, the caterer should deal with the same local supplier. As this supplier becomes familiar with the caterer's needs, he will often be in a position to make worthwhile suggestions, or to advise when particularly good secondhand equipment becomes available.

F. Tables and Chairs

Folding tables and chairs that can be stacked in a minimum of space are necessary even for a beginner in the catering field. The most popular table size is 10 feet. This will seat 10 people if the tables are placed separately. Eight people will be seated comfortably if the tables are placed end to end. The starting caterer will find that in many of the halls, churches and other places where he has his functions scheduled, tables and chairs will be part of the equipment furnished to him. Tables and chairs may be rented if lack of funds prevents the caterer from purchasing them at the start of his business.

G. Proper Use and Maintenance

The proper use and maintenance of all kitchen equipment (ranges, ovens, slicers, grinders, knives, etc.) is taught in all good schools of cooking. Since most kitchen equipment is expensive, proper handling is necessary to insure that the equipment will give good service and last for a long time.

2-2 TRUCK PURCHASE AND MAINTENANCE

A. Types of Trucks

Two types of trucks are in common use for mobile unit catering. The first type is a two-piece truck and body. A ¾-ton truck costs from $1800–$2000, and the body costs approximately $2000. Terms of purchase can be arranged through local banks or with the sales company. [See Fig. 2–4(A) and (B).] An article from *Vend* Magazine describes such a truck.

"The exterior of the truck bodies is fashioned from highly polished scored aluminum panels attached to a sturdy steel frame. The interior is equipped with stainless steel. The sides and back have massive single section doors which raise vertically, providing shade and shelter from the elements and easy accessibility to the truck's contents.

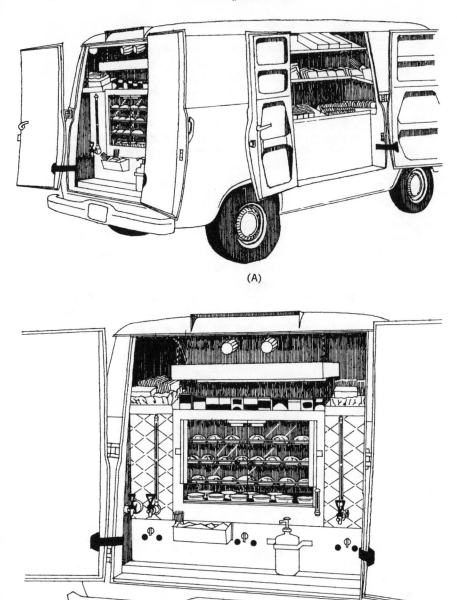

(A)

(B)

Fig. 2–4. (A) Single-unit mobile caterer's truck, opened and ready to serve. (B) Back of truck showing heating units loaded with individual portions of various foods, coffee urns, and easy to reach paper cups (top center) with stirrers and individual packets of sugar in deep shelf at lower left. Cream is in a plastic dispenser bottle. Everything is set up for easy rapid service. (Courtesy of Ford Motor Co. and Chef's Catering, a Div. of The Charles Corp.)

"The rear section of the truck is equipped with two 5-gallon coffee urns and a warming oven. These units are maintained at proper temperature by butane gas-fired burners. The right side of the truck has four roomy shelves to accommodate the various types of merchandise carried in stock. Beneath these shelves the ample refrigeration section keeps beverages and cold foods at correct serving temperatures.

"Several permanently attached bottle and can openers make it easy for customers to serve themselves.

"Openings at the bottom panels conceal waste containers for used paper cups and containers.

"Customers are served only from the right side of the truck. In this way customers are not exposed to the hazards of traffic while being served at a curbside location."

The second type of extensively used mobile unit is the one-piece car and body. This type of truck, like the first, is equipped with stainless steel coffee urns and ovens in the rear. Shelves may be built in on the curb side, and a stainless steel compartment used for milk and other cold beverages. Storage space would be on the driver's side, in the rear.

B. Maintenance

Every fleet operator has a somewhat different arrangement for truck maintenance. Some of the variations are as follows.

1. The fleet owner has complete responsibility for maintenance of trucks owned by him and operated by driver–employees. Drivers may be responsible for gas or trucks may be gassed up daily at the commissary.

2. The daily-lease driver (on a one-time deal) is responsible for gas. The fleet owner is responsible for truck maintenance, as with driver–employees.

3. Regular lease drivers may be responsible for minor repairs, as well as for gas. For a small daily fee, the fleet owner will do all repairs, minor and major, on the truck.

4. On lease-to-purchase, the responsibility for maintenance is covered in individual agreements. The driver is responsible for gas.

The fleet owner should carry sufficient insurance to protect his investment in addition to any vehicle motor insurance that is required by local law. The independent driver is responsible for complete maintenance, licensing, and insurance on his truck. Under all of the existing arrangements, periodic checkups will help keep the trucks in excellent running condition.

2–3 LIGHT EQUIPMENT

The light equipment used by the caterer refers to all equipment for the guest service, as well as other portable equipment. It also includes linen, paper goods, and novelties.

A. Equipment for Guest Service

All such equipment should be ordered from open stock, to avoid the problem of matching replacements.

Dishes: The starting off-premise caterer often does not have the money or the facilities to store his own dishes. He may not have a call for them often enough to warrant their purchase. Renting dishes would then prove more economical. Another point to remember is that most club and public facilities that have kitchens usually have their own dishes, glasses, flatware, and, very often, pots and pans.

When the caterer has to bring dishes and other equipment into a private home or a club, he should charge the host for any rental costs. When any equipment brought in by the caterer is rented, a very clear notation should be made on the contract to avoid any misunderstanding. The caterer might include the rental charges in the price and give the host one all-inclusive price. In that case the following line should appear on the contract: "The price shown includes rental of tables, chairs, linen, plates, cups and saucers, and flatware, as enumerated on reverse side of this contract."

Another method of billing is to list the food, service, and rental as three separate items. In either case it should be clearly stated that there are rental fees involved, whether they are included or shown separately.

In the banquet hall operation the customer cannot be charged for the use of the dishes except for the gold service (see *Gold Service* in this section).

For the banquet hall caterer, dishes in large quantities are absolutely necessary. When the caterer has arrived at the point of opening his own hall, he should know exactly what type of service is to be offered and therefore exactly what type and assortment of dishes will be needed.

If a banquet hall seats a maximum of 300 in the major room, with two smaller rooms that seat up to 100 in the first and 50 in the second, then the caterer must have sufficient dishes on hand to serve 450 meals at one time.

Minimum banquet service will require the following:

Service plates	Fish plates (might be same size
Dinner plates	as salad plates)
Luncheon plates	Cups and saucers
Salad plates	Relish trays
Bread and butter plates	Platters
Soup bowls	Ramikins
Bouillon cups	Sherbet cups
	Ash trays

Also necessary are dishes for any "specialty of the house." The caterer specializing in one particular type of food might not need all of the above. Regardless of the type of food to be served, there should be sufficient dishes on hand to serve everyone at the same time.

There was once a time when no discerning hostess, good restaurant, or fine catering service would allow plastic dishes on the table. Now, however times have changed. Plastic dishes have been improved to the point where they are generally accepted for luncheons, informal receptions, and similar affairs. Formal dinners, and the like, still require traditional china. Plastic dishes are available in all standard dish sizes and in a wide variety of colors and patterns. For the off-premise caterer who wishes to have all of his own equipment they solve many problems. They are lightweight, easy to handle, and practically indestructible. When dishes have to be carried from job to job and packed and repacked constantly, the breakage on regular dishes mounts up.

Silver: *Silver* here refers to display items used on buffet tables, serving and display trays, and candelabra, as discussed below. Flatware, which is often referred to as silverware, is discussed elsewhere in this chapter.

1. *Chafing dish (Fig. 2–5):* A chafing dish is a five-piece unit for keeping food hot on buffet (stand, heating unit, water pan, food pan, and cover), available in 2-, 4-, and 8-qt sizes. The larger sizes should be used whenever possible to eliminate unnecessary refilling, particularly if a large group of guests is to be served.

2. *Champagne ice bucket and stand (Fig. 2–6):* It is a two-piece set with sturdy free-standing single-bottle coolers. One set is needed for each banquet table. Buckets can also be placed directly on the table. Cardboard paint mixing tubs or wax-lined paper buckets may also be used as coolers.

Fig. 2–5. Round chafing dishes, whether silver or copper usually hold only 2 or 4 qts. For larger quality service, the oval or oblong chafing dishes are used. (Courtesy of Abbey Rents.)

Fig. 2–6. Champagne ice bucket and stand.

3. *Champagne or punch fountain:* see *Champagne* on page 15.

4. *Compotes:* Compotes are footed candy, nut, and bonbon dishes.

5. *Creamer and sugar sets:* These may be part of the tea service. Glass creamer and sugar sets may be placed on each table for dinner service. Both kinds will be needed in sufficient quantity to serve the maximum number of tables.

6. *Candelabra:* Assorted sizes and styles for the different types of functions to be catered. The quantities needed will be determined by the type of catering service that is offered:

(a) large five-arm candelabra for ornate buffet or cake table,
(b) three-arm candelabra for smaller tables,
(c) single candelabra for individual table settings.

7. *Display Trays:*

(a) Round, oval, or oblong for passing hot hors d'oeuvres, etc., and for the buffet table.
(b) Sectioned trays for formal French service.
(c) Trays should range in size from 14 × 20 to 20 × 20 in.

Round trays for buffet should range from 18 to 24 in. across. Smaller trays clutter the table and demand constant refilling, which slows the service considerably. Trays should have an attractive border and handles, and also be footed, except for trays used to pass food.

Large sectional Lazy Susans are used very effectively on all size buffets. (See Sec. 9–2B.)

Gold service: Most first-class hotel and banquet hall catering services offer *gold service*. This is limited to dinners of over a specified price that varies with each operation. All dishes and flatware are gold and the glasses are very fine crystal with gold rims.

The gold service is most often used for elegant formal French dinners, served by a full complement of trained service personnel. The menu must be the very finest, usually completely French. This service is available for

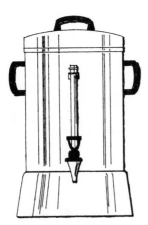

Fig. 2–7. Coffee urn with easy-to-use handle and spout. Available in 35 or 85-cup models.

anyone who wishes to use it, but because of the high cost and the menu requirements, it has a limited appeal.

Flatware: The same problems apply to the purchase or rental of flatware as apply to dishes. The off-premise caterer should consider, before making any purchases, that a simple design with no initial would suit his purpose best. No hostess is going to want her table set with flatware bearing the caterer's initials.

The banquet hall caterer might have an attractive initial on the flatware, since it will be used in his hall. While the initialed flatware is acceptable, it might be very costly to replace, if lost. Therefore, open stock design might be more practical in the long run. Basic flatware needed are

Dinner fork	Luncheon knife
Entree fork	Butter spreader
Salad fork	Soup spoon
Fish fork	Creamed soup spoon
Dessert fork	Teaspoon
Dinner knife	Iced teaspoon

The serving pieces needed will be determined by the type of service, but all caterers will need a good supply of the following:

1. salad tongs, or salad forks and spoons;
2. large serving spoons for hot food from chafing dishes;
3. large salad forks for cold sliced meat, cheese, etc.;
4. cake knife and cake server sets.

Glasses (See also Sec. 11–1): The banquet hall caterer will need a full complement of dining room glasses, in addition to the bar glasses if there is a bar on the premises. The dining room glasses include

1. fruit juice glass—5 oz,
2. water tumbler or goblet—8–10 oz,
3. general beverage glass—9 oz,
4. iced tea glass—12 oz,
5. wine glass—2–4 oz,
6. champagne glass—4–5¼ oz,
7. supreme glass and liner*,
8. parfait glass*.

The off-premise caterer may need a quantity of champagne glasses. If much of his catering calls for setting up a small bar, he might also have a supply of hi-ball and "on-the-rocks" glasses. As with dishes, he may include the rental charge in the job price, add it on to the price of the food, or list it separately. The host should be charged for guest breakage.

Coffee Urns (Coffee Makers): The second cup of coffee is as natural to any meal as the main course. Banquet hall kitchens have special *coffee*

---

* These two items are usually considered as dishes since they are used for the meal rather than for beverage service.

bank areas, just off the serving pantry or in the serving pantry, but not connected directly to the kitchen operation. The salad man or assistant cook usually prepares the coffee in adequate time for service with the scheduled meal.

For off-premise jobs, portable coffee urns may be needed. Some clubs have coffee urns in their kitchens. Many offices have small coffee makers, but nothing adequate for quantity service. New portable coffee urns or carriers are light, easy to clean, and turn out a good cup of coffee. When in doubt about the size urn needed for a job, take the larger one.

In private homes where any amount of entertaining is done, there is often at least one 30-cup coffee maker.

The off-premise caterer should have enough portable urns to make two cups of coffee for the largest number of guests he can serve (Fig. 2–7).

All mobile unit catering trucks have coffee urns at the back of the truck (Fig. 2–4).

Coffee Serving Urns: Large decorative coffee servers have self-contained heating units using canned heat, and easy-to-use handles and drop-free spouts. The coffee must be made in the kitchen in a coffee urn, and then poured into the server while it is still hot. These servers range in size from 35 to 100 cups (Fig. 2–8).

Pitchers: For coffee service to the seated guest, coffee pitchers should be insulated, if possible, and have heat-resistant handles. Silver pitchers are

Fig. 2–8. Decorative coffee serving urn, sugar, creamer, and tray may be placed on a buffet for served or self-service meal. (Courtesy of Abbey Rents.)

most attractive, but they are not insulated and are heavy. Some of the newer alloy pitchers are extremely light and easy to handle. All pitchers should hold approximately 2 qt.

The same style pitchers may be used for pouring both coffee and tea, although a thin-necked pitcher is preferable for tea. Water pitchers might be glass, clear plastic, or a colorful metal alloy. All pitchers should be of simple design and easy to clean and store (Fig. 2–9).

Tea Service (Samovar): The tea service includes:

1. tea pourer (containing essence),
2. pot with boiling water (kept over warming unit),
3. a cream and sugar set.

These are usually of silver or fine china, set on a silver tray. The tea service is most commonly seen at teas and similar functions where an "honorary hostess" pours. (See Sec. 9–2D.)

Trays: Regardless of the time or location of a catered meal, trays are always a necessity. Display trays are discussed in *Silver* in this section.

Utility trays include waiters' trays, kitchen trays, and bar trays. These should be made of heavy-duty metal or plastic. They should be large, without decorative borders or handles. The following are approximate dimensions of various types of trays:

1. waiters' trays — 28 × 22 in., oval,
2. kitchen trays — 15 × 20 in.,
3. bar trays — 12–14 in., round, cork-lined.

If bar trays are not cork-lined, a cloth napkin should be placed on the tray to prevent glasses from sliding and to catch any spillage.

Busboxes: These are utility boxes of metal or plastic from 12 × 18 to 18 × 24 in., 5½ in. deep. They are used to carry dirty dishes and flatware from the dining room to the kitchen.

Fig. 2–9. Pitchers of various designs.

B. Portable Equipment

Carrying Cases: Except for the heavy cooking equipment in the kitchen, all equipment of the off-premise caterer should be portable. As such, it must be packed in suitable carrying cases (Fig. 2–10). These include the following.

1. *Glass boxes:* Champagne glasses, bar glasses, punch cups, and punch bowls require heavy-duty cardboard or wooden boxes, fitted with dividers and shelves, as packed by the manufacturer. Boxes should be marked, *Glass—Fragile.*

2. *Tray boxes:* Heavy-duty cardboard or plywood boxes are required for all silver trays, which should be wrapped in cloth bags before being packed in boxes. Utility trays can be packed in ordinary cardboard boxes for transportation.

3. *Candelabra boxes:* If these boxes are not cloth-lined, then the separate pieces of the candelabra should be placed in cloth bags before being packed. The boxes should have dividers to prevent the pieces of the candelabra from being banged about. Sufficient space should be left for a supply of candles.

4. *Chafing dish boxes:* Light wooden boxes are needed to fit the various sizes and shapes of chafing dishes, with space for canned heat. If chafing

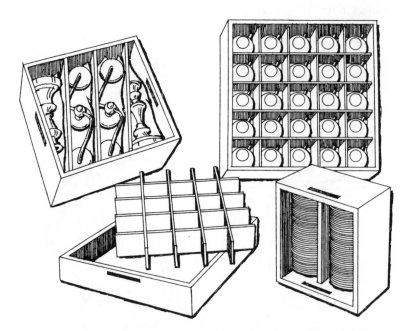

Fig. 2–10. Individual cases for caterer's equipment. All caterer's equipment used off premises should be packed in individual packing cases with strong dividers and tight-fitting covers. These serve a two-fold purpose: prevents breakage and makes immediate sight inventory simple.

dishes are silver, they should be wrapped in cloth before being packed in the carrying cases.

5. *Heavy-duty cardboard boxes:* Heavy-duty cardboard boxes are used for the following:

1. flatware,
2. linen,
3. kitchen utensils,
4. pots and pans,
5. pitchers,
6. coffee urns (if silver, they should be handled as chafing dishes),
7. all other equipment that might be needed off premises.

Portable Equipment for Cooking and Carrying Food: Many off-premise caterers have been doing business for years and have never owned one piece of portable cooking equipment. They limit their catering to locations where facilities for cooking are available or they do all the cooking in their own commissary.

Good equipment is not cheap, but in the matter of portable equipment it is most important to buy the very best, as this equipment must withstand constant and often rough handling. No staff member will be as concerned about a piece of equipment as the man who has paid for it.

Electric frying pans and roasters can be used where there is no stove available. This is a common occurrence at office parties. These electric heating units are compact and easy to carry, although they do limit the amount and type of food that can be heated or cooked at one time. After the food is heated, it should be placed in a chafing dish for service.

Foremost on the list of other portable equipment for the off-premise caterer are insulated food carriers. Ice chests and heated units with fitted trays and pans to accommodate the type of food to be served (Fig. 2–11) are also important.

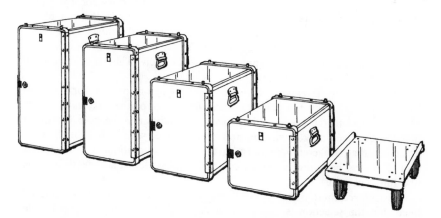

Fig. 2–11. Hand-lift cabinets in various sizes. (Courtesy of Cres-Cor.)

C. Linen (Banquet Hall)

The term *linen* refers to cloth coverings for tables as well as guest napkins. Today the finest restaurant and catering service linen is actually made from cotton fabrics, although the term *linen* is still used. Cotton fabrics can withstand rough treatment and constant laundering in strong detergents and bleaches. Real linen, being a finer fabric, does not stand up as well.

To Buy or Rent: The initial purchase price of fairly good grade table linen, including a supply of napkins, is not very high, but the upkeep is. All linen must be washed, dried, and ironed after every use. It is often more economical and a lot easier to rent linen, except for the specialty linen (see *Speciality Linen* in this section), on a regular basis.

Most linen rental houses will arrange for regular delivery and pickup. The cost of rental guarantees delivery of clean, ironed, and properly folded linen. Even when linen is used only sporadically, as by the starting caterer, the linen rental house offers the same service. Most linen rental houses can also supply cook's whites and waiter's jackets.

The average banquet hall table is 29 or 30 in. high, with considerable variation in length and width. Linen should be ordered in sizes to cover the tables and allow even drop on all sides. (See Tables 2–1 and 2–2.)

Specialty Linen:

1. *Buffet cloths:* The buffet cloth should be at least one and one-half times the width of a regular banquet table cloth, i.e., at least 80 × 120 in. One such cloth will cover 10 ft of buffet table which are visible to the guests. (See Sec. 9–2B.)

Because of their unusual size, these cloths are not regularly carried by most linen rental houses, since they would have to charge a premium for laundering. The caterer might do well to purchase these and arrange to have them laundered at a small local laundry that has facilities for individual handling.

2. *Lace covers for buffet:* Lace, nylon, or net covers for the buffet should be approximately 54 × 120 in. in order to cover the top of the table and also allow a short even drop on all sides of the table. They might be 80 × 120 and be used floor length. These covers are expensive, but they add considerably to the appearance of the table. They should be hand laundered with the utmost care.

3. *Overskirts:* Overskirts may be of satin, nylon, or any form of fine lace or netting. They are placed around the buffet or the cake table. They can be pinned to the regular table cover. Overskirts may be floor length, or half length. They may be draped and held in place with ribbons or flowers, in colors that are complimentary to the room decoration. The overskirts should always be white, although the buffet table cloth underneath may be of a different color.

4. *Colored table linen:* Many linen rental houses do have some colored linen, but the selection is limited. If a catering service offers colored table linen, it should make arrangements to have that linen laundered where

TABLE 2–1. STANDARD SIZES OF TABLE LINEN

Size, in.	Table Coverage
44 × 44 square	32-in. bridge
54 × 54	48–50-in. bridge or round
64 × 64	60-in. round
72 × 72	68-in. round
81 × 81	77-in. round
90 × 90 (square banquet)	84-in. round
44 × 64	5-ft oblong table, but leaves only 4-in drop
54 × 72	5-ft oblong
54 × 96	7-ft oblong
54 × 120	8-ft oblong
⎰54 × 144 or ⎱72 × 144	10-ft oblong
80 × 120*	8-ft oblong buffet
80 × 144*	10-ft oblong buffet

* The last two sizes are not standard. These are one and a half as wide as a regular banquet cloth. They are used for buffet tables and will cover the tables and reach the floor on one side. Usually two or three oblong tables placed end to end will be used to make one long buffet.

TABLE 2–2. STANDARD SIZES OF LINEN NAPKINS

18 × 18 in. square	Luncheon napkin
20 × 20 in. square	Dinner napkin

there are facilities for individual handling. Laundering colored linen requires special care to prevent fading and bleaching.

Colored linen should be used in strict rotation. This prevents some cloths from being used and washed more than others. Otherwise, after a dozen uses, all the cloths will no longer be the same shade.

The colors most frequently seen on buffet tables, besides white, are

(a) pale yellow,
(b) pale pink,
(c) blue: light, medium, electric,
(d) red: bright or vibrant for Valentine's Day and Christmas,
(e) fiesta shades: bright yellow, orange, or green for special informal occasions.

Formal service demands white or a very pale pastel linen. Informal service may have any color desired by the host or the committee. White napkins can be properly used with all colored buffet linen; the reverse, white buffet linen with colored guest napkins, can also be very attractive.

5. *Kitchen linen:* Kitchen linen is very important. A cook without a potholder or a clean cloth can be in serious trouble. If a dishwashing machine is available, then it may not be necessary to handle dishes, glasses, and flatware. Nevertheless, a supply of the following should always be in every kitchen:

(a) potholders: large, heavy duty;
(b) dish towels for wiping pots and pans (if necessary);
(c) hand towels or clean rags for general cleanup and for wiping silver trays and chafing dishes;
(d) bar rags: small, clean hand towels;
(e) mopup rags: clean rags for general use to be disposed of after the job. No matter how careful the staff is, some things are bound to be spilled, and rags should be available for quick mopup.

D. Paper Goods

Perhaps automation has pushed us into using as much paper goods as we do. Yet, for informal parties, the paper service leaves very little to be desired. Paper goods include containers such as cups and bowls of waxed paper, styrofoam, or cardboard; paper plates that are cardboard or plastic lined; plastic or wooden spoons, knives, and forks; and table cloths and napkins.

Many starting off-premise caterers will try to avoid the use of paper, preferring the traditional china service. However, if his clients are vitally concerned with the expenses involved, the rental of dishes and glassware might make the catered affairs too costly. For reasons of economy, therefore, the caterer might turn to paper goods.

Dishwashing can be a very serious problem for the off-premise caterer when a location has limited facilities. Using paper goods may make it possible to serve and clean up in what would otherwise be an impossible situation.

For the banquet hall caterer, dishwashing may not be a problem at all. His kitchen should be equipped with proper dishwashing units. Since these units are capable of washing huge numbers of dishes per hour, the use of paper goods may be limited to cocktail napkins, doilies, and similar items.

Mobile unit caterers would be out of business without paper goods.

Single-Service Units: Paper plates, cups, table covers, and napkins are inexpensive, universally available, and decorated with designs for practically any occasion. As they have a long shelf life, they may be bought in large quantities to effect savings.

All paper goods are considered single-service units. As such, they should be stored, handled, and dispensed in a sanitary manner, and disposed of after a single use.

1. *Plates:* Plastic-coated paper plates, with a smooth porcelain-like finish, are available in all popular plate sizes. They come in white or pastel

colors, or printed with floral patterns or wedding, anniversary, or holiday designs. These plates are excellent for light luncheons and buffets, or for coffee and cake services held at informal wedding receptions. They should be placed on the buffet exactly as any other plates, china, or plastic would be placed.

Unlike the rental of china dishes and glassware, the price of paper plates is very low and may therefore be included in the job price.

2. *Cups:* Paper cups come in a wide variety of sizes, styles, shapes, and colors and can be imprinted in huge quantities. Imprinted cups are used by the mobile unit caterer or by the restaurant using paper in standard service.

Imprinted cups, like imprinted cocktail napkins and match books, are not good advertising spots for banquet hall or off-premise caterers. Catering is often done in a private home or a club, and the paper goods used should carry a design in keeping with the theme of the party and not serve as advertising for the caterer.

Unless the off-premise caterer does a highly specialized type of catering, he will need a 5- or 6-oz cold cup to be used for punch. Hot cups should be the same size, either of cardboard, with fold-out handles, or of insulated styrofoam.

The number of paper cups for punch taken for an off-premise job should be twice the guest count to eliminate the possibility of running short. For coffee cups, a 10–15 percent average will be sufficient. While a guest may take a single cup of coffee and hold on to it, he might have two or three cups of punch before the reception is over. He will probably hold on to a champagne or highball glass and return to the bar for a refill. This is not so, however, with paper cups. He will often dispose of the paper cup before returning for a second or third serving of punch. When the menu has champagne for the adults and punch for the youngsters, allow three paper cups for each child at the reception.

The mobile unit kitchen will need very large quantities of all paper goods, since all food is individually wrapped in single-service units. As with all catering services, the menu determines exactly what is needed. The following are commonly used:

Coffee (hot) cups	Salad cups with covers
Stew bowls	Printed sandwich labels
Sandwich wrappers or bags	Straws
Napkins	Plastic or wooden forks and
Glassine or plastic bags	spoons
Cold cups	

A cup count will immediately let the driver know how much coffee has been sold. Since the truck is freshly loaded daily, the driver merely counts the total number of paper cups at the beginning of the day, and subtracts the number remaining at the end of the day. The difference is the number of cups of coffee sold. The same counting method can be applied when any similar paper items are used.

The following is an example of this method:

	Morning Count	Night Count	Portions Sold
Coffee cups	100	56	44
Stew bowls	50	37	13

3. *Paper Napkins:* A fine grade of paper napkins may be used for all semiformal, informal, and outdoor parties. Standard paper napkin sizes are

1. breakfast or luncheon—18 × 18 in.,
2. dinner—20 × 20 in.,
3. cocktail—from 9 × 9 to 12 × 12 in.

There are other sizes and a wide variety of folds. These listed above are all folded in even quarters.

While linen napkins might be used for any meal service, cocktail napkins are almost always paper, even at private parties held in the home. Cocktail napkins can be plain white or printed with a wide variety of designs, cartoons, or decorations. They may also be printed with the names of the persons celebrating and the date of the function.

Wedding napkins come in a variety of designs in the sizes listed above. The decorations may be wedding bells, wreaths and doves, wedding rings, or lilies of the valley. They are printed lightly in gold or silver. The name of the bride and groom and the date of the wedding are then overprinted in the same color ink. Other colors are available at specialty shops and on special order from local paper houses.

Holiday napkins for New Year's Eve, Christmas, Easter, Halloween, and St. Patrick's Day are usually available just before the holidays noted.

Birthday and anniversary napkins are available at all times. These are colorful and add much to the festive mood of both the table setting and the room. Table covers in various sizes to match the holiday napkins are also available.

Mobile units can use a dispenser–fold paper napkin, with the dispenser placed so the customer can help himself. These napkins could be part of the regular paper supply picked up at the commissary and placed in the dispenser, at the beginning of each day's run. The dispenser should be refilled as often as needed.

4. *Paper table covers:* Like the paper napkins, paper table covers can be bought in all solid colors or imprinted with motifs and designs for various holidays and occasions. Individual sets include table cover and matching napkins, although the number of napkins in the set is generally too small for quantity service.

The use of paper table coverings is determined by the type of service and the price. On a buffet table, however, the paper cloth presents a problem for the caterer. The buffet table might have to stand for a number of hours, and in most instances, paper is too fragile to withstand that much wear. When anything is spilled, even the smallest amount, the paper tends to disintegrate. When guests rub against the table, the paper cloth tears very quickly. This can spoil the appearance of the table for the balance of the evening. Therefore, even at an affair where paper is being used throughout the room, the caterer should consider the use of two or three linen buffet cloths. At a relatively small cost, these will insure a buffet table that will look lovely throughout the evening.

5. *Place mats:* Paper place mats are considered part of the regular place setting in many restaurants and restaurant chains. These are designed with the name and address of the restaurant, along with other information, such as a list of restaurants in the same chain or the menu itself.

These advertising pieces are wonderful for the restaurant but not for the caterer, with certain exceptions. For a breakfast or luncheon in a public meeting hall or a church, it is acceptable to use a place mat with the caterer's name, providing it has an attractive design. The banquet hall caterer might use place mats for breakfast or luncheon served on his premises.

The banquet hall caterer would not use place mats for dinners, however. Likewise, for any meal served in a private home, a place mat with the caterer's name and address would be in extremely bad taste. Generally, caterers pass up place mats completely in favor of more useful paper items and more meaningful advertising.

6. *Paper doilies:* Paper doilies come in a great many sizes, shapes, colors, and designs. An assortment of the most commonly used sizes will be needed by all caterers.

A 5- or 6-in. doily, called a *liner,* is placed under the fruit cocktail or sherbet glass on the serving plate. A liner is also placed under any individual dessert tart on the serving plate and under a finger bowl.

A doily covering the entire surface, except the border, should be placed on any tray on which dry finger food is to be served. This includes hot canapés and hors d'oeuvres, finger sandwiches, cookies, sliced cakes, petit fours, etc. When an empty tray is returned to the kitchen to be refilled, a clean doily should replace the soiled one before any new food is put on the tray. Paper doilies are single-service items.

White doilies are most commonly used. Silver, gold, and various colored doilies are available for special occasions. Gold or silver doilies, folded in half, can be rolled around the exposed end of the drumstick, when a turkey is placed on a buffet.

As the service expands, the individual caterer will learn exactly which sizes and styles of doilies he uses most. These should be ordered in large quantities.

For the mobile unit, the doily is too dainty and fragile and is not generally used.

Paper (Cardboard) Boxes: Some catering services have no need for paper boxes (single-service items) at all. Others do volume business in takeout items and therefore need a great many boxes.

The banquet hall caterer may use fairly large cake boxes for the top tier of the wedding cake. Aside from that, paper boxes generally are not needed.

Mobile units do not need any boxes on the trucks, except those in which additional supplies and staples are packed.

The off-premise caterer needs a great many boxes of various sizes, shapes, and weight capacities in addition to insulated food carriers. The banquet hall caterer working off premises needs the same assortment of paper boxes used by the off-premise caterer.

Heavy-duty boxes are needed to carry packaged items to be cooked on the job, canned goods, staples, etc. Kitchen equipment such as pots and pans and utensils can be carried in these boxes as well. Common box sizes used by caterers are

1. flat (pizza) box: 12 × 12 × 1½ in. up to 16 × 16 × 1½ in. (for storage of hors d'oeuvres in freezer and for delivery of same);
2. pie box: 9 × 9 × 3 in. (for assorted food items);
3. cake box: 12 × 12 × 6 in.;
4. loaf box: 9 × 5 × 5 in.

When large quantities of boxes are needed, they can be imprinted with the caterer's name and address. For smaller quantities, the caterer may stamp his name and address on each box as he uses it. He can also order printed gummed labels to be pasted on the top of each box.

E. Novelties and Extras

Candles: A supply of candles, to fit the various sized candelabra, should be on hand. When using three- or five-arm candelabra, the candles should be approximately the same height as the candelabra. White candles are appropriate for all occasions. The caterer might however offer a selection of the most popular pastel colors: white, pink, yellow, blue, or green. The caterer should charge for any special colors that must be purchased separately for the job.

Colored candles in harmony with room decorations and floral arrangements are most often supplied by the florist.

Gifts for Departing Guest: The ancient custom of distributing gifts to the departing guest is still practiced today. These include the following:

1. *Jordan almonds or sugar-coated nuts:* At Italian weddings the host can present guests with these confections in tiny ceramic or plastic shoes, or wrapped in small squares of colored net.

2. *Cake:* Slices of the occasion cake or individually wrapped pieces of the groom's cake and the bride's cake might possibly be considered in this same category.

3. *Rice:* A small amount of rice, wrapped in fine net and tied with a ribbon, may also have a gift card attached. These can be placed in a decorated basket or on a small silver tray on the guest register table. The guest then helps himself when he signs the book. He may also take some rice as he leaves the reception hall to bid farewell to the newly married couple. Many reception halls forbid the throwing of rice inside the building,

as this may constitute a hazard. The rice is not intended as a gift, but is a symbol of fertility and is showered on the departing couple. The gift card is then saved as a reminder of the date and the occasion.

4. *Other gifts:* Local merchants often contribute samples or small packages of their products in support of various public functions. Cigarette lighters and holders, small compacts, rain bonnets, key chains with various charms, etc., are distributed to the guests or are put on the table at each place setting. This is a modern merchandising practice that is perfectly acceptable.

CHAPTER 3

Kitchen and Commissary

3–1 THE KITCHEN

A. Banquet Hall

Unlike the restaurant kitchen that is opened and in operation every day, the banquet hall kitchen operates only when there is a specific job to be catered. The kitchen arrangement will vary according to the size of the dining room, the total number of guests to be served at one time, and the type of service to be offered. In all cases, however, the kitchen should be set up for rapid quantity service. Rapid service means that food goes out of the kitchen so as to serve all guests as quickly as possible. The floor plan for a typical banquet kitchen setup is illustrated in Fig. 3–1.

In addition to the kitchen, the banquet hall may have a service pantry, a small area just off the main dining room. The pantry usually contains a small refrigerator and sink, and it can be equipped to facilitate rapid meal service by eliminating the need for frequent trips to the kitchen for certain items. The coffee urns and a supply of linen, glasses, and service trays may be kept in the service pantry. Just before the meal service begins, the bread, butter, coffee, tea, cream, sugar, sliced lemons, and various other necessary condiments may be brought in and stored in the pantry.

B. Off Premises

The off-premise caterer's kitchen is apt to be much simpler than that of the banquet hall caterer. Although the kitchen might eventually be enlarged, a small operation can also be efficient and extremely productive. (See Fig. 3–2.)

Regardless of the size and shape of the kitchen, it should be painted a light color, have good ventilation, with screened windows and doors, and good lighting. It should contain a minimum of movable items such as chairs, unattached tables, and coat racks, which should be kept in another room or in a screened-off area. (See Sec. 3–3.)

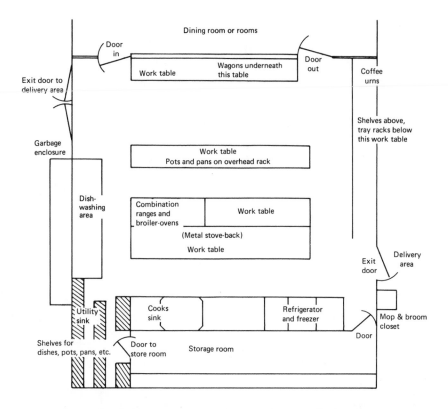

Fig. 3–1. Floor plan for banquet hall kitchen. Kitchen is approximately 40 × 40 ft and capable of serving 400 guests. Flow line goes from delivery area past work tables, then to refrigerators, freezers, and store room. As food is needed, it is removed from storage to work areas. Two doors to store room eliminate necessity of going completely around the room, against flow, to get supplies. Not shown are exhaust hood over ovens and ranges, shelves, cabinets, windows, and drawers in work tables.

"On location," the kitchen may be anything from a tiny home kitchen to a very large, completely equipped, club arrangement. The caterer, or a member of his staff, should familiarize himself with the physical arrangements of the work area before the time of the food delivery. Questions to ask when catering in a location include the following:

1. Do all the stoves and ovens work?

2. Is the refrigerator operating properly? If not in constant operation, arrange for it to be turned on a few hours before the cold food will be delivered. If in a private home, request that it be emptied, if necessary.

3. Are proper sizes of pots and pans available? The caterer may have to bring his own. Measure ovens to be sure caterer's pans will fit.

4. Are cutting boards available?

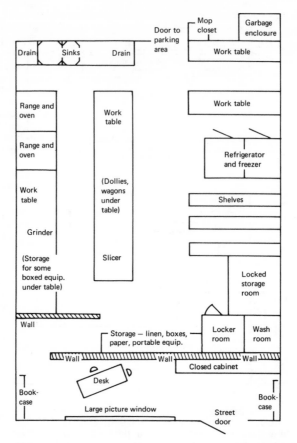

Fig. 3–2. Floor plan for off-premise caterer's kitchen, commissary, and office, combined. This efficient arrangement features work tables near ranges for hot food preparation and other tables near refrigerators for cold food preparation. Central wide aisle is large enough to move boxed equipment which may be stored in various places as cabinet space permits. Not shown are hood over ovens, and various shelves and cabinets, windows, and drawers in work tables.

5. Soaps and detergents—who is to supply them?

6. Dish towels, if needed—are they available, or does the caterer supply them?

7. Does the dishwasher operate according to instructions on its side, or is a custodian needed to operate it? If so, arrange for him to be in attendance.

8. Are all serving pieces, dishes, flatware, glasses, etc., in easily accessible areas, or must a custodian bring them out of storage?

9. Same for chairs and tables.

10. Will the work areas be clean when the caterer comes in?

11. The caterer will leave the kitchen clean, but will the custodian replace all equipment, or does the caterer's staff do it?

C. Mobile Unit

Most mobile unit caterers, or fleet owners, will purchase almost all of their food in portion-controlled packages. Therefore the kitchen will be a highly specialized operation for preparing large quantities of those few items that are not prepackaged, i.e., sandwiches and certain baked goods. (See Fig. 3–3.) These will be made fresh daily to fill the orders placed by the drivers at the end of the previous day's run. The kitchen is separate from the commissary (Fig. 3–4) where the drivers make their daily pickups.

Practically every mobile unit caterer, regardless of how large or small, will purchase much of his food from wholesale suppliers. To meet the

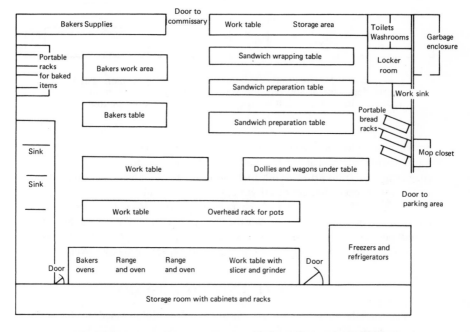

Fig. 3–3. Mobile unit caterer's kitchen floor plan. Kitchen divided roughly into three areas: bakery, hot food preparation, and cold food preparation with easy access to parking lot and commissary. Work flow line goes from parking area to store room or refrigerator and freezer. Food would come out to work area and when finished through door to commissary. Small store room door to left of bakers ovens would allow baker and cook to get needed supplies without going completely around ranges and ovens.

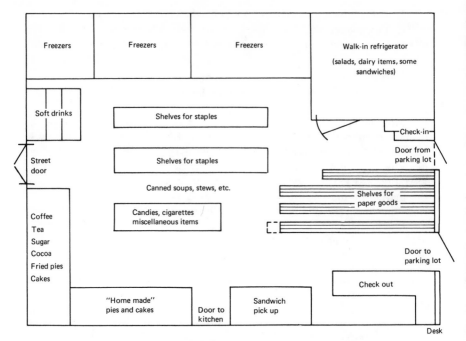

Fig. 3–4. Mobile unit caterer's commissary floor plan. Separate doors for *in* and *out* and supermarket type of setup enable drivers to pick up supplies with least waste of time or motion.

growing demand for individual portions, many national companies now put out a variety of food items in small sizes. These include soups, stews, chili, spaghetti, and franks and beans, and more items are constantly being added to the list. Frozen dinners of all varieties are also available.

Packaged baked goods may be purchased from local bakeries. A fleet operator who feels that it is worth the trouble might produce his own baked goods, although he then runs into the need for professional bakers and specialized equipment including large and expensive baking ovens.

3–2   MOBILE UNIT COMMISSARY

The mobile unit commissary must be carefully planned to facilitate rapid delivery and pickup of food.

A. Basic Procedures

The commissary generally operates under the following basic procedures.

1. Drivers (both lease drivers and independents) hand in their order slips at the end of each day's run.

2. Drivers return unsold perishable items.

3. Drivers clean their trucks.

4. Drivers are due at the commissary the next morning early enough to check trucks and put ice in the ice chest and water in the coffee makers.

5. Inside the commissary, drivers pick up the order sheet and all items ordered, load the truck, and leave. Time for loading the truck will vary from one-half hour to an hour depending on the efficiency of the commissary and the speed of the driver.

To avoid the necessity of extra commissary personnel, each driver comes into the commissary, takes his order sheet and a loading basket or wagon, and walks around the commissary picking up the items that he needs, much like a supermarket setup. Among the items that should be within easy reach are paper goods; individually wrapped candy bars; cigarettes, cigars; soft-drink cans, packaged coffee, tea bags, and powdered hot chocolate. Large freezers should also be easily accessible for the various frozen items that are placed right in the heating unit on the truck to be hot when needed at the various stops.

A commissary man might load the perishables, specialty items, and sandwiches into smaller boxes with the driver's name and number. These boxes are picked up at a counter near the checkout desk.

Since route stops are the same every day, the amount and type of items carried should be the same (with the exception noted below) and should always be packed in the same place on the truck. This is of the utmost importance since the customer expects to find certain items in certain places and the whole mobile unit operation is based on rapid self-service, with the driver merely taking cash and making change.

B. Forms for the Driver

At the checkout desk all items taken by the driver are checked against his order. The driver then signs the checkout slip. (See Figs. 3–5 and 3–6.)

A wholesale route sheet lists all items available at the commissary including staples and paper goods. This may serve as the driver's order form to be filled out daily. Fig. 3–7 has a total of 164 items. As with all caterer's menus, the choice of items is determined by the type of service and the client's desires.

The individual load slip or checkout slip which lists everything that is actually taken from the commissary can also be used as the cost sheet for daily accounting.

On the checkout slip all items are under group headings. All items of one group that sell for the same price are listed as one, such as salads or cigarettes. The actual breakdown of exactly how much of each specific item appears on the wholesale route sheet. The listing on the wholesale order sheet must be exact as to type of food, size of portion and cost, but on the checkout slip the general classification is sufficient.

The checkout slip is signed by the driver when he picks up his order.

DATE_____19____   P & F – LOAD SHEET

Mon. Tu. Wed. Thur. Fri. Sat.

DRIVER_____ROUTE_____19___

ITEM	COST	ON TRUCK	LOADED	DUMPED	RETURNED	SOLD	AMOUNT		
CIGARS	.06								
CIGARS	.08								
CIGARS	.10								
CIGARS	.35								
CIGARETTES	.30								
TOBACCO	.20								
CANDY	.10								
CANDY	.05								
CANDY	.02								
GUM-SAVERS	.05								
GLASS SODA	.10								
CAN SODA	.15								
SODA	.20								
NEAR BEER	.30								
MATCHES	.00½								
ALKA SELTZER BROMO SELTZER	.15								
VICKS CLORETS	.15								
TUMS	.12								
PAPER CUPS 6 OZ.	.02								
8 OZ. CUPS	.02								
12 OZ. CUPS	.02								
8 OZ. SOUP BOWLS	.02								
SUB-TOTAL TAXABLE									
SANDWICHES	.65								
SANDWICHES	.50								
SANDWICHES	.45								
SANDWICHES	.40								
SANDWICHES	.35								
SANDWICHES	.30								
HAMBURGER	.35								
HOT DOG	.35								
DINNERS	.60								
DINNERS	.55								
DINNERS	.45								
TAMALES	.35								
CHICKEN PIES	.50								
BURRITOS	.35								
SOUP	.25								
CHILI BEANS	.40								
STEW	.40								
PECAN PIES	.25								
MAPLE BARS	.12								
MUFFINS	.12								
CINNAMON ROLLS	.15								
PIE	.20								
DONUTS	2/.25								
DONUTS	.10								
SNAILS	.20								

		CREDITS				
		Check No.				
		Check No.				
		Check No.				
		Total Checks				
		Currency				
		Silver				
		1.00				
		.50				
		.25				
		.10				
		.05				
		.01				
		Total Silver				
		Total Cash				
		Add Paid Outs				
		Charge Sales				
		Sales				
		Less Rec'd on Acct.				
		Sales				

Sub-Total						
Credits						
Sub-Total						
Sales						
Over (Short)						
Resales						
Taxable						
Food						
Total						
Charge						
Paid on Acct.						
Deposit						

I had sufficient time to check my truck_____minutes.
I have received everything charged to me on this slip.

Date	Signed	Witness

Fig. 3–5. This load or checkout sheet is in triplicate form. First copy goes to office, second to packing room or is left at checkout desk, and third is retained by driver.

DRIVER'S NAME _____

NO. _____ DATE _____   NO. _____ DATE _____   NO. _____ DATE _____

SANDWICHES			PASTRIES			MILK		
BUNS			BANANA			QTS. MILK		
HAM			VANILLA			PTS. MILK		
BEEF			ASS'T CAKE			1/2 PTS. MILK		
BEEF AND CHEESE			CHOCOLATE					
HAM AND CHEESE			CRUMB			QTS. CHOC. MILK		
BAR-B-Q BEEF			COCONUT			PTS. CHOC. MILK		
BAR-B-Q HAM			PLAIN			1/2 PTS. CHOC. MILK		
HAMBURGER ROYAL			POWDERED SUGAR					
CHEESEBURGER			CINNAMON			PTS. BUTTERMILK		
CHILIBURGER			ORANGE			1/2 PTS. BUTTERMILK		
HAMBURGER			CHERRY					
HAM AND EGG			CHOC-COCONUT			1/3 QTS. BUTTERMILK		
SAUSAGE AND EGG			GLAZED			1/3 QTS. MILK		
BACON AND EGG			CHOC. GLAZED			1/3 QTS. CHOC. MILK		
DENVER			SUGAR RAISED					
						QTS. 1/2 AND 1/2		
STEAK			BRAN MUFFINS			PTS. 1/2 AND 1/2		
DAGWOOD			TOASTED COCONUT					
SUPER BURGER			LONG JOHNS CHOC.			COTTAGE CHEESE		
SIZZLERS			LONG JOHNS FILLED			1/2 PTS. NON-FAT		
SPEC. KAISER			MAPLE BARS					
			NUT MAPLE BARS			1/2 PTS. ORANGE JUICE		
BAR-B BURGER			GLAZED BISMARK			PTS. ORANGE JUICE		
KAISER			CHOC. BISMARK			1/2 PTS. CONES		
FISH STICK			WHITE BISMARK					
WESTERN STEAK			OPEN JELLY					
TUNA & EGG			OPEN LEMON			TOTAL		
SUPREME STEAK			TWISTS			CREDITS		
SLOPPY JOE			BUTTERFLIES			Total Milk		
SPEC. TRIANGLES			LONG APPLE T.O.					
			APPLE T.O.					
			APPLE SLICES					
TRIANGLE ASSORTED								
			CRISPIES					
SPECIAL FLATS								
			MARY ANNS					
			APPLE SAUCE RD.			Truck Rental		
RYE PLAIN ASSORTED						Total Confections		
						Total Tobacco		
RYE COMB. ASSORTED						Total Sandwiches		
						Total Pastries		
TOTAL			TOTAL			Total Milk		
CREDITS			CREDITS			Total Sundries		
Total Sandwiches			Total Pastries			TOTAL Pay This Amt.→		

Fig. 3–6. Load or checkout single sheet. This is used by driver to pick up items, then left at checkout desk, and finally sent to office.

C. Other Commissary Forms

The commissary quantity order forms are simple and list only items that move well. From time to time these forms should be updated.

All items from the local bakery (Fig. 3–8) are "individual" and placed in glassine bags at the bakery. When ordering, the caterer will indicate whether items such as brownies and doughnuts are to be packed one or two to a bag.

01 Whether the kitchen is part of the operation or a separate company, the *daily sandwich order sheet* is needed (Fig. 3–9). This tells what the kitchen can actually make. This list should also be updated periodically as items "wear out," new stops are added to the routes, and specific requests come in from regular customers at the old stops. There are 135 items on this current list. The lower part of this list covers the baked or fried pies as well as salads. The pies are purchased locally from a commercial bakery. They are individually wrapped and labeled and are easy to handle. The salads may be made in the kitchen or ordered fresh daily from dairy companies.

D. Storage

All food items in original manufacturer's containers should be stored in a cool place, except for frozen foods, which must be kept in freezers.

Prepared foods such as sandwiches and salads that are made daily must be refrigerated. Pies and cakes may or may not have to be refrigerated, depending on the ingredients and fillings or icings. All baked goods should be covered.

Packaged goods such as candies should be stored in a cool place and the stock rotated so the oldest stock is used first. Paper goods should be stored in a cool dry place and the stock rotated so the oldest stock is used first.

Storerooms and storage areas should be inventoried regularly so that old stock and slow-moving items cluttering the shelves may be eliminated.

Staples and frozen items should be ordered periodically, so that a supply is always on hand. The commissary should never run out of any of its regular items, but neither should it be overstocked with nonessentials.

In this business space as well as time represents money.

DATE | P & F CATERERS | NUMBER

CIGARETTES	R-BEER-CHERRY	PAPER BOATS .75	PEANUTS BOX .85	TV DINNERS .30
CIG. KING	ORANGE GRAPE-UP	PAPER BAGS .25	PEANUTS BAG .08	P & F DINNERS .35
	DAD'S R.B.	NAPKINS—BROTH .45		TV DINNER .45
ROI TAN	COKE-DR. PEPPER	NAPKINS—BOX .16	COOKIES TOM .65	
HAVA TAMPA	PEPSI- CANS		RAISINS .86	ENCHILADAS .20
GOLFER	BAR NONE	PLASTIC LIDS (100) .60	COOKIES BAG .07	CHILI RELL. .28
DUTCH MASTER	CO_2 TANK	CUP LIDS (100) .40	APPLE CR. .14	TAMALE G. .22
WM. PENN	CAN FLAVORS	12 OZ. CUP LIDS .75	CUP CAKES .11	TOM,MAC & CH. .25
KING EDWARD	CAN COKE-PEPSI BUBBLE-UP	PLASTIC CUPS .85	P & F PIES .11	CONNIES' .39
COPENHAGEN	CAN DR. PEPPER	MEDALLION CUPS .80	FRIED PIES .11	EGGS .07
DAYS WORK	Sm SODA BOTTLE	12 OZ. CUP COLD 1.15	CAKE SLICES .11	TAMALES .14
HOLIDAY	Lge. SODA BOTTLE	14 OZ. CUP 1.25	HELEN MAJOR .12	BURRITOS .17
BEACH NUT	BARQ'S	9 & 10 OZ. CUP / 12 OZ. HOT 1.00	MILLER CAKE .10	PIES CH. & BF. .33
PIPE TOB.	SUNNYLAND	CONE X CUP 1.05	PECAN TWIRL .11	FR. CHICKEN .49
WHITE OWL			TARTS .07	Sm. SALAD .10
ROBT. BURNS	TOTAL	PLASTIC SPOONS 3.15	COFFEE CAKE .11	Sm. CHEESE .11
MURIEL AIR TIP CORONELLA	CREDIT	STICKS .90	PERSIAN ROLLS .09	6 OZ. SALAD .15
	TOTAL CONFECTIONS	STRAWS .95	FANCY PASTRY .15	Lge. SALAD .18
	BREAKFAST C.	SPOON BAGS .45	PASTRY .12	FANCY TRAYS .26
TOTAL	CH & SANBORN	SALT IND.—Med. .30		TRAYS .20
CREDIT	MOCHA JAVA	SALT Sm. .18		Lge. CHEESE .19
TOTAL TOBACCO	SANKA	SALT Lge. .15	JUICE MED. .13	COTTAGE F. .20
R-AIDS-CLORETS	HOT CHOC. 1.90	PEPPER BX. 1.75	JUICE Sm. .08	SHRIMP COCKTAIL .26
5¢ GUM-COUGH DR. REEDS-CHARMS LS	TEA Sm. .15	SALT BX. 1.45	APPLE JCE. Lge. .18	
CANDY FIVE	TEA Lge. 1.05	SUGAR #5	APPLE JCE. Sm. BERRY .13½	PEPPER GAL. 1.80
CANDY TEN	MARYLAND 1.80	SUGAR C2#	McCOMBERS .12	GAL. MUST. .90
CANDY TOM	MILK Lge. .15	SUGAR C4#		GAL. RELISH 1.85
TOMS PATTIE		CATSUP .20	SOU & BNS HEINZ .11	PICKLES-GAL. 1.30
10¢ CHARMS 1.30	MATCHES .17	MUSTARD .12	STEW HEINZ .23	
	TOWELS .07	HOT SAUCE .15	HEINZ .15	METRECAL .31
10¢ CANDY BAGS	NEW TOWELS .27	HOT SAUCE PIC. .19	CHILI CON CARNE .20	
2¢ MINTS		RELISH .28	V.SAUS.-CB HASH .25	
BC & ALKA	CAN OPENER Lge. .25	PEPPERS .48	OYSTER STEW .25	
BROMO SELTZER	CAN OPENER Sm. .10	PICKLES-POL.S. .12	SIL SKILLET .21	SERVICE CHG. 1 50
TUMS	SUGAR DISP. .55			(ICE-HOT WATER, CARTS, ETC.)
CERTS	MUST.& CAT.DISP. .35	CHIPS .07½	CHILI & BEANS .20	
VICKS LUDEN C.D.	CLEANSER-SPOUTS .15		STEW .22	
		CRACKERS .01½	SPAG. SAUCE .20	
TISSUES, SINGLE	FRUIT .09	KRAFT CRAX .08		TOTAL
TISSUES, DOUBLE	APPLES	CHIPS .10		CREDIT
SUCRETS 2.65		SLIM JIMS 1.30		TOTAL CHARGE
		BEEF JERKY 1.20		

Fig. 3–7. Wholesale load sheet.

BAKERY

WHOLESALE

2135 Washington Avenue

Name _____

	- - - - 1971	
Danish		
Jelly		
Custard		
Apple		
Pineapple		
Butterhorn		
Raisin		
Bear Claw		
Figure 8		
PUFF PASTE		
Apple Turnovers		
Apple Strips		
Cream Horns		
Napoleons		
Puff Pockets		
Brownies		
DOUGHNUTS		
Maple Bars		
Chocolate Bars		
Persians		
Custard		
Jelly		
French		
Twist		
Raised Chocolate		
Raised Glazed		
Raised Sugar		
Old Fashioned Plain		
Old Fashioned Glazed		
Cake, Plain		
Cake, Chocolate		
Cake Toasted Coconut		
Cake Plain Coconut		
Cake Cinnamon		
Cake Crumb		
Cake White Iced		

Fig. 3–8. Bakery wholesale order sheet lists items most frequently ordered in quantity from bakery if no baking done by caterer.

CODE NO.

Name

GOLD CROWN	TRI		Cater-Spec.	Gold Crown
TRIANGLES		P-Nut-Jel.		X
CATER'S SPEC.	X	HAM		
POOR BOY	X	Hm. & Ch.		
BAR-B-Q BEEF FRENCH	X	CND. BF.		
STEAKS		SALAMI & CHEESE		
D. D. CHILI	X	BF. & CH.		
MUSTARD DOG	X	BEEF		
WIENER GRANDE		SW. CH.		
D. D. CH. & ON.		BOLO		
D. D. MUSTARD		L. M. & CHEESE		
CHILI DOG		SALAMI		
HAM FR.		AM. CH.		
BAR-B-Q HM. FR.	X	CHICKEN SALAD		
HAM & CH. FR.		HAM SALAD		
BEEF & CH. FR.		EGG		
MEAT LOAF FR.		TUNA		
ITALIAN		CHEESE SPREAD		X
BEEF FR.				
PASTRAMI FR.				
FRENCH BURGER				
BEEF & ONION				
BEEF BUN				
BAR-B-Q HAM BUN				
BAR-B-Q BEEF BUN				
HAM & CHEESE BUN				
HAM BUN				

CLUBHOUSE	
BR. VEAL CUTLET	
T.K. PASTRAMI	
T.K. BEEF & CH.	
T.K. BEEF	
T.K. HAM	
T.K. HAM & CH.	BEEF
KNOCKWURST	POT.
JUMBO-COMBO	BEAN
BIG BOY	CHEESE
GRINDER	EGG
PENN. SAUSAGE	RED
STEAK MARIO	PORK
VEAL MARIO	CHICKEN
KNOCKWURST MAR.	PIC.
SHEEPHERDER ST.	WIENER
TOTAL SAND.	
BURRITTO	
PIES B	APPLE
FRIED	PIN. AP.
TAMALES	COC.
CHICKEN PIES	PEACH
BEEF PIES	APRICOT
CHEF SALAD	CHERRY
PIN. & COT. CH.	BERRY
JELLO	RAISIN
POTATO	MINCE
MAC.	LEMON
PUDDING	BLUE BERR. FRENCH APPLE
	CHOC.
	TOTAL

Fig. 3–9. Sandwich or "kitchen" order sheet. This is a daily order sheet from commissary to kitchen.

3–3 SANITATION

A strict sanitation program is necessary to protect food against contamination, to ensure the wholesomeness of food, and to meet customers' expectations of quality. All food operators have the normal responsibility of preventing any possibility of food poisoning or even minor illness, which can occur when high sanitation standards are not maintained.

All employees, in any part of the food industry, must be made aware of the importance of obeying the rules for good sanitation. Whether they are full-time, part-time, or temporary, *all* workers should wear clean outer clothing. When working around food, the outer garments should be easily launderable uniforms and aprons.

All food service workers should wash their hands *thoroughly,* both before starting work and as often as necessary during working hours. No employee should ever resume work after visiting the toilet room without first washing his hands. Smoking should never be permitted in any area where food is being prepared. *No Smoking* signs should be prominently displayed.

A. Toilet Facilities

Adequate, conveniently located toilet facilities, lockers, and dressing rooms should be provided. All toilet facilities, including bowls, basins, fixtures, and waste receptacles, should be kept clean. Doors to all toilets should be self-closing. Lavatories should be equipped with sinks having hot and cold running water, hand soap or detergent, clean cloth or disposable paper towels, and toilet tissue.

When proper facilities are available, it is easy for the staff to maintain a high standard of personal cleanliness and to minimize the possibility of food contamination.

B. Kitchens, Commissaries, and Storerooms

All floor surfaces in kitchens, commissaries, and storerooms should be of smooth, nonabsorbent, easily cleanable material. All walls and ceilings should be kept in good repair, be painted a light color, and have washable surfaces up to the highest point possibly reached by splash or spray. Local ordinances in some areas permit only white paint in kitchens or in places where food is prepared. The light color is an aid in the even distribution of light and facilitates thorough cleaning.

It is assumed that all public kitchens (club, meeting hall, etc.) used by caterers will have been inspected and will have met with local board of health standards. Responsibility for these kitchens belongs with the club management.

Kitchen garbage and rubbish containing food waste materials should be kept in leak-proof, nonabsorbent containers with tight-fitting lids. Methods of storage of garbage prior to disposal should be checked with local authorities. All garbage should be disposed of frequently enough to prevent accumulation.

All garbage containers, whether metal or plastic, must be thoroughly cleaned after being emptied and before being reused. Food waste grinders or disposal units should be of the type that comply with all applicable state and local plumbing and sanitation laws, ordinances, and regulations.

In kitchens where there is a commercial dishwashing machine, the dishwashing area should never be used for food preparation. In a small kitchen, there is a temptation to set up cold preplated food, salads or desserts, on the drainboard area. This practice should be avoided.

Once a meal is in progress, the dishwasher should be at his station. If there is no "silverware sink" at one end of the dishwashing area, then a large pot or busbox, half full of hot water with soap or detergent, should be placed at the edge of the dishwashing area. This should be used for dirty silverware only.

As the waiters bring in used plates, they or the dishwasher should separate the silverware and drop it into the busbox. All dirty dishes should be placed on the board, with glasses in a separate area. The dishes should be scraped, rinsed, and stacked according to the method required by the dishwashing machine. The dishwasher should start to work immediately and not wait until the end of the meal. Whether the dishes are done by machine or by hand, the general procedure is as follows:

1. Separate the dishes, silverware, and glasses.
2. Scrape, rinse, and stack the dishes in washer racks.
3. Wash and rinse the dishes. Let drain.
4. Sanitize or sterilize them according to the type of washer used.
5. When all the dishes are done, do the silverware.
6. Repeat step 4 for silverware.
7. Wash the glasses.
8. Repeat step 4 for glasses.
9. Replace all used equipment in the proper racks, cabinets, and drawers.
10. Clean the balance of the kitchen. Sweep the floor.
11. Remove the garbage.
12. Make sure the kitchen is clean and ready for the next day's work.

C. Mobile Units

It is not sufficient that sanitation standards apply to the food, the methods of preparation, and the personnel involved. They should also apply to the source of the food and to the methods of transportation.

Special attention should be given to mobile unit trucks. In order for these units to conform to local sanitary requirements, it is sometimes necessary for them to operate out of an approved depot or commissary. These locations have proper facilities for disposal of waste material as well as equipment for washing and sanitizing the equipment and utensils used on the truck.

Board of health rulings concerning mobile unit trucks and their drivers differ widely from one area to another. In some cities, the board of health requires that the mobile unit truck be inspected, just like a restaurant, and issued a permit to operate. Depending upon the local regulations, a driver may or may not have to pass certain board of health standards before he is permitted to operate a food truck. When in doubt, check with the local board of health.

D. Transporting Food

Transportation of food, even for short distances, also requires special care. All food should be transported either in heated or refrigerated covered containers (see Fig. 3–10), or, as in the case of canned goods, in the original container from the processing plant.

Rules for the Road was compiled by *Vend* Magazine and is reprinted below by permission of the magazine. However, since it concerns the transportation of food, it is listed here as an additional reminder to all food operators that they are working with highly perishable items. The health and safety of the customer rests with the food operator.

Rules for the Road

- Keep perishable foods hot or cold while in transit to locations—45°F for cold holding, 140°F for hot holding.
- Do not attempt to transport perishables without provisions for holding the legal temperature levels until the last stop.
- In scheduling route deliveries, food comes first. Nonperishable stops are last.
- Do not expect winter weather to substitute for refrigeration.
- Make monthly checks on the temperature of food when it reaches the location. Use a thermometer to check temperatures.
- Prechill perishable ingredients, including bread, while making sandwiches in the commissary. Return perishables to refrigeration after packaging.
- Assemble foods in boxes for route delivery in the walk-in cooler as near delivery time as possible.
- Do not leave perishables out at room temperature on a location while servicing other machines. Use supplementary refrigeration if there is a time lag between delivery and stocking.
- Take extra precautions in hot weather. Use two trucks instead of one to ensure safe, prompt delivery.
- Clean interiors and exteriors of food carriers frequently with soap and hot water or chlorinated detergents.
- When a container leaks and spills over onto other products in a carrier, do not take a chance. Instruct route personnel to go back to the commissary for a fresh supply of products.
- Do not pack sandwiches and other foods tightly in a carrier or box. Cool air should be allowed to circulate around the products.
- When buying foods from an outside caterer, check with the local board of health for an appraisal.
- Make a personal, unannounced visit to the supplier's commissary when foods are being assembled. Look for sanitary surroundings, well-groomed and careful employees.
- Schedule food sanitation training sessions for route and commissary personnel, once a month.

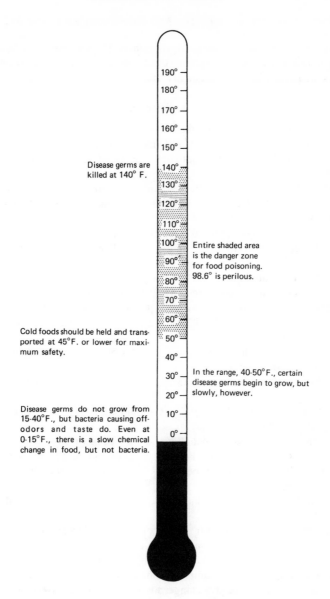

Fig. 3–10. Thermometer used in caterer's kitchen. (By permission of *Vend* Magazine.)

3–4 ACCIDENT PREVENTION

Just as an efficient sanitation program is good business, so is an effective accident prevention program. Common sense and strict attention to the job at hand will keep accidents to a minimum.

A. Kitchen

While there are many danger areas in a kitchen, too many warning or caution signs tend to confuse and distract the workers. One basic check list can be used instead. It would include all of the following, where applicable:

1. Smoking is not permitted at any time in any area where food is being prepared. A lit cigarette left carelessly on the edge of a work table represents a great hazard.

2. A fully stocked first-aid kit should be easily accessible.

3. All cuts and burns, no matter how slight, should receive first aid immediately.

4. All sharp implements—knives, cleavers, skewers, etc.—must be kept in one specially designated area. They should never be left lying around on work tables or dropped into a sink full of soapy water and left for someone to wash. They should be washed and returned to their proper place as soon as they are not in use.

5. Pot holders should be used at all times when handling anything from the ovens or ranges.

6. Floors should be kept clean and dry, and all spills mopped up immediately.

7. Boxes, cartons, and containers should be kept off the floor and out of the path of traffic.

8. All drawers and cabinet doors should be kept closed.

9. Glass items should be kept to a minimum in the kitchen. Broken glass should be swept up immediately with a broom and dustpan (never picked up by hand).

10. Dollies or hand trucks should be used for loading and moving heavy items.

11. All workers must wear proper clothing, including uniforms, aprons, work shoes, and hats (or hair nets, for women).

12. All work areas should be well lighted and well ventilated.

In addition, dangerous equipment should be used with care. The electric slicer should be considered a dangerous tool and must always be switched off when not in use. Inexperienced help should not be allowed to use the slicer. Great care should be exercised in cleaning the machine. Since the slicer blade is extremely sharp, serious accidents may occur even when the machine is not operating; it should therefore be covered when not in use.

The food grinder is also a dangerous machine when not used properly. Use only the wooden pusher to push food through the machine. The same rules apply to the grinder as to the slicer: it should be used by experienced personnel only and must be switched off and covered when not in use.

B. Dining Room

The basic rules to be followed are as follows:

1. Use proper doors for entrance and exit to and from the dining room.
2. Leave sufficient space between tables for waiters to walk with loaded trays.
3. Beware of chairs left out in the aisle.
4. Do not overload trays with food or dirty dishes.
5. Carry glasses on a cork-lined tray. If these special trays are not available, place a clean cloth or small towel on the tray before loading it with glasses. This will prevent slipping.
6. All spills should be mopped up immediately.
7. Proper work shoes should be worn.
8. Smoking should not permitted at any time while working in the kitchen or dining room.

Specific cautionary instructions should be issued to each staff member to cover each specific serving situation. All serving personnel should use care, caution, and common sense to keep accidents to a minimum.

C. On the Road

For accident prevention on the road, pay attention to the following:

1. Drive with utmost care and caution.
2. Park the truck so that customers will no be endangered by passing traffic or by hazards on the roadway (puddles, holes, high curbs, etc.).
3. Do not leave bottles or cans in the parking area.
4. Allow sufficient time to get from one stop to the next, so that speeding will not be necessary.

CHAPTER 4

Staff

4-1 BASIC STAFF REQUIREMENTS

In any catering service, the number of people and the capacity in which they will work in depend on the size of the facility and the type of service being offered.

A. Banquet Hall

In a banquet hall the staff would consist of the chef, the cook, an assistant cook, the pantry or salad man, the kitchen man, the waiter (waitress), the busboy, bartender, a banquet manager, an office staff, and a maintenance crew.

The banquet manager or the caterer in a small operation would be responsible for booking the jobs, following up on all leads, working out the menu with the client, writing the contract, securing the deposit, and arranging all details of the affairs—linen, staff, etc.

The office staff does the paper work as required by the operation. A bookkeeper or accountant keeps the books in order

The size of the maintenance crew will vary depending upon the requirements of the banquet hall.

B. Off Premises

In addition to the staff listed above, the off-premise caterer must have drivers for the cars and trucks that will transport the food. Often a staff member or the caterer himself may drive, but it is necessary to schedule the drivers for each job. If the driver is not to work on the specific job, then he must know the time for his return and pickup.

Often, when catering at a club or a civic center, for example, the caterer will use the club's own janitorial service and utility men. These men know how to operate the dishwasher and know where clean equipment and dishes should be put. The janitorial staff should then be paid by the caterer for doing the dishes. As a public relations gesture, he might also offer them dinner, if the committee in charge of the dinner is not doing so.

When the caterer specializes in "delivery only," then he will need full-time drivers and delivery men as required by the size of his operation.

Responsibility for truck and car maintenance belongs to the caterer. However, any dependable driver will alert the car owner when service and minor repairs are needed to prevent major repairs later on.

In most cases when given adequate notice and instructions, the service staff should be able to get to the location by themselves. If there is a particularly large staff, or if the location is difficult to find, arrangements for transportation might be made. The staff could meet at the commissary and then travel in the caterer's car, or merely follow his car to the location.

C. Mobile Unit

The fleet operator who supplies all food and nonfood items must know basic and quantity cooking, with particular stress on salads and sandwich making. Since he will be directly involved in the operation of many trucks, he should know something about automotive maintenance. He might have trained mechanics on his staff or he might find it more economical and more practical to make definite service arrangements with the agency from which he buys his trucks. This arrangement should cover all maintenance as well as periodic car checkups.

The mobile unit driver must be punctual, able to do rapid over-the-counter selling, and able to make change quickly. He should like to be outdoors and to work independently of others. Above all, he must have an excellent driving record.

4-2 STAFFING A DINNER

Once the menu and type of service is decided upon, then the staff required and the responsibilities of each staff member can be determined.

Table 4–1 can be used as a guide for the staff needed under normal conditions to serve the number of guests indicated at each of the different types of affairs. The given number of persons should be sufficient to set up the room, to serve, and clear tables within a reasonable amount of time.

This chart does not include the staff needed to cook the meal in advance, or, in the case of the off-premise caterer, the staff needed to transport food to the location.

A. Responsibilities of Staff Members

Caterer: This is his business, so he will want to oversee the entire affair. He is responsible to the host to perform all that was agreed upon in the contract. He is responsible for the actions of his staff, whether they are full-time, part-time, or temporary help. In assigning responsibilities, he

TABLE 4-1. NUMBER OF SERVICE STAFF PERSONNEL NEEDED UNDER NORMAL CONDITIONS

No. of Guests	Staff	Cocktail Reception	Breakfast	Wedding Breakfast	Family Style Dinner	Ladies Lunch	Buffet Served Dinner	American or Banquet Dinner	Formal French Dinner
25	Cook	1*	1	1	1	1	1	1	1 Chef
	Waiter	1	1	1	1	2	2–3	2	3
	Bartender	1		1			1	1	1
	Busboy	1	1	1	1	1	1	1	1
	Dishwasher		1	1	1	1	1	1	
50	Cook	1	1	1	1	1	1	1	1 Chef 1 Cook
	Waiter	2	2	2	2	4	3–4	4	6
	Bartender	1		1			1	1	2
	Busboy	1	2	2	2	2	2	2	1
	Dishwasher	1	1	1	1	1	1	1	
100	Cook	1	1	1	1	1	2	2	2
	Assistant Cook		1	1	1	1			
	Waiter	3	4	4	3	8	6	6	
	Bartender	2		2			2	2	
	Busboy	3	3	3	3	4	4	4	
	Dishwasher	1	2	2	1	1	1	1	
500	Cook	1+1*	2	2	2	2	3	3	
	Assistant Cook	1+1*	1	1	1	1	2	2	
	Waiter	10	10	10	10	25–30	20–24	20–24	
	Bartender	5–6		5–6		5–6	8–10	8–10	
	Busboy	5	5	10	10	10	10	10	
	Dishwasher	2–3	2–3	2–3	2	2–3	2–3		

* For cocktail parties, a garde-mangé or salad man may be used instead of the cook. Busboys will pick up glasses and return them to the bar as needed.

should be sure that the persons taking on the various jobs know what is expected of them.

Chef and First Cook: The chef (chief cook) may actually do the cooking in a small organization, or supervise the entire kitchen operation in a larger organization. He should have complete knowledge of menu planning, food purchasing and preparation, and methods of service and storage. He (or she) might be called upon to answer questions by the host regarding specific foods and methods of service. Today's chefs have formal training in schools of cooking and at various colleges throughout the country and the world. (See Appendix B.) The cook prepares the food called for on the menu and serves the food onto platters or serving trays.

Assistant Cook(s): The assistant cook assists the cook and chef in food preparation and serving. He may be a student apprentice.

Caterer's Assistant: One of the regular waiters or waitresses can be the caterer's assistant. When there is a buffet, he is the general supervisor. He is responsible for arranging and setting up the buffet table. This includes the linen, decorations, and placement of centerpieces. When the meal is in progress, he checks to see that food trays are replenished as needed. He will alert the staff to keep the table neat and attractive at all times. This person might also instruct other staff members in methods of serving and general procedures of operation. When there is a served meal, the caterer's assistant will generally act in a supervisory capacity, arranging the setting up of the room, etc.

Waiters (Waitresses): Their responsibility is to serve the meal properly. They must know the different methods of serving. When they serve from a buffet, they should remove empty trays to the kitchen for refilling. They set the tables, serve seated guests as required by the menu, and clear the tables at the end of the meal.

Bartender: His job is to serve liquor, wine, or champagne as the menu requires. He should know all popular mixed drinks, the proper amounts to pour, and which glasses to use. Setting up the portable bar and cleaning up his work area may also be part of his duties.

Busboys: Busboys are usually youngsters learning to be waiters or studying various other phases of the catering or restaurant industry. They may pass rolls and pour coffee at a served meal, but may not serve food to the guests. They can assist at the buffet table by bringing out refilled trays as needed. They should help set up the room in advance and clear the tables when the meal is over.

Pantry or Salad Man: The pantry or salad man prepares the cold salads, appetizers, and hors d'oeuvres. He might also make the coffee and prepare other nonalcoholic beverages.

Kitchen Man: The kitchen man washes dishes. However, he might also help dish up food from the serving counter and help move food and equipment to and from the storeroom.

Dishwashers: Not only do the dishwashers wash dishes brought in by the waiters and busboys, but they also place all used equipment in its proper place. No equipment that has been used for cooking or serving should be left unwashed at the end of a meal. The dishwashing area should be completely cleaned up when all other work is finished.

Conversation between staff members and guests should be discouraged, since it can slow the service. If a guest has a question, he should be referred to the caterer or to the caterer's assistant. Staff members should be polite at all times, but should concentrate on the work at hand. Long conversations with guests or with other members of the staff should be avoided.

4–3   UNIFORMS

A. Banquet Hall

Attractive uniforms always make a good impression. Even for the starting caterer, who must depend on part-time and temporary waiters and waitresses, it is imporant that his staff be in uniform.

Chef, cooks, and kitchen men should wear whites (Fig. 4–1). In many kitchens, grey denim work trousers are also acceptable, but white shirts, cooks coats, and aprons are necessary. All uniforms should be spotlessly clean. Hats should be worn by all kitchen employees. If the meal is to be cooked off premises, an extra set of clean whites should be supplied to the kitchen staff. Once the meal is cooked, the staff should change into them before starting to serve.

Fig. 4–1. Chef's coat and hat. (Courtesy of Shane Uniform Co.)

Linen rental houses stock all necessary whites and aprons. Renting these items is not expensive, and guarantees the cleanliness and uniform appearance of the staff.

Busboys should wear white jackets [Fig. 4–2(A)]. Solid colored jackets are also available, but usually not used, unless the organization is quite large and has a permanent staff. All part-time help will have their own uniforms, although large organizations may supply them to guarantee uniform-ity on the floor.

Waiters jackets [Figs. 4–2(B) and (C)] are available in both traditional and contemporary models, in various colors. Often waiters jackets and vests are matched to the waitress uniforms.

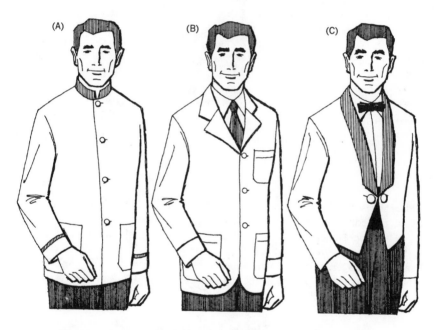

Fig. 4–2. (A) Busboy's jacket. Traditional white military collar coat. Trim can be in colors to match waitresses' uniforms. (B) Traditional waiter's jacket. Available in white or solid colors. (Courtesy of Shane Uniform Co.) (C) Traditional Eton jacket with collar. White with gold lapels or various other color choices. (Courtesy of Angelica Uniform Co.)

The traditional waitress uniform is a black dress with white tea apron (Fig. 4–3). Collars, cuffs, and head bands are optional. Even when all the tea aprons are not the same, as with part-time help, the uniformity of the black dress and the general style of the tea apron make all the variations perfectly acceptable. For informal service, or when the members of the organization will be serving, as at charity affairs, simple black skirts and

Fig. 4–3. Traditional black uniform for waitress with white apron, collar, and head band. Available in various colors. (Courtesy of Angelica Uniform Co.)

white shirts are appropriate. String bow ties or small silk kerchiefs tied under the collars add a touch of color.

The importance of a properly uniformed staff should not be over-looked. Guests at a catered affair may not see or talk with the caterer or banquet manager, but they will see members of the staff. It is vital to the growth of the business that the impression made by the staff is good. Proper uniforms will help.

B. Mobile Unit Drivers

The drivers for a fleet operator usually wear the uniform provided by the company. If no uniform is provided, the fleet operator might require white shirts, work trousers, and jackets or sweaters, depending on the weather. The independent driver should be aware of his physical appearance as a selling point and wear clean work clothes.

Women drivers usually wear slacks which fit well without being too tight. A white blouse or tailored shirt and a comfortable sweater or jacket completes the uniform. Good taste should dictate the amount and type of perfume and makeup to be worn by the woman driver. As with all food service operators, only a minimum of jewelry should be worn.

4–4 ADDITIONAL STAFF

A. Taking Tickets

The method of handling the door will vary with each affair. The caterer is advised to leave this to the committee planning the dinner.

The most common and widely accepted methods of "handling the door" for paid affairs, as opposed to invited affairs, are as follows:

1. *Pre-paid reservations only:* A list of the paid-up members is at the place card table. Committee members will staff the table, check guests as they come in, distribute place cards, and direct guests to their tables.

2. *Reservations but pay at the door:* The list of reservations is at the place card table. The committee handles the door as above, in addition to taking the money and making change as needed.

3. *Pay at door—no reservations necessary:* This method can be disastrous for the organization as well as for the caterer, if the planning committee does not have a good idea of how many guests to expect. Committee members handle the door as above.

B. Check Room

This room should be close to the reception room, in the outside hallway or lobby. It might be serviced by the caterer's staff or by the organization staff. Arrangements should be made for this service prior to the date of the affair.

C. Police and Detective Protection

If the host or the committee in charge at a private affair feels extra protection is necessary, special officers can be engaged through most local police departments.

For civic affairs or community activities, the local police department will be most cooperative. Private protection agencies can also be used.

A uniformed man at the door will discourage unwelcome visitors. All functions that are open to the general public should have some sort of special police protection.

D. Other Staff

For arrangements that the caterer should make with musicians, photographers, etc., see Sec. 10–3.

CHAPTER 5

How to Start a Catering Business

5-1 TRAINING AND BACKGROUND

This section applies to banquet hall and off-premise operations only, as no special training or background in food preparation is required for the mobile unit caterer.

Any previous food service training offers a background for the catering business. The ideal approach is through formal training at one of the recognized schools teaching cooking and food services. Local chamber of commerce and board of education offices can supply a list of all such courses being offered in their cities. (See Appendix B.) After school, work with a recognized caterer, restaurant, or other food service operation is recommended. Practical experience in quantity cooking cannot be gained at home, but must be done in the field.

Most of the schools that teach cooking and related subjects have employment services for their graduates. Caterers will often call on these schools for additional and part-time help. These part-time jobs offer an excellent opportunity for the student to gain practical experience.

Cooking as a hobby, combined with a study of interesting dishes, menus, and methods of serving, is also a good background. The hobbyist who volunteers his services for club and informal functions finds that there are more and more demands for his services. This is the "accidental" method of going into business. Many retired couples who enjoy cooking find that they are in the catering business after doing a series of hobby and volunteer meals for local club meetings.

The ability to cook well can be learned through practice and study. Proper training in the rules of food preparation, combined with the use of modern tested quantity recipes, guarantees consistently excellent food and it is in this that the good cook takes pride.

5–2 SETTING UP A CATERING BUSINESS

A. Banquet Hall

Unless there is a sizable amount of ready cash on hand to build, rent, or lease a facility, and equip it fully, it is best to start by working for an established caterer or in a large hotel with catering facilities. As experience and background increase, many other possibilities will present themselves:

1. When a new hotel is being planned or an old hotel is expanding, there is the possibility of offering a new catering service if none exists there, or of working with the new increased service.

2. Many older and smaller hotels with good kitchen facilities have not yet moved toward full-time catering services. Often this is due to a lack of trained capable catering personnel. There is a good possibility for an ambitious starting caterer.

3. Local clubs (golf clubs, yacht clubs, country clubs) as well as public and private meeting halls that have kitchens but no permanent kitchen staff offer very good possibilities. It is best to cater one or two affairs at the club in question to become familiar with the facilities and to let the management see what services you can offer. Discuss with the management the possibility of taking charge of the kitchen and offering a complete catering service with the aim of bringing more outside affairs into the club.

4. Start as an off-premise caterer, and when the volume of business warrants it, expand to banquet hall operations.

B. Off Premises

For the starting off-premise caterer, a small store can be turned into an attractive, efficient kitchen, with space left for an office.

Wherever food is to be prepared for sale, it is necessary to check with the local board of health and the local licensing bureau. Specify that no food will be consumed on the premises, since that would make the operation a restaurant or banquet hall, which it is not. Once the store is located, verify that:

1. the area is zoned for the type of operation desired;
2. proper licenses are available and that the building will pass board of health requirements;
3. gas and electricity lines are available for the projected use;
4. a water heater with temperature controls is available;
5. the room will accommodate stoves, refrigerator, freezer, slicer, and grinder;
6. space and plumbing exist for two sinks—one large enough to be used as a pot sink;
7. facilities exist for washrooms and toilets;
8. the door to the loading or parking area is wide enough to admit caterer's portable equipment.

All the equipment listed in Fig. 3–2 is not necessary on the opening day, but the range, refrigerator, freezer, and slicer are practically essential. The grinder and mixer may be home models. Used with care, these should do until the volume of business warrants buying the larger commercial machines. The type of transportation (car, station wagon, etc.) needed will be determined by the type of service offered. The type of containers used for transporting food will vary as well. Some catering services will need insulated food carries while others will use only cardboard boxes and cartons. (See Chap. 2.)

The takeout and delivery only are physically the easiest of all the catering services. These are ideal for the beginner, since the staff can be kept to a minimum. However, extensive advertising is necessary to make the company known.

There are many large catering organizations that specialize in this type of service. They offer a variety of freshly prepared foods, including trays of canapés and hors d'oeuvres, as well as various meats and salads. They offer no other service, and no additional service staff such as waiters, bartenders, etc.

The menus might be somewhat limited, but the caterer must decide what the best selling items are in his particular area and for the clientele being served. Changes should not be made often, but do consider all suggestions made by the customers. If it is found that an item is not moving, it is dropped and something else is substituted.

All food is delivered in plastic bags, cardboard boxes, or aluminum foil pans, or on heavy, disposable, foil-covered cardboard trays. There is no return or pickup of equipment, since all packaging is done in single-service disposable units.

C. Mobile Unit

One of the great attractions for the beginner is his ability to start with a very small outlay of cash. If there is an opening, he can start as a driver for an established concern and work toward the lease and purchase of his own truck. He can continue to expand his service as far as his ability and initiative will carry him.

No specific training or background is required. General business knowledge, financial responsibility, and some experience in retail sales are helpful. The ability to keep accurate though simple records is also helpful. The beginner should be an excellent driver. He should like to work with people and do over-the-counter selling. He should be able to make change very quickly. He should also be aggressive enough to increase sales whenever possible.

Age is no barrier. Many personnel and plant managers prefer the more mature driver who will transact his business quickly, efficiently, and pleasantly. He should leave the premises where he makes his stops promptly, not detaining the workers any longer than the recognized break or meal period. Many women are very successful independent operators.

This is not difficult work, but it is physically demanding. A good driver may cover upwards of 60 miles a day on a very tight time schedule. Some routes cover long distances out into the suburbs, while others chalk up their mileage by operating within a small area.

This type of work allows for considerable independence and a better-than-average potential income. Outsiders are not aware of this fact, although all fleet owners are. Therefore they choose their drivers with great care.

The methods of actually starting depend on the arrangements that can be made with the fleet owner. These include:

1. *Driving a truck for an established catering concern:* The driver for an established concern is on a salary, with bonus or commission based on volume of sales. The fleet owner is responsible for all licensing, maintenance, and supplying of food, as well as establishing the routes and time schedules.

The employer will verify any credit and personal references, with particular attention to the applicant's driving record.

2. *Truck lease with no option to purchase:* This driver leases the equipment on a regular basis and purchases supplies as needed. He may purchase his supplies and food elsewhere, but in most cases it is wiser to do it from the same concern from which he has leased the truck. The driver can follow the fleet operator's route suggestions, find his own stops, or combine the two. He can increase his income more rapidly than the regular driver, without the problems of the independent driver or the fleet owner.

3. *Truck lease with option to purchase:* Since mobile unit equipment is expensive, an excellent method of starting is the pay-as-you-go plan. The driver leasing a truck and paying for it while working toward building independent routes and schedules. When leasing with an option to purchase, it is good business to continue to buy food and supplies from the original fleet owner.

When leasing equipment, the terms of the lease should be clearly understood by both parties. The exact cost and method of payment should should be written out in order to prevent misunderstanding. The responsibility for maintenance of the truck during the time of the lease should be clearly established. Continued availability of food and staple items should be guaranteed to the driver.

As his service increases, the independent driver might establish his own commissary, purchasing staples, paper goods, and other items, in quantity from wholesalers. He might continue to order fresh food items from the fleet operator's kitchen. Expansion and extension of services can ultimately lead to the independent driver's becoming a fleet operator himself.

When an independent driver begins in this business, he should check with the local licensing board to determine the type of license he will need. Some cities differentiate between "catering" and "peddling."

The independent operator will look for customers in the same general area as the fleet owner and in that respect becomes a competitor. The independent operator cannot do large-volume business, and he should seek out the smaller companies or less crowded locations. If a small company should expand its operations, then the independent driver should be able to increase his services to meet the increased demand for food. Many independent drivers who have reached the maximum capacity that they can handle by themselves are content to continue on the same level. However, the independent driver who wishes to increase his business is always looking for newer and larger areas to service.

City maps put out by the Chamber of Commerce show all streets and roads, with notations about those under improvement as well as proposed new highways and freeways. A drive along any of these construction areas will show where the work crews congregate and where the operations office will be located. Food service for these locations is not always arranged for out of the main office. In many instances, no food arrangements at all are made, because these are not permanent locations. Sometimes locations change as frequently as every three months, and sometimes they remain in the same place for as long as two years. These are excellent route stops. Road work crews start very early in the day and sometimes work very late at night. Consequently, their mealtimes do not coincide with the regular mealtimes that would be scheduled at production plants and offices. The ambitious independent driver can almost double his daily sales and income by going after these out-of-the-way stops.

Other possibilities for the independent driver are

1. train stations,
2. bus terminals,
3. office buildings (for early-morning, midday, or midafternoon coffee breaks),
4. loading areas of dock and freight yards,
5. small airports, landing strips, and heliports.

Many of these can be covered on a regular schedule. The daily newspapers carry a list of incoming and outgoing ships. At such times dock workers can make good use of the mobile unit caterer.

New production plant openings which are usually listed in the local papers, are another possibility for the independent driver as well as public events such as band concerts, parades, and regattas which are open to the general public. Many city-operated parks and recreation areas do not allow mobile unit caterers into the parks because the city operates the snack facilities. However, for big public events, the existing facilities are generally not adequate, and public pressure may force the city management to relax that prohibition. In cities which do not have this prohibition, the area is open to any mobile unit caterer.

Midget racing is a new, rapidly growing sport attracting fairly large crowds. These tracks are open on weekends during the summer months, with big final race days at the end of the summer season. A drive around the outlying areas of any town will show the tracks, and often the name and address of the local sponsoring organizations.

Plain and FANCY Caterers

Route # _____ Driver _____

Area _____

(See individual customer sheets attached for additional information on each stop.)

Stop #.	Arr.	Lve.	Company	Address	Remarks

Time spans the Arr. and Lve. columns.

Fig. 5–1. Office record of route stops. Office record forms will differ with each operation, but Route Stop Sheet should have at least all above information.

To map a route for a new driver, on a sheet of blank paper, draw the lines for only major streets and crossings. Where long distances are to be driven on the same street, freeway, or thruway, indicate only the distances. Print major street names and any special points to be noted. Indicate the order of the stops and the time the driver is due to arrive at and leave each route stop. As the driver becomes familiar with the route, such a map is no longer needed, even when a new stop is added. The fleet office will keep an accurate record of each route and all the stops. Any changes should also be noted (Fig. 5–1).

It is advisable that the new driver, accompanied by an experienced driver, make a few practice runs under normal traffic conditions as well as in bad weather. He must maintain a rigid schedule to cover his route completely. Once he has learned his route and the routine of selling, he will not need anyone to accompany him.

CHAPTER 6

Selling the Service

The caterer must understand what is desired by the client or what is needed in the community and be able to fill that need. In order to do this the caterer must have a complete knowledge of every phase of his catering service: cost, work, equipment, and staff involved in the preparation and serving of any menu that he offers. He should be prepared to answer all questions relating to his service as well as many concerning various fringe services. His advice will be sought by clients as to the proper type of service and menu for different occasions. (See Sec. 8–2.)

The caterer's staff represents the company. When on the job, they should refer all questions to the person in charge of the particular affair. The staff should be trained to sell the service by being efficient, gracious, and courteous at all times.

6–1 ADVERTISING

A. Banquet Hall

Since the customer must come to the banquet hall, various forms of advertising are necessary to bring the service to his attention.

Newspaper Advertising: In catering, as in all businesses, newspaper advertising should give just enough information to whet the customer's interest and make him want to know more. It should aim to convince him that this caterer can give him exactly the service he wants (Fig. 6–1).

Leads: An excellent method of finding the potential customer is through the help of related or "fringe" services. These fringe services should be familiar with the caterer's work and should be able to lead prospective customers to him. Some of the fringe services are

1. bridal shop, since these might be the first stop for the prospective bride,
2. photographers,
3. florists,
4. bake shops,
5. society columns and women's pages in the local papers.

Need a Room For a Party?

Beautiful Ballrooms
of Various Sizes
Available for Rent for
Your Next Social Function
Accommodating 25 to 300

Plain and FANCY Caterers

123 MAIN ST.

PHONE NO.   NAME

Fig. 6–1. Newspaper advertisement for banquet hall caterer. Small ad might be used at regular intervals to keep caterer's name before public.

Plain and FANCY Caterers

Dear Mr. and Mrs. Long,

May we offer our congratulations on the forthcoming wedding of your daughter Marilyn, and at the same time may we offer our services.

Our Banquet Rooms can accommodate parties of from twenty to 300 for any type of meal or reception that you desire.

We invite your inspection of our premises at your convenience.

Very truly yours

P & F caterers

Fig. 6–2. Personal note offering congratulations sent by banquet hall caterer.

The business of leads is a two-way street, and the caterer should be prepared to suggest various fringe services when asked. Since many committees and private parties will engage the caterer first and then set about to make arrangements for the other services, the caterer should be able to recommend other services with which he is familiar. The caterer should also be prepared to give these leads to various cooperating businesses. This cooperative exchange of leads helps build good business relationships and should preclude the necessity for any "paid-for leads."

Direct Mail: Direct mail is the best method of following through on these leads. A personal note offering congratulations on the forthcoming occasion is a good opener (Fig. 6–2). This note, sent directly to the home of the interested parties, should be followed up with a phone call within a week or ten days. At that time an appointment should be arranged for the earliest possible time that is mutually convenient. This is very personalized service and one on which the caterer can build good will.

B. Off Premises

Direct mail and free samples (Sec. 6–1D) are the best advertising for the off-premise caterer, because they go directly to the potential customer and show his wares. Flyers and throwaways are also good. Letters to personnel managers of large offices in the vicinity might be more effective than throwaways or flyers. Suggested letter and sample throwaway are shown in Figs. 6–3 and 6–4.

Local newspaper ads should indicate clearly that the caterer can cater anywhere (Fig. 6–5). Local radio and television are very expensive. However, a spot announcement just prior to major holidays might bring sufficient business to warrant the expense. The station advertising manager will be in a position to know.

Special advertising might be aimed at medium- and small-sized offices for holiday parties, and at church groups and organizations that meet regularly in public meeting halls. These groups already have the location for an affair and would be apt to use a caterer who could work in their own facility.

Telephone directory listings and space advertising should be considered as part of the regular advertising campaign.

An attractive sign and window decoration will invite passersby to stop in to inquire about your service.

C. Mobile Unit

The fleet owner or his sales representative must make the initial contacts for all stops and work out the details with the parties concerned. For regularly scheduled stops, the sales representative will seek out industrial plants, factories, and suburban office buildings. Large construction companies often arrange for stops at construction sites; however, individual drivers may service these and make the necessary route changes to accommodate the work crews as they move to new locations.

Plain and FANCY Caterers

Mr. R. L. Remington, Personnel Manager
Production Plant
Broadway
City, State

Dear Mr. Remington,

When office personnel is relieved of other-outside problems —
the efficiency and morale will go up.
May we offer our services in this regard?
Our new complete line of "take-home" prepared foods at reasonable prices will relieve many (we hope a great many) of the
office personnel of the "What Shall I Cook Tonight?" problem.
May we ask that the enclosed card be placed on the employees
bulletin board?
You are cordially invited to visit the commissary and be our
guest for a "take-home" dinner for two.
Thank you for your kind interest.

Very truly yours,

Enc.

Fig. 6–3. Sample of individually written letter for takeout
business. Letter should be addressed directly to some person
in charge, individually typed, and mailed first class to achieve
the individual attention and suggest personalized service
offered.

The fleet owner should not depend on his sales representative exclusively for all new business but should plan an advertising campaign to bring
the service to the attention of the public. The problem here is that the potential customer market is as close as the garage on the corner and as far
as the production plant some 35 miles outside the city limits. Telephone
directories as well as trade and union publications and the business sections
of the local Sunday newspapers, give most desirable coverage. (See Fig.
6–6.) Once an inquiry is received, the sales representative will follow up
immediately.

Throwaways and flyers can be used successfully, but the operator
should be sure that they are not actually thrown away and littering the
parking area of a potential customer. The independent operator should not

---

Plain and FANCY Caterers

123 MAIN STREET • PHONE 000-0000

We Cook To YOUR Order — or Take Home Our Specialty.

ALL FOOD READY TO HEAT AND SERVE.

SPECIAL THIS WEEK

Casserole for Two

Chicken Cacciatore

(8 Luscious pieces of Plump Chicken cooked in Rich Italian Sauce. Side orders of Spaghetti)

Only $0.00

MANY MORE CASSEROLE DISHES TO CHOOSE FROM.

Open daily from 8:00 am – to take orders until 7:00 pm – so you can pick up at your convenience.

CALL 000-0000 ANY TIME OF DAY.

Fig. 6–4. Bulletin board card or throwaway should be commercially printed; can be distributed with outgoing orders and as enclosure with all written estimates. It should be changed and brought up-to-date from time to time.

lose sight of the fact that advertising is essential to the growth of business.

When an operation is small, advertising should be aimed directly at the individual potential customer. With no sales representative, the independent driver must use the personal letter (Fig. 6–7) or phone calls and visits at other than route stop times. This specific advertising can increase the volume of business in keeping with the operator's ability to handle it.

With the strict limit on space, it is difficult for the mobile unit operator to vary the menu as much as other caterers, but a variety of sandwiches will keep regular customers coming back. Good food is its own advertisement, and catering to the particular needs of specific stops—e.g., hearty

Cocktail Party?
Office Party?

Let us plan your Complete Party

Suggested Menu

1. Hot and cold hors d'oeuvres
2. Hot and cold buffet
   • Roast turkey and chicken • Delightful salad trays
   • Decorated cold meat platters • Mountains of rolls
   • Colorful relish trays • Pepper, salt, mustard, mints
3. Coffee, cake, cookies, peanuts
4. Soda, ice, flowers, fruit centerpiece
5. Service, china, glasses, linen, etc.

FREE DELIVERY

For a complete party brochure call

CATERER'S NAME

ADDRESS   PHONE NO.

Fig. 6–5. Newspaper advertisements should stress variety of locations where caterer can work, or can emphasize caterer's specialty such as home weddings or office parties. *Note:* Free gift can be small tray of open-face decorated canapés or box of cookies or candy. It should be something in the food line.

soups and meat dinners for work and road crews, and salads for clerical and office workers—will help increase sales to regular customers. Observing all good business practices, including cleanliness and punctuality, is of prime importance.

Once a contact is established and the route serviced on a regular basis, it might be advantageous to talk with the personnel or plant manager about making additional stops at other locations for the same company or servicing the same area at additional times such as

1. morning coffee, before the plant operations begin,

Industrial Catering
SERVING THE ENTIRE AREA

Let specialists
serve your
factory — office —
plant construction
site, etc.

Our efficient operation saves
valuable plant time...Day or Nite

Fresh food daily delivered in our spotless
stainless steel trucks

Hot and cold sandwiches— coffee—salad—desserts
fountain service—soup—inplant feeding

Latest Modern Equipment • Call for information
000-0000 • If no answer call 000-0000
"We have our own modern commissary"

Fig. 6—6. Picture of mobile unit truck is keynote of most fleet operator's advertising. All advertising should stress mobility of service.

2. mid-morning coffee break,
3. lunch,
4. afternoon coffee break,
5. dinner for late shift or night workers,
6. special stops during rush seasons, inventory taking, or holiday seasons, etc.

Plain and 𝕱𝔄𝔑𝔆𝔜 Caterers

Mr. R. L. Standard, Personnel Manager
Production Company
Main Street, City

Dear Mr. Standard,

The Daily paper yesterday carried an article about the proposed expansion of your Company. Since the new plant will cover
a great area with the dining room facilities only at the north end
of the plant may we offer the services of our Mobile units for
coffee breaks.

The time needed to get from the work area to the dining room
and back might take up much of the break time, and there will
probably be long lines. We can help relieve that situation by bringing the coffee and snack right to the back door of the plant.

We offer a varied menu including hot and cold foods, maintain
a rigid time schedule and police the area assigned to us. There is
no charge to management for our services and we like to consider
our services as morale boosters. We will gladly furnish names of
other companies that we serve.

May we call for an appointment at your convenience to discuss
this matter in further detail.

Very truly yours,

Fig. 6–7. Personal letter (advertising) from independent
driver.

D. Free Samples

There is no better method of advertising than giving free samples.
However, be forewarned that these are expensive and must be consumed
when fresh. The methods of distribution are as follows.

1. *Drop-in customers:* In the kitchen or commissary keep a small tray
of sample items in the front section of the ice box. These can be offered to
customers who come into the store to inquire about the caterer's service.
A pot of coffee can be kept on a small table near the desk.

2. *Business offices:* Check with personnel managers to be sure that this
practice is allowed. Verify the time of your delivery. If possible, make it
just before a coffee break. Avoid delivering during the lunch hour, as many
employees leave their desks at this time.

3. *Luncheon meetings:* Check with the food committee and offer an
item that fits with the rest of the meal. Contribute dessert rather han appetizer. At the end of the meal and before the program begins, the chairman
should announce something to the effect of: "We wish to thank the P and F

Caterers, who have just opened for business at 123 Main Street, for the delicious dessert which they so graciously contributed to our luncheon today."

4. *Favorite civic groups or charities:* Send a party box of cakes and cookies regularly to your favorite charity, local orphanage, or old folks home. Check with the director for the best delivery times.

5. *Carnivals and bazaars:* Often such fund raising affairs will have raffles, auctions, and floor prizes, and this is an excellent place to put some free samples. The caterer presents a card (Fig. 6–8) which invites the winner or highest bidder to come to his store (banquet hall or commissary) to pick up his prize. At that time the caterer can advise the winner of other services offered, but not really push for any additional cash sales. The purchaser has already paid for the food. If he is pleased with the sample, he will be a return customer.

Present this card at the

Plain and FANCY Caterers

123 Main Street

any time between 8:30 am and 5:30 pm within one month of the date of the closing of the LOCAL CHARITY BAZAAR and receive FREE OF ANY CHARGES

Your choice of

1 tray of 100 Assorted Hot Hors d'Oeuvres
(ready to heat and serve)

OR

1 tray of 100 Open Face Decorated Canapés

VALUE $12.50

Please allow 48 hours after placing order before calling for pick-up. Call XXX-XXXX at your convenience.

This card contributed by the

to the Local Charity Bazaar May 5 —10 19XX

_____   _____
Winner's Signature   Caterer's Signature

Fig. 6–8. Unlike bulletin board card, this contribution or charity card can be individually typed with exact information. These cards should be numbered, signed by caterer, and a careful record kept of each card given away.

Be sure that you sign and date every card. Keep a record of how many cards are distributed and to which organizations. When the customer signs a card for merchandise received, it is your record to be kept for tax purposes. A tax deduction is allowed on all such contributions to charity affairs; otherwise, they can be charged against advertising expenses.

A charity bazaar, or similar affair, is not always a money-maker for the caterer. This is because part of the food preparation is usually done by a bazaar committee. Such an event can, however, be an excellent showcase for future business, as organizations that sponsor bazaars also sponsor other affairs. Many of these functions will require the services of the professional caterer.

6–2 PUBLIC RELATIONS

In all dealings with the public, the caterer should keep in mind that catering is a service business. If the customer is not satisfied with the service, he has only to look around to find another company whose services will please him. With the increased competition for catered jobs, the customer can expect more and better service.

This is not to say that the customer is never wrong. Sometimes he is, but whether he will admit his error or not does not matter. Do not dwell on any customer's mistake. Try to correct what is wrong as quickly and efficiently as possible and go on to something else. Do not embarrass the customer unnecessarily.

Where food and services are concerned, some people are never satisfied, regardless of how fine the service is. When the customer makes impossible demands, it is wiser for the caterer to refuse the job than to take on more than he can handle. One job badly done will be remembered long after a dozen or more excellent jobs are forgotten.

A. Customer Loss

Prices: Higher prices may be due to wasteful purchasing, careless food production, or using excessive "on the job" staffs. Prices which are too low might indicate buying inferior food items or being short of help on the job (*Possible solutions:* Check all food orders for quality and quantity. Watch actual preparation and eliminate any "deadwood" from the staff. Hire some young ambitious help.)

Monotonous Menus: Lack of imagination in menu planning may become a problem. Except in the very large cities where the entire business may run very well on drop-in inquiries, most catering companies build on repeat business and recommendations. The same people might be guests at several affairs done by one caterer. If the same thing is served every time, many guests will look elsewhere for their catered affairs. (*Possible solutions:* Keep up to date with trade publications. Read cook books, including quantity cook books. Be alert to clients' suggestions. Suggest different—possibly foreign—foods. Most of all, use your own imagination.)

Poor-Quality Food: There is no excuse for poor-quality food. The cause may be an incompetent staff, purchasing low-grade food, or poor preparation or storage. Improper storage can ruin the best of foods. (*Possible solutions:* Follow through on actual ordering, storage, and food preparation. Always buy the best quality possible. Cheap food is no bargain.)

Faulty and Incompetent Service: The regulars on the staff might be getting careless and the newcomers might not know what they are expected to do. (*Possible solutions:* Set up a brief training program. Check to be sure that each staff member knows exactly what his responsibility is. Take time to teach newcomers. Impress upon all members of the staff that good public relations is sometimes more important than good family relations.)

Unsanitary Conditions: As with poor-quality food, there is no excuse for unsanitary conditions. The reason may be lack of proper working space, lack of time, or inadequate facilities for cleanup. (*Possible solutions:* Allocate time for cleanup. Impress upon the entire staff the importance of sanitary working conditions. No caterer can afford the possibility of food poisoning. Have soaps, detergents, clean rags, and all other items necessary for making cleanliness in the kitchen easy.) (See Sec. 3–3.)

Poor Room Arrangement: While the host or committee in charge will have final say, if the room is poorly arranged it will hamper the service and interfere with the guests' enjoyment of the evening. Unfortunately, the caterer will be blamed. (*Possible solution:* Work out a few good table arrangements for the room to be used. Try to convince the host or committee to use one of them.)

Promotional Activities: Promotional activities linked to an advertising campaign will bring the service to the attention of the public. Lack of time for such outside activities is no excuse. (*Possible solutions:* Pick a local civic group you support. Work with the group whenever possible. Food can always be donated or contributed to the worthy cause, with the attendant publicity.)

Lateness: When a route stop is for a coffee break with a 10–20 minute limit, the driver cannot afford to be five minutes late. Once the route stop is established, it is vital that the driver be on time. (*Possible solutions:* The driver should be aware of alternate routes in case of accidents, tie-ups, or heavy traffic which might result in delay. He should know how long it takes to service each stop. Customers should be allowed to serve themselves immediately and then move away from the truck. Drivers should avoid lengthy conversations with customers as this tends to hold up the line. Long waiting discourages sales.)

B. Protocol

The caterer should be familiar with the proper etiquette and protocol for any affair he caters. Parties concerned with the ceremony will not always know proper procedures. When a question arises, the caterer might be called upon for the correct answer. The most common questions asked concern the wedding reception line.

Wedding Reception Line: The line usually starts at the door, in this order:

1. mother of the bride (first to greet the guests),
2. father of the groom,
3. mother of the groom,
4. father of the bride,
5. bride (on the groom's right),
6. groom,
7. maid (or matron) of honor,
8. ushers,
9. bridesmaids (stand in front of ushers).

Other arrangements might be used as required. If the groom is in military uniform, the bride stands on his left. If the arrangement of the room makes it necessary for the bride to stand on the groom's left (whether in uniform or not), the reception line should be directed in such way that it passes the bride before the groom. Various other conditions may require the father of the bride to step out of the line. For any arrangement other than the usual, see Appendix D.

The caterer should discuss the receiving line with all parties concerned before the day of the affair. At the affair, all parties should be able to take their places as quickly as possible, so that the guests may be greeted without unnecessary waiting.

Seating Arrangements for Honored Guests: Honored guests should be seated so they can be seen by all other guests in the room. When a head table is used, guests should be placed on one side of the table only. No one at the head table should ever be seated with his back to the room.

Other Receiving Lines: Whether or not to use this line is up to the host of the committee in charge of arrangements. If used, it should be kept short, and the order is usually the following:

1. announcer (just inside the door or space designated),
2. hostess for the day,
3. guest of honor,
4. host for the day,
5. second guest of honor,
6. committee chairman.

Other Ceremonies: For all other ceremonies, the caterer will be guided by a committee in charge of ceremonies. Most organizations have such committees or historians who are well versed in the proper procedures for their particular group. They will advise as to welcoming committee lineups (receiving lines), seating arrangements, etc. It is important for the caterer to work very closely with these committees in order to know exactly how much time will be needed for any ceremony planned for the evening. Speeches of welcome to the guests, Grace, presentation of officers, etc., all take time. A wise caterer will take this into consideration when planning the time for serving scheduled meals.

CHAPTER 7

Business Practices

7-1 INSURANCE AND LICENSING

All legal information should be obtained from a lawyer. National laws and rules concerning insurance, workmen's compensation, and liability are interpreted in Washington by trained government lawyers. Local laws and regulations can be defined and explained by local lawyers or personnel in the local offices.

It is of the utmost importance that a competent lawyer check the local and national laws under which you will be working.

A. Insurance

Banquet Hall: The banquet hall will require the following types of insurance.

1. *General business insurance* against fire, theft, etc., is necessary here, as in any business.

2. *Workmen's compensation* as required by the state is needed to cover all employees whether full or part-time.

3. *Accident and liability* covers accidents to guests while on the premises.

4. *Products insurance* covers against anyone becoming ill as a result of eating poor or contaminated food.

Insurance for Off-Premise Caterer: The off-premise caterer would also need a *floater policy* insuring the equipment that goes from job to job. This type of insurance covers all the equipment (enumerated in the policy) that the caterer takes with him on any job. The floater policy does not cover the equipment except when it is being used on job location.

Equipment rental houses carry insurance to cover all equipment while on their own premises, but there is no "third party" insurance to cover rented equipment in the client's home or on his premises. Once the rented equipment is delivered, it is the client's responsibility to see that the equipment is not damaged or destroyed. Rented equipment that is damaged or destroyed at the home of the client must be paid for by the client. The client may, if he feels it necessary, obtain special coverage for the rented equipment while it is on his premises. This is quite expensive and rarely done.

Mobile Unit: The mobile unit kitchen and commissary will have to be covered in much the same manner as any caterer's premises. However, the floater policies are not necessary.

The trucks, whether part of a fleet or independently owned and operated, should have the following coverage:

1. commercial truck accident insurance,
2. liability to cover accidents that occur to persons near the truck while being served,
3. products insurance, which should be carried by the producer of the food as well as the seller, since both parties are responsible.

Weather and Rain Insurance: Insurance against rain for a specified date and time of day can be obtained, provided that the rain will cause a definite financial loss to the parties covered. A college may insure the date of an outdoor concert or a sports event to which tickets are sold, if rain at the time of the event would mean a financial loss to the parties concerned. The exact time of the rain and the amount must be specified and verified by the weather bureau.

A caterer wishing to insure a day against rain would likewise have to prove the possibility of financial loss, rather than the inconvenience to guests, if rain forced a scheduled garden party or wedding to move indoors.

In theory, anything can be insured. There must be proof, however, of possible financial loss against which the insurance is to be written, before any responsible company will consider it.

B. Licensing

Every locality has its own licensing requirements. A partial list follows of catering activities that might require licensing. The abbreviations refer to banquet hall (BH), off premises (OP), and mobile unit (MU).

1. License to do business: BH, OP, MU, local—city or county.
2. Board of health permit for kitchen and commissary: BH, OP, MU.
3. Preparation of food for public sale to be consumed on the premises: BH, board of health—local.
4. Preparation of food for public sale not to be consumed on the premises: OP, MU, board of health—local.
5. Board of health permit for MU truck (see Sec. 3–3).
6. Liquor license for liquor to be consumed on premises: BH—state.
7. Caterer's liquor license, issued only in connection with a regular liquor license—state.
8. Driver's license: OP, MU—state.

Since taxes are collectable on some food items, it is necessary to check with the local tax bureau or state board of equalization. Board of health and sanitation rules vary widely from area to area. The local board of health will cooperate supplying information.

Do not try to guess the law; it can be very costly. Check with the department or the office of the board concerned. There is never any charge for information from any city, state, or national service bureau.

7–2 BOOKKEEPING

A. Keeping Records

In the matter of keeping the books, it is wise to have professional help from the start even if it is a small catering business. A simple day-by-day record of expenditures and sales kept by the caterer can then be given to an accountant for a monthly entry, payment of bills, statements, and any additional paper work required.

B. Job Envelope

Most caterers use the *job envelope* filing system, which is simple, effective, and efficient. Copies of all job estimates, menus, bills, and correspondence should be carefully kept.

When an inquiry comes in, a 5 × 8-in. file card is filled out. The job envelope, which is a 9 × 12-in. manila envelope or file folder, is not filled out until the job is booked. When the job is booked, then the card, known as a follow-up card, can be placed in the envelope or in a file for possible future jobs.

All papers, menus, contracts, notes, and correspondence, as well as bills specifically charged to this affair go into this envelope. After the affair, the original contract signed by the host is removed and placed in a permanent office record book. If a duplicate of the contract is used, then the signed original is placed in the contract book immediately upon its receipt.

The following information should appear on the follow-up card, as well as on the job envelope:

Host's name _____ Date _____ Place _____

Address _____ Phone _____

Occasion _____ Approx. no. of guests _____

Deposit received (date) _____ Acknowledged (date) _____

Remarks _____

The off-premise caterer would indicate the place, such as host's home or yacht club. The banquet hall caterer would indicate which room was to be used.

The job envelopes are kept in an active file according to date. After the job is completed, the caterer might wish to make a few notations concerning the affair. His comments and remarks would be for his own reference for future jobs. This folder is then placed in the completed job file and kept for tax and other references.

C. Establishing Credit

Supplying good credit references is the quickest way to get additional credit, whether for food or other items. However, the person starting in business for the first time may not have any previous business credit references. Although bank references are acceptable, some companies might want other commercial references. Credit may be established in various ways. First, all equipment can be bought on time. Promptness in meeting installment payments will aid in establishing a good credit rating.

Paying bills promptly also helps to establish credit. The starting caterer should take the time to talk with credit managers of various companies with which he will be doing business. Various terms and methods of billing and payment can be discussed.

Many small businessmen make the mistake of assuming that cash payments for all deliveries will establish credit over a period of time. This is not so. Although purchasing for cash has the advantages of eliminating follow-up bookkeeping and offering occasional quantity price savings, it has the disadvantage of leading to a sloppy or inaccurate bookkeeping system. Cash purchasing should generally be done only when necessary, and a very careful record should be kept.

The same good business practices that apply to any other business apply to catering as well.

D. Deposit

Advance Deposit for the Catered Job: Take-home orders by phone or delivery only orders usually do not require a deposit, since the amount involved is generally small. However, when a contract is written, and where the total cost is apt to be substantial, a deposit should be paid by the host. This guarantees the date for the host and binds the caterer to perform as stated in the contract. The deposit may vary from one-fourth to one-third of the estimated total. The amount of the deposit should be clearly marked on all copies of the contract and deducted from the total amount when the final bill is presented. All deposits should be acknowledged in writing.

Loss of Deposit: If the customer cancels an affair, the caterer should ascertain the reason before deciding whether or not to return the deposit. If the cancellation is due to conditions beyond the control of the customer, such as death in the family, a severe illness of a major participant (bride or groom), or necessity of departure of a major participant on government orders, the caterer must accept these as legitimate reasons.

In the case of a death in the family, most caterers will return the deposit in full. In the two other cases, each caterer works differently; some return the deposit, some return part, and some wait to see if the room can be rented for the cancelled date before they think of returning the original deposit. In all cases, an earnest effort is made to rerent the room for the date in question.

The following are considered insufficient reasons for returning a deposit:

1. The couple broke up.
2. The club decided not to hold the annual dinner.
3. The committee did not have sufficient support from the general membership.
4. The customer has certain personal reasons for cancelling the affair.

The fact that the bride and groom decided not to follow through on their marriage plans should not entail any loss for the caterer.

The other reasons usually do not stand up under close scrutiny. Often, the expression "personal reasons" is an excuse used when a host or committee has placed deposits on every room in town. They assume that all deposits should be refunded cheerfully, regardless of the inconvenience they may have caused.

When a committee finds the membership lax in supporting a proposed function, their first thought might be to retrieve the deposit. The caterer has two alternatives. He may offer to return the deposit only if he can rerent the facilities for the day in question. This sometimes causes the membership to get to work to make the proposed affair a success, rather than lose whatever money was initially put down. If the lack of support is the result of some unfortunate event within the organization, the caterer might then return the deposit as a public relations gesture, hoping the organization will come back when planning their next function.

Policies concerning the return of deposits should be flexible enough to allow the caterer to use his own judgment. Each request for the return of a deposit must be handled individually and always tactfully, even though the customer appears to be completely wrong.

Balance Due: The balance is due at the end of the affair. Some of the large catering halls and hotel catering services are affiliated with the credit card companies, and billing is handled in the manner established by those companies. Whether the credit card is used or not, a bill should be presented at the end of the affair.

The simplest method of billing is to use carbon copy of the original order form (Fig. 7–1). On delivery only orders, where the order is a set package, only one notation, as follows, is necessary:

Selection of a buffet for 20—$00.00. Delivery date_____.

The tape from the cash register can be used for any take-outs.

When a contract is drawn up and the entire menu and all services are enumerated, then a separate bill should be presented. The regular business letterhead or a printed bill form can be used. The bill should be made up in duplicate or triplicate, depending on the bookkeeping method used. The third copy of the bill might go into the job envelope, the second copy to the bookkeeper, and the original be presented to the host for payment

Plain and FANCY Caterers

Name _____ Phone # _____

Deliver to (Address) _____

Date of Delivery _____ NOT LATER THAN _____ am _____ pm

Kindly check selection. Where choice is offered, please indicate every item.

: :

Selection A	Selection B	Selection C
International Buffet	Cosmopolitan Buffet	Royal Buffet
++++++++	++++++++++ !	++++++
Continental Canapes	Continental Canapes	Continental Canapes
Assorted Smorgasbord	Assorted Smorgasbord	Assorted Smorgasbord
(Select 4)	Deviled Eggs, Stuffed Celery	Deviled Eggs, Stuffed Celery, Liver Pate with Crackers
—Wild Rice Turkey Rolls	(Select 6)	
—Neopolitan Ravioli	Any from Selection A, or	(Select 8)
—Beef & Sausage in Hot		Any from Selection
Sauce	—Tongue Polonaise	A, B or
—Chicken Chow Mein	—Chicken Cacciatore	
—Viennese Rolled Cabbage	—Veal Scallopini Marsala	—Sugar Cured Ham, sliced
—Roumainian Pastrami,	—Mandarin Egg Roll	—Duckling bits a la
Sliced		Orange
—Spare Ribs – Duck Sauce		—Beef Stroganoff
—Creole Deep Sea Fish		—Southern Fried Chicken
Casserole		—Pepper Steak
—Wheat Pilaf – Mushrooms		

All Buffets include Dinner Rolls, Hawaiian Fruit Tray and Miniature Pastries. This does not include any personnel or service save for the delivery as ordered. Minimum order for 10. Price includes delivery within city limits. Price per guest: Selection A $X.XX Selection B $X.XX   Selection C $X.XX

Kindly send (indicate selection) _____ for _____ number of guests @ $X.XX per
 guest for a total of $ _____

 Misc. Charges or Tax _____

 Deposit _____

 Balance due on delivery _____ . Rec. _____

Customer's
Signature _____

Fig. 7–1. Order form used as bill (off premises).

Plain and ꞩ₳ℕ₵Ɏ Caterers

Date: _____

To:
Dr. & Mrs. R. Dark
129 Hillrise Road
City
Open House Reception – New Year's Day for
   100 guests   @ $5.50 per guest $550.00
                 4% sales tax   22.00
                                     $572.00
         Rental of 100 champagne glasses
            @ $.12 each   12.00
                                       $584.00
         Less deposit rec. 10/1/XX   150.00
              Balance due $434.00
It is a pleasure to serve you.

Fig. 7–2. Bill for off-premise catered affair.

(Fig. 7–2). Upon receipt of payment, the bill should be marked *paid* with the date and initials of the person receiving payment. This signed bill remains in the possession of the host.

E. Work Sheets

Work sheets, such as those illustrated in this section, are used for all phases of the banquet hall or off-premise caterer's job. Some of the forms used are not printed, but simply prepared as needed. Often, a large sheet of paper with the organization name and the date written across the top will be sufficient for lists of staff, equipment to be moved, etc.

The banquet or party prospectus (Fig. 7–3) is used by most banquet hall caterers, while the simpler menu–contract (Fig. 7–4) is used for off-premise catering. Actual practice will determine which form is best for the particular service being offered. The accountant should be able to suggest the best form of bill for the services rendered. For an example of a completed contract, see Fig. 7–5.

Take-out and delivery only business can use one combination menu–order–bill with a carbon copy being kept for office records.

Mobile unit drivers use an order form and load–check-out sheet. This check-out sheet, signed by the driver, becomes the bill for which he is responsible at the end of the day's run.

Work sheets may be distributed according to the following outline.

Plain and FANCY Caterers

BANQUET OR PARTY PROSPECTUS

Nature of Function

Day　　　　　　　　　Date　　　　　　　　　Time

Room　　　　　　　　　　　　　　　　　　　Rent $

Name of Organization

Address　　　　　　　　　　　　　　　　　Phone

Name of Engagor

Address　　　　　　　　　　　　　　　　　Phone

Responsibility of Party　　　　　　　　Credit Approved

Price per Person $　　Number Expected　　Number Prepare For　　Number Guaranteed

EXTRAS: Wines ☐　Liquors ☐　Corkage ☐　Cigars ☐　Cigarettes ☐　Music ☐　Flowers ☐　Decorations ☐

OTHER EXTRAS:

MENU	BUFFET
	WINES
	Cigarettes Cigars Liquors Waters

Copies To:

Notify Dept. Heads

　REMARKS:

Date Taken

By

Approved

Fig. 7-3.　Banquet or party prospectus.

Plain and FANCY Caterers

To: Mr. H. W. Exxxxxx, Chairman
Charity Drive
Civic Center, This City

Dinner for 150 guests at Civic Center as per contract
dated _____ @ $X.xx per guest $XXX.xx
                                    X% sales tax   XX.xx
Additional chgs: None $XXX.xx
                                    Less Deposit   XXX.xx
                                    Balance due $XXX.xx
Paid: _____ Date _____
Received by _____

It is a pleasure to serve you.

Fig. 7–4. Bill for catered dinner. Tax on this type of meal only applies in various parts of country. If this dinner were held in caterer's banquet hall, he would indicate name of room instead of Civic Center, although all other information might remain the same.

1. *Contract–menu or banquet prospectus (four–five copies prepared):*
(a) One copy remains with host or person signing the contract.
(b) Four copies go to the caterer. The original goes in the permanent file.
(c) Two copies remain in the job envelope until time to start work on the job. One copy is then forwarded to the head of any department involved in special arrangements for the affair (bar, wine steward, custodian, etc.)
(d) The final copy remains in the job envelope as a work and reference copy.

2. *Floor plan (two copies prepared) (Fig. 7–6):*
(a) One copy goes to the chairman in charge of room arrangements.
(b) One copy remains in the job envelope until the day of the affair (or time to set up).

3. *Food requirements (one copy prepared):* This list remains in the job envelope until the time to prepare purchase orders.

4. *Purchase orders (three copies prepared):*
(a) One copy stays in the job envelope.
(b) One copy goes to the office for actual ordering.
(c) One copy goes to the storeroom to be used as a check-in slip and is then returned to the office.

5. *Work schedule (two copies) (Fig. 7–7):* Copies are made up about two weeks prior to date of the affair.

Plain and FANCY Caterers

Phone no.   Street
                                         City   State

Organization: Local Charity Drive   *Location* Civic Cntr   *Date* _____
                                         Number
Time: 6:00 - Midnight   *of Guests* _____

Cocktails 6:30, Dinner 7:30

MENU

Assorted hot and cold hors d'oeuvres to be passed for the cocktail hour.

Served Buffet

       Coq au Vin (Chicken in Wine) from chafing dish
         Parisian Potatoes from chafing dish
       Cold sliced meat trays – Corned Beef – Tongue – Ham
       Large Shrimp Salad Bowl garnished
       Tossed Green Salad with Chef's Dressing
       Relish Tray: Carrot Sticks, Celery Fingers, Olives,
         Radish Roses, Pickles
       Fruit Platters (fruit in season) garnished
       Dinner Rolls   Butter
       Individual Fruit Tart with Whipped Cream
        Coffee – Tea

In addition to the above the caterer agrees to supply:

Linen for buffet table   Linen for guest tables
Silver chafing dishes as needed   Silver serving trays as needed
Cocktail napkins
Staff: Waitresses (*), Kitchen staff for cooking and clean-up.
Price: $X.XX per guest (plus X% sales tax)
Committee for Dinner will set up tables and chairs (diagram attached), will
arrange for floral decorations for tables and buffet table, will have complete
charge of bar; set-up, service and clean-up.
(*) Number of waitresses to be determined by final number of guests.
Waitresses will set tables prior to cocktail hour and pass hors d'oeuvres
for cocktail hour.
It is understood that host has made arrangements for use of hall, kitchen,
kitchen facilities. Host to supply liquor and/or champagne.
Glass Rental: .$.12¢ ea. Replacement for guest breakage. Champagne glasses:
$.50¢ ea. Bar glasses: $.10¢ ea.
Extra: Bartenders: $20.00 ea.   Waitresses: $9.00 ea.
Note: Waitresses to be included in price shown above.
DEPOSIT $ _____ (date) _____   _____
Balance due date of affair (shown above)
Minimum guarantee by: _____   _____
    "   " 10 days prior to date of affair.

P & F Caterers

Fig. 7–5.   Completed contract–menu form.

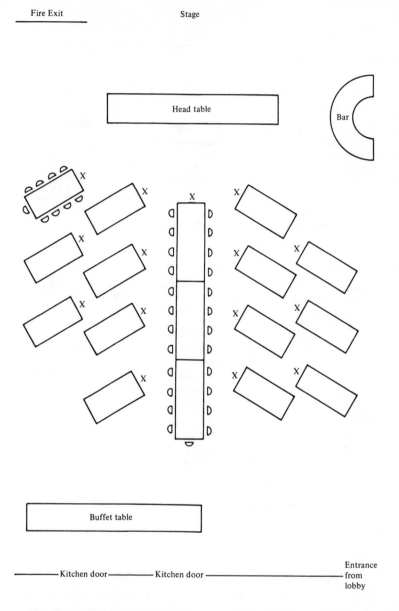

Stage

Head table

Bar

Buffet table

Kitchen door — Kitchen door

Entrance
from
lobby

Fig. 7–6. Caterer's floor plan for charity drive dinner approved by committee. Head table seats 8, 14 tables of 9, and center table seating 25; 159 actual seats.

	Serving	(Location or)
Organization: _____ DATE _____ Time _____ Room _____		

Special Attention: _____

Monday	Tuesday	Wednesday

Order all food
 	
Check food in
  storeroom
 	
Assign staff:
  Waiters
  Waitresses
  Busboys
  Cook & Ass't
  Dishwasher from CC
	Order Flowers
	
	Check all equipment
	  at CC
	
	Order linen
	  for delivery to
	  CC Friday
		Make hors d'oeuvres
		  for freezer
		
		Pack and mark all
		  equipment for CC
		    Service trays
		    Candelabra
		    Special linen
		    Cocktail napkins

Thursday	**Friday**	**Saturday**

Check that all
food is in the house
 	
Check Dinner
Committee about
room: set-up, etc
	Cook corned beef
	Cook tongue
	Cook ham
	Cook shrimp
	
	Make Relishes
	
	Check all food
	preparation
	
	Check room at CC
	
	Check dishes,
	  flatware,
	  glasses,
	  chairs & tables
	
	Linen del.
	
	Deliver equipment
	to CC before 5:30 pm
		Cook chicken
		Slice all cold
		meat
		
		Make shrimp
		salad
		
		Make all other
		salads
		
		CHECK MENU AND
		PACK ALL FOOD
		FOR DELIVERY AT
		CC AT 4:00 pm
		
		Fruit platters
		  to be made at CC

Fig. 7–7. Work schedule or work sheet.

(a) One copy stays in the job envelope.

(b) One copy with a copy of the menu is placed in its proper sequence on the kitchen bulletin board.

6. *Cost sheet (four copies):* The cost sheet should list all costs as they appear on all the work sheets, including

(a) food requirements,

(b) staff,

(c) special equipment (or charges for the use of house equipment),

(d) transportation,

(e) special items and incidental expenses.

7. *Bill (three copies prepared):*

(a) One copy is presented to the host for payment, marked *paid,* and is retained by the host.

(b) One copy marked *paid,* goes with the money to the office.

(c) One copy remains in the job envelope.

The estimated price will be based on previous similar menus, allowing for any changes in food costs. Using the cost estimator, it is possible to estimate accurately the actual cost of each portion of food to be served. All other costs—staff, equipment, overhead, etc.—are already known. These expenses can be added to the estimated cost of the meal. Thus the actual cost of the job can be determined.

These estimates should be made when the menu is first prepared, so that a proper charge can be made for the meal. The precise cost of all services cannot be figured until the job is finished. This total cost should be figured out as soon after the job as possible.

If taxes have been collected, the amount should be noted in the manner established by the accountant. The final estimate as well as the actual cost for the job should be placed in the job envelope for bookkeeping purposes and future reference.

F. Contracts for Mobile Unit

When this industry was new, a simple verbal agreement between a driver and a plant personnel manager was sufficient to guarantee the route stop. However, with the increased number of operators and individual drivers, there is greater competition for each location. Sales representatives as well as plant managers prefer a written agreement signed by both parties. The following items should be specified in the contract:

1. the exact times when the truck will be wanted;

2. the approximate number of people who will be available to make purchases;

3. the exact area where truck or trucks are to park;

4. a suggested menu to be offered with changes made as needed (Fig. 7–8);

5. the amount of time allowed for each stop (truck must leave or close up at the exact time specified);

6. the disposal of waste (all trucks have space for disposal of waste, but but the plant may provide additional refuse cans in the parking lot).

There are no set forms for this type of agreement, but the general information contained therein would be much the same for all locations.

Once the details are worked out and agreed upon, plant or section managers often allow the personnel to line up a few minutes before the truck is due to arrive, so that purchases can be made as quickly as possible.

7–3 MENU

A. Banquet Hall

The banquet hall caterer should be able to offer a wide menu variety (see Chap. 15) and to prepare any foods that the client wants. Foreign foods, which often frighten cooks, are no more difficult to prepare than American dishes. In France, for example, the traditional Thanksgiving dinner as we know it, is considered a delectable foreign meal.

Menus and recipes are available from a large variety of sources. (See Appendix C and Chap. 16.) Any food that is prepared and eaten regularly anywhere in the world can be prepared by the food caterer. His only limitations are the acceptability of the food by the guests, and the ease with which a particular dish can be served. For example, the Greek Islands are famous for their goat's milk cheese, which is eaten with a very dark, coarse bread. However, in preparing a Greek dinner, it would be wise to suggest something else, such as the rice cooked with grape or cabbage leaves. Goat's milk cheese and dark bread, while authentic Greek dishes, would not be generally acceptable and therefore have no place in the caterer's menu file.

A special file of foreign dishes that are acceptable as well as a number of complete foreign menus are great sales boosters, as they offer the host a more interesting selection for his catered dinner. It is up to the individual caterer to decide the type of service and menu that he wishes to offer.

B. Off Premises

The off-premise caterer should have the widest possible selection of menus and menu items to offer, since the menu must be tailored not only to fit the specific desires of the host, but also the facilities at the location.

When the location is the client's home, his individual likes and dislikes are of the utmost importance. Persons with specific food requirements are much stricter about what they eat and serve in their own homes than when they eat in public places. (See Sec. 8–2.) Special attention should be given to serving guests with special food requirements, as requested by the host. While this individualized attention means extra work, it will bring favorable comment and recommendations. Much future business may result from this personalized service.

C. Mobile Unit

The average mobile unit truck will carry approximately 20–25 varieties of food. The choice of items to be carried on each truck will be decided upon ultimately by the customers' preference. The items that sell well will be given prime place and those that do not will be dropped. The time of year, the weather, and the type of clients will help in determining the menu items to be carried.

As *Vend* Magazine puts it: "To be successful, the driver must be thoroughly familiar with the preferences of his clientele. At the end of each day he places his order for his food requirement for the following day. As the wholesale value of his load will run from $350 to $500, he must exercise extreme caution and superior judgment in ordering perishable items. Average markup on food products is 28 to 30 percent. His acumen in this regard helps determine his net income which averages from $135 to $165 weekly."

Hot dishes that can be offered include sandwiches, soups, stews, chile, and spaghetti. In the winter season, more space will be given to these items and less to cold sandwiches.

If the route services office buildings where there are more office workers than laborers, the menu might feature salads and beef pies rather than the more starchy hot dishes.

Pies, cakes, cookies, and approximately 50 other staples such as candy, gum, cigarettes, cigars, bottled and canned soft drinks, coffee, tea, and cocoa are regular items on practically all routes all year round.

7–4 PURCHASE OF FOOD

Purchasing for catering is different from the average restaurant operation in that most caterers (except mobile units) do not have a set menu that repeats day after day and week after week. Since the caterer must make up his orders according to individual menus, he can seldom anticipate future needs.

As in any food operation, the procedures for food purchasing should be guided by need and by the amount of proper storage space available. All food purchasing should be the responsibility of one member of the staff. In a small business, the caterer himself should oversee this most important operation.

When possible, staples should be purchased in quantity to take advantage of quantity prices and stored for future need. However, since the "shelf life" of all staples varies, nothing should be bought that will not be used within the individual shelf life of the item.

All food producers, or their wholesalers, will gladly discuss the shelf life of their products, since it is to their advantage that items be purchased and used when they are at their best. No wholesaler is anxious to have the caterer buy huge quantities of their products, only to have them spoil.

Except for staples such as flour, oil, shortening, or seasonings, many caterers do not order anything else until a job is in the house, i.e., until the menu–contract is signed. This sometimes means last-minute purchasing and in small quantities and is one of the reasons it is important to establish good contacts with various producers and food wholesalers.

Portion-controlled, precut, and frozen meats and fish are more expensive than raw items, but sometimes using them can effect a savings in preparation costs. This is particularly true for the small operator.

Since competition in all phases of the food business is great, any savings that can be effected by careful purchasing should not be overlooked. The food suppliers will gladly discuss actual needs and make suggestions for alternate choices as well as guarantee deliveries at times desired.

All perishables should be purchased for delivery as near to the using or serving time as possible.

7–5 INVENTORY

A running inventory of all supplies is urgent in any well-run business. Periodic checks will help keep shelf losses to a minimum.

Perishable items should be inventoried more frequently than staples. All equipment should be inventoried every time it is moved to a job and replaced on the shelf. Periodic inventories of supplies, staples, paper goods, etc., should be part of the business routine, with reorders placed before existing supplies are exhausted.

Whether banquet hall, off premises, or mobile unit, the storeroom is the heart of the business. It should be clean, sensibly arranged, equipped with open as well as closed shelves, cool, well ventilated, and well lighted. In addition, it should be inventoried regularly and locked when not is use.

All shelves should be metal with movable trays and on legs approximately 6 in. off the floor. Nothing should ever be stored directly on the floor.

Closed cabinets should be used for small items as well as the more expensive specialty items such as spices and seasonings, and wines and liquors used in cooking.

Locked cabinets should also be used to store any items purchased for a specific affair. All such items should be marked with the name and the date of the affair for which they were purchased. This is done simply by pasting a piece of tape over the face of the package with an indication such as "Haverson Wedding 2/26." This will ensure that the item is not used for some other affair. It will further ensure that the item is not overlooked when preparation for that affair is started. When the customer has ordered and paid for a specific item, he as well as the caterer wants to be sure that it is used.

All paper goods should be stored on shelves in a cool dry area. Linen, flatware, and table items used most frequently should be stored in easily accessible closets, shelves, or bins.

Silver trays, chafing dishes, candelabra, and other large buffet table items should be stored in individually designed cloth-lined boxes, labeled with the contents. These boxes should be stacked in such a way that they can be moved out quickly and replaced without having to move other equipment out of the way.

Portable items such as heating units, insulated carrying chests, ice chests, and any other equipment used for off-premise jobs, should also be labeled carefully and placed in easy access to the loading area. All portable equipment should have the caterer's name marked very clearly on one visible and one covered surface.

CHAPTER 8

Arranging the Affair—I

8-1 ESTIMATING COSTS

It is essential to be able to estimate one's costs in order to make proper charges to the customer for food and services.

The price of raw food and the cost of service personnel vary widely from one part of the country to another, and from one time of year to the next. However, a suggested method of pricing can be shown here. Since every catering operation is different, each must establish methods of pricing its services that will allow for a margin of profit and still be competitive and within the acceptable market price.

A suggested percentage breakdown of a catered meal is as follows:

1. Price: $4.50 per guest, based on preparation for 100 guests
2. Food costs: 24.44 percent
3. Preparation and service: 26.66 percent
4. Overhead (includes general operating expenses, rent, advertising, etc.): 20.00 percent
5. Profit: 28.90 percent

These figures are taken from a medium-sized operation. Each individual caterer must make the adjustments to suit his particular type of service.

To estimate the cost of any catered meal it is necessary to have the actual cost of the following:

1. the total amount of raw food to be used;
2. kitchen help for complete preparation and dishing up;
3. equipment to be used (buffet silver, trays, candelabra, etc.);
4. the total service staff (besides kitchen staff), including waiters, busboys, bartenders, special janitorial staff, and, drivers;

5. overhead (gas, electricity, rent, insurance, advertising, and miscellaneous);
6. the anticipated profit.

This total figure then must be divided by the number of guests to be served. This will give the figure to be charged for the menu and services shown.

8–2   HOW TO PREPARE A MENU

There are five key questions that form the basis for the menu preparation for all catered affairs. Even if only partially answered, they will help immeasurably in practical party planning.

A. Occasion

In the first conversation with the client, the reason for the party and the theme, if any, should be established as a guide in selecting menu items. Where a men's fund-raising dinner would call for steak and all the trimmings, a salad plate might be more appropriate for a ladies' luncheon. A housewarming might call for a barbecue, and so on.

B. Number of Guests

Every guest must be served the full meal. There are no exceptions. Therefore, the menu should be one that will have universal acceptance. Food items such as highly spiced vegetables, should be eliminated as the guest list increases. The menu selected should be one that can be served properly to the anticipated number of guests.

C. Location

Facilities at different job locations will vary. A caterer should not accept someone else's word that the kitchen at a certain club is very large, or that the room is more than adequate for the affair under consideration.

People mean well, but the caterer should go see for himself. Once a contract is signed, it is the caterer's responsibility to produce the meal contracted for. It is too late then to discover that the club kitchen has only one home-type stove and oven combination, and the contract calls for *prime ribs of beef au jus* for 150 guests.

A careful check should be made of the kitchen, dining area, as well as the areas for loading and parking, before a contract is signed.

D. Time of Service

In the first conversation with the host it is important to establish the time of the party. (See Sec. 10–1.) The following is a standard listing of times for various occasions:

1. Breakfast: From very early in the morning until about 11:30.
2. Brunch (including wedding breakfasts): 11:30 to 1:00. (Allow slightly later serving times for Sundays.)
3. Lunch: 11:30 to 2:30.
4. Tea (ladies only): 2:00 to 4:30.
5. Cocktails (including all cocktail receptions): From 5:30.
6. Dinner: Any time after 6:30.
7. Midnight supper: Any time after 11:30.

Any good book on etiquette will stress the importance of punctuality, particularly when the food is a "time" item such as *prime ribs of roast beef*. Guests should go in to dinner at the scheduled time to ensure the very best dinner possible, although one of the major problems for the caterer is to convince the client that there is a proper time for serving various types of food. If the time of day indicates a meal, then the guest expects a meal to be served. If only light, snack-type foods are served at a meal hour, the guest may go away hungry and disappointed. The caterer will be the person blamed, even if he served exactly what was ordered. If the host does not wish to serve a meal, the caterer should try to convince him to move the reception to a nonmeal hour. It is the caterer's responsibility, and in his own interest, to be sure that the menu is appropriate to the time of day. The caterer's reputation rides on every job.

E. Food Preferences

Ask the host if he has any specific food preferences or dietary requirements at the start of the menu planning session. Make a note of all specifications.

Special religious and ethnic requirements should be given careful consideration. When a host expresses a preference or a taboo, regardless of how silly or peculiar it may seem it cannot be ignored. If the requirements are such that the caterer cannot fulfull them, then the job should be refused politely but immediately.

The caterer should be familiar with local dietary preferences. If specific information is required for religious food requirements, a visit to the local clergyman for that denomination will supply all the answers. The following is a general breakdown of various food preferences and includes a discussion of certain religious food requirements.

Allergies: Violent illness may result if an allergic person eats even the smallest amount of some specific food. This has nothing to do with the method of preparation or quality of the food. Special care should be taken to eliminate such foods from the menu, in accordance with the host's request. The following sentence might be added to the bottom of the menu–contract to reassure the host: "No (food named) to be used on this menu."

Dietary (Weight Reduction, Diabetic, etc.): This type of food preparation requires special training and is generally not the concern of the general caterer. However, if the caterer can offer tasty and attractive low-calorie dishes for ladies' luncheons, he might find his services in great demand.

Personal Preferences, Peculiarities, and Idiosyncracies: A good host will generally not inflict his personal preferences on his guests. However, the good guest is often aware of his host's preferences and will abide by them. A strict vegetarian believes that it is morally wrong to kill animals and to eat their meat. The caterer in this field can learn to make tasty, attractive dishes and plan whole menus around fruits and vegetables.

Religious: The largest group of commonly known food requirements and restrictions are the religious. These are not difficult to follow, but they are important.

1. *Catholic:* Parties and celebrations are not planned for fast days or days of abstinence.

2. *Church of Jesus Christ of the Latter Day Saints (Mormon):* According to the teachings of the Church, the use of alcoholic liquors, tobacco, coffee, and tea is not permitted.

3. *Episcopal:* There are no dietary laws which are obligatory for all members although many members do not eat meat on Friday.

4. *Jewish*:* The Jewish faith is classified into three major divisions: Orthodox (traditional), Conservative (not as strict in other matters, but with the same food requirements as Orthodox), and Reform (generally no food restrictions.) The dietary rules are not complicated. Briefly, *Kosher* is anything which is fit by Jewish law to be eaten and enjoyed. Only animals that chew their cud and have split hooves are considered edible.

All other animals, including pigs, are prohibited. Also prohibited are animals that have died a natural death or have been killed in any way other than that prescribed by Jewish law.

(a) Fish: Only fish that have both scales and fins are permitted to be eaten. All others, including lobster, oysters, and shrimp are prohibited.

(b) Fowl: All birds are permitted to be eaten except birds of prey.

(c) Mixture of meat and milk products is forbidden by the Bible.

5. *Lutheran:* There are no dietary laws which are obligatory for members of the Lutheran Church.

6. *Methodist:* There are no requirements that prohibit the eating of particular foods.

7. *Society of Friends:* There are no specific rules, but abstinence from tobacco, narcotics, and alcoholic beverages is customary.

8–3   HOW TO ESTIMATE QUANTITIES

All good quantity cook books will indicate the size of the portions, and all packaged food items indicate the total weight of the package. Ultimately, it is for the caterer to determine if the portions indicated are what he

---

* Taken from *Lessons in Jewish Living,* compiled by S. Colodner, Block Publishing Co., New York.

wishes to serve. If not, then he must make the necessary adjustments. The size of the portion should be determined by

1. the occasion,
2. the time of service,
3. the age and sex of guests (young, old, all men, etc.),
4. the appearance of the portion on the plate (or in the package).

For example, very young children eat very little and a small variety of mildly spiced foods. At parties, they eat ice cream, cake, and cookies, and drink milk, punch, and some soft drinks. Teenagers eat more than any other age group. They eat practically anything and everything, and the spicier the better. People from their mid-twenties to mid-fifties have sophisticated tastes. They are apt to eat in moderation and good taste. People past sixty eat much the same as the middle group, except for a lessening of the sharp and spicy foods.

For the mobile unit, the major food processing companies do all the figuring of portion sizes. They supply portion-controlled individually packaged foods. For the sandwiches made by the mobile unit caterer, the above guides can be applied.

Using turkey as the main food item, Table 8–1 suggests the difference in the size of portions for the various groups.

TABLE 8–1. DIFFERENCE IN SIZE OF PORTIONS

Occasion	Time	Item	Portion Size
Children's party	Noon	Turkey plate Dressing	2-oz meat with gravy 2-oz
Sweet 16 dinner–dance	8:00 p.m.	Turkey sandwich supreme*	4-oz meat with wine sauce Two slices bread
Men's club lunch	Noon	Hot turkey sandwich	6-oz meat with gravy Two slices bread
Thanksgiving dinner	7:30 p.m.	Turkey plate Dressing	6-oz meat with gravy 4-oz dressing
Mobile unit	Noon	Turkey salad sandwich*	1½-oz chopped meat with dressing, celery, relish

* See Chap. 16 for recipe.

When hors d'oeuvres are to be served, the following outline suggests a suitable number, all of which are considered generous servings:

1. At a four-hour reception, regardless of the starting time—12 per guest.
2. Cocktail hour, to be followed by dinner—four per guest.
3. Wedding reception, from 2:30 to 5:30—eight per guest.
4. Cocktail reception, from 3:00 to 6:00—eight to ten per guest.
5. For all other occasions, estimate four per guest per hour for the first two hours, and two per hour after that.

These figures include both hot and cold hors d'oeuvres and canapés. They do not include relishes and dips.

For an open house, housewarming, or office party that is scheduled for all day or all afternoon, the number of hors d'oeuvres is based on the length of time the average guest will remain. (Although the party may last for six hours, the average guest may remain only one and a half to two hours.)

A. Self-Service vs. Served

Sometimes when guests serve themselves they tend to be very generous; at other times they may be very timid. For a self-service buffet allow slightly more than if the same buffet is to be served by waiters. Guests do not always take more themselves, but since they do not always know how to serve properly, more food is wasted.

To estimate other quantities, the following items will prove helpful. Fig. 8–1 ilustrates how many cups various can sizes will yield. Table 8–2 estimates the number of servings one can expect from different size frozen vegetable packages. Table 8–3 illustrates the various substitutions that can be made from one size can to another. Table 8–4 illustrates how to estimate the cost per portion when buying meat, poultry, or fish.

8–4   FOOD REQUIREMENTS

Working from the actual menu that will be used, the first list is a comprehensive list of all the food items that will be needed. A notation should be made at the same time concerning ordering. Quantities needed will be determined from the Recipe file before actual orders are placed.

TABLE 8–2. APPROXIMATE NUMBER OF SERVINGS—FROZEN VEGETABLE PACKAGES

Ounces per Serving	Package Size		
	2-lb	2½-lb	3-lb
2	16	20	24
2½	13	16	19
3	10	13	15
3½	9	11	13
4	8	10	12
4½	7	9	10
5	6	8	9

TABLE 8–3. SUBSTITUTING ONE CAN SIZE FOR ANOTHER

1 No. 10 can = 7 No. 1 cans
1 No. 10 can = 5 No. 2 cans
1 No. 10 can = 4 No. 2½ cans
1 No. 10 can = 3 No. 3 cans
1 No. 10 can = 2 No. 5 cans

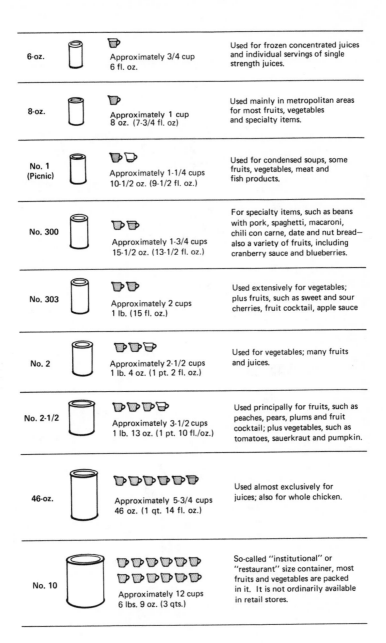

6-oz. — Approximately 3/4 cup 6 fl. oz. — Used for frozen concentrated juices and individual servings of single strength juices.

8-oz. — Approximately 1 cup 8 oz. (7-3/4 fl. oz) — Used mainly in metropolitan areas for most fruits, vegetables and specialty items.

No. 1 (Picnic) — Approximately 1-1/4 cups 10-1/2 oz. (9-1/2 fl. oz.) — Used for condensed soups, some fruits, vegetables, meat and fish products.

No. 300 — Approximately 1-3/4 cups 15-1/2 oz. (13-1/2 fl. oz.) — For specialty items, such as beans with pork, spaghetti, macaroni, chili con carne, date and nut bread— also a variety of fruits, including cranberry sauce and blueberries.

No. 303 — Approximately 2 cups 1 lb. (15 fl. oz.) — Used extensively for vegetables; plus fruits, such as sweet and sour cherries, fruit cocktail, apple sauce

No. 2 — Approximately 2-1/2 cups 1 lb. 4 oz. (1 pt. 2 fl. oz.) — Used for vegetables; many fruits and juices.

No. 2-1/2 — Approximately 3-1/2 cups 1 lb. 13 oz. (1 pt. 10 fl./oz.) — Used principally for fruits, such as peaches, pears, plums and fruit cocktail; plus vegetables, such as tomatoes, sauerkraut and pumpkin.

46-oz. — Approximately 5-3/4 cups 46 oz. (1 qt. 14 fl. oz.) — Used almost exclusively for juices; also for whole chicken.

No. 10 — Approximately 12 cups 6 lbs. 9 oz. (3 qts.) — So-called "institutional" or "restaurant" size container, most fruits and vegetables are packed in it. It is not ordinarily available in retail stores.

Fig. 8–1. A guide to common can sizes. (Courtesy of American Can Co.)

TABLE 8-4. PORTION COST CALCULATOR FOR MEAT, POULTRY, OR FISH

50¢ to $1.25

| Per lb. | 0.50 | 0.55 | 0.60 | 0.65 | 0.70 | 0.75 | 0.80 | 0.85 | 0.90 | 0.95 | 1.00 | 1.05 | 1.10 | 1.15 | 1.20 | 1.25 |
Per oz.	0.031	0.034	0.039	0.041	0.044	0.047	0.05	0.053	0.056	0.059	0.063	0.066	0.069	0.072	0.075	0.078
3 oz	0.09	0.10	0.11	0.12	0.13	0.14	0.15	0.16	0.17	0.18	0.19	0.20	0.21	0.22	0.23	0.23
4 oz	0.12	0.14	0.15	0.16	0.18	0.19	0.20	0.21	0.23	0.24	0.25	0.26	0.28	0.29	0.30	0.31
5 oz	0.16	0.17	0.19	0.20	0.22	0.23	0.25	0.27	0.28	0.30	0.31	0.33	0.34	0.36	0.38	0.39
6 oz	0.19	0.21	0.23	0.24	0.26	0.28	0.30	0.32	0.34	0.36	0.38	0.39	0.41	0.43	0.45	0.47
7 oz	0.22	0.24	0.26	0.28	0.31	0.33	0.35	0.37	0.39	0.42	0.44	0.46	0.48	0.50	0.53	0.55
8 oz	0.25	0.28	0.30	0.32	0.35	0.38	0.40	0.42	0.45	0.48	0.50	0.52	0.55	0.58	0.60	0.63
9 oz	0.28	0.31	0.34	0.37	0.39	0.42	0.45	0.48	0.51	0.53	0.56	0.59	0.62	0.65	0.68	0.70
10 oz	0.31	0.34	0.38	0.41	0.44	0.47	0.50	0.53	0.56	0.59	0.63	0.66	0.69	0.72	0.75	0.78
11 oz	0.34	0.38	0.41	0.45	0.48	0.52	0.55	0.58	0.62	0.65	0.69	0.72	0.76	0.79	0.83	0.86
12 oz	0.37	0.41	0.45	0.49	0.53	0.56	0.60	0.64	0.68	0.71	0.75	0.79	0.83	0.86	0.90	0.94
13 oz	0.41	0.45	0.49	0.53	0.57	0.61	0.65	0.69	0.73	0.77	0.81	0.85	0.89	0.93	0.98	1.02
14 oz	0.44	0.48	0.53	0.57	0.61	0.66	0.70	0.74	0.79	0.83	0.88	0.92	0.96	1.01	1.05	1.09
15 oz	0.47	0.52	0.56	0.61	0.66	0.70	0.75	0.80	0.84	0.89	0.94	0.98	1.03	1.08	1.13	1.17
1 lb	0.50	0.55	0.60	0.65	0.70	0.75	0.80	0.85	0.90	0.95	1.00	1.05	1.10	1.15	1.20	1.25

$1.30 to $2.00

| Per lb. | 1.30 | 1.35 | 1.40 | 1.45 | 1.50 | 1.55 | 1.60 | 1.65 | 1.70 | 1.75 | 1.80 | 1.85 | 1.90 | 1.95 | 2.00 |
Per oz.	0.081	0.084	0.088	0.091	0.094	0.097	0.10	0.103	0.106	0.109	0.113	0.116	0.119	0.122	0.125
3 oz	0.24	0.25	0.26	0.27	0.28	0.29	0.30	0.31	0.32	0.33	0.34	0.35	0.36	0.37	0.38
4 oz	0.33	0.34	0.35	0.36	0.38	0.39	0.40	0.41	0.43	0.44	0.45	0.46	0.48	0.49	0.50
5 oz	0.41	0.42	0.44	0.45	0.47	0.48	0.50	0.52	0.53	0.55	0.56	0.58	0.59	0.61	0.63
6 oz	0.49	0.51	0.53	0.54	0.56	0.58	0.60	0.62	0.64	0.66	0.68	0.69	0.71	0.73	0.75
7 oz	0.57	0.59	0.61	0.63	0.66	0.68	0.70	0.72	0.74	0.77	0.79	0.81	0.83	0.85	0.88
8 oz	0.65	0.68	0.70	0.72	0.75	0.78	0.80	0.82	0.85	0.88	0.90	0.92	0.95	0.98	1.00
9 oz	0.73	0.76	0.79	0.82	0.84	0.87	0.90	0.93	0.96	0.98	1.01	1.04	1.07	1.10	1.13
10 oz	0.81	0.84	0.88	0.91	0.94	0.97	1.00	1.03	1.06	1.09	1.13	1.16	1.19	1.22	1.25
11 oz	0.89	0.93	0.96	1.00	1.03	1.07	1.10	1.13	1.17	1.20	1.24	1.27	1.31	1.34	1.38
12 oz	0.98	1.01	1.05	1.09	1.13	1.16	1.20	1.24	1.28	1.31	1.35	1.39	1.43	1.46	1.50
13 oz	1.06	1.10	1.14	1.18	1.22	1.26	1.30	1.34	1.38	1.42	1.46	1.50	1.54	1.58	1.63
14 oz	1.14	1.18	1.23	1.27	1.31	1.36	1.40	1.44	1.49	1.53	1.58	1.62	1.66	1.71	1.75
15 oz	1.22	1.27	1.31	1.36	1.41	1.45	1.50	1.55	1.59	1.64	1.69	1.73	1.78	1.83	1.88
1 lb	1.30	1.35	1.40	1.45	1.50	1.55	1.60	1.65	1.70	1.75	1.80	1.85	1.90	1.95	2.00

Note: Starting at the price group (top line), find the cost per pound that applies, then read down to the portion size to find the exact portion cost.

Open-face decorated canapés
Assorted hot hors d'oeuvres

Chicken	order Monday for Friday delivery (for chicken preparation)
Celery	for Thursday delivery
Onions	in
Shortening	in
Mushrooms	
Sherry	in
Parsley	for Thursday delivery
Potatoes	in
Ham	for Friday delivery
Tongue	for Friday delivery
Mustard	in
Shrimp	for Thursday delivery
Mayonnaise	in
Carrots	order Monday for Thursday delivery
Radishes	order Monday for Thursday delivery
Olives, ripe and green	in
Pickles	in
Fruit	
Melons	order Monday for Thursday delivery
Grapefruit	order Monday for Thursday delivery
Oranges	order Monday for Thursday delivery
Maraschino cherries	in
Greens: lettuce	for Thursday delivery
Red cabbage	for Thursday delivery
Butter	for Friday delivery
Cream	for Friday delivery
Coffee	in
Tea	in
Sugar	in
Lemons	for Friday delivery
Rolls	for Saturday delivery to CC
Fruit tarts	for Saturday delivery to CC.

When the list is completed, all items marked *in* are in the house and are checked off, then a purchase order is prepared for each of the different categories: meat, produce, dairy, and baked goods. At that time every item needed for this meal should be accounted for, either in the house or on an order sheet. All orders should be placed in sufficient time to guarantee delivery on the date needed. The work schedule for the week preceding the job should be made up ten days to two weeks prior to the job.

CHAPTER 9

Arranging the Affair—II

9-1 ARRANGEMENT OF THE ROOM

A. Who is Responsible

At a banquet hall the caterer is responsible for the arrangement of the room, in accordance with the wishes of the host or committee. In public halls and private clubs, the caterer makes up a floor plan for the approval of the host or committee. The setting up of the room, i.e., the arranging of chairs and tables, should be done by the janitorial staff of the building. The host or committee is responsible for having this completed in time for the caterer to make the necessary place settings, etc., before the serving of the meal.

B. Room Decorations

The committee or the host usually knows what sort of room and table decorations are wanted and what the budget will allow. Except for the suggestion that these decorations should not interfere with the meal service, the caterer should leave the decorations to the person in charge of that activity.

If the banquet hall is attractively arranged, additional decorations may not be necessary. Many large halls do not allow decorations, since the management feels that these detract from the elegance of the room. However, if additional decorations are desired, any of the following may be used.

Buntings: Any form of brightly colored buntings, ribbons, or organizational flags may be draped on the walls and placed around the room. If buntings are to be used, they should be tightly secured to the walls and pillars. They should be put up at least the day before the affair, so as not to interefere with the setting up of tables and chairs on the day of the affair.

Floral Decorations: Large floral pieces set in stands around the room make attractive decorations. However, unless these are secured to the posts against which they stand or set in large solid pots, they represent a hazard and should be avoided. They should always be placed on the platform or out of the general line of traffic.

The American Flag: The American Flag is never used as a bunting or a decoration. It should be placed on its staff in a flag stand behind the main speaker or to the speaker's right, if space permits. It should be in clear view of everyone in the room, particularly if the Pledge of Allegiance is to open the program. The flag is never draped, folded, pleated, or tied.

The Head Table: If the head table is on a platform or a dais, the cloth covering it should reach the floor. This cloth might be covered with an overskirt, floral chains, simple satin ribbon drapes, or decorations in keeping with the rest of the room.

Dais and Speakers Stand: Buntings and wide, colored ribbons, or organizational flags, make appropriate decorations for the speaker's stand. A small low floral piece might be placed on the stand, if this will not distract the attention of the guests.

C. Floor Plans (Arrangement of Tables)

Like the room decorations, table arrangements are usually the decision of a committee. The caterer should work closely with this committee, to be certain that the table arrangement chosen leaves room for the waiters to serve the meal as required by the menu–contract.

A certain amount of table space must be reserved for each guest. The following gives some idea of the space required:

1. *Buffet:* Allow ten feet of buffet table to serve each 60 to 75 guests. A heavy menu, such as a dinner, might require additional table space. For table place settings, allow 18–20 in. between covers. Ten guests can be seated at an 8-ft table; four on each side and one at each end.

2. *Dinner, served:* Allow 20–24 in. per guest.

3. *Formal French service:* Allow 24–30 in. per guest. Additional space is required, because the food is served on trays to the seated guests.

The floor plans in Figs. 9–1 through 9–5 allow adequate space for guests to be seated comfortably, for waiters to pass between the tables, and for waiters' stands. These stands can be set up immediately after the guests are seated.

These floor plans are arranged so that none of the guests are seated with their backs to the head table. These plans can be expanded or reduced, depending on the number of guests and the size and shape of the room.

D. Table Decorations (Theme of the Party)

The type of table decoration and whose responsibility it will be should be decided when the contract is signed. At a private home, the hostess will generally want to do the table decorations herself, whether for a served meal or a buffet. At large civic functions, there will be a committee in charge of decorations. At smaller club functions, there may or many not be such a committee.

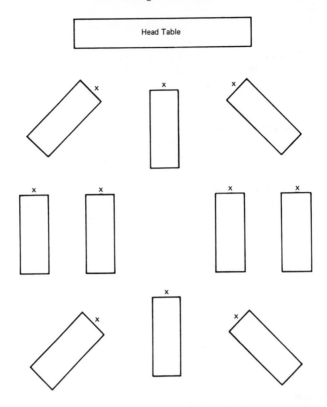

Fig. 9—1. Floor plan to seat 100 guests. No bar and no dancing. 10 tables of 9, plus 12 at head table (102 actual seats).
No seating where marked ✕ so that no guest sits with his back
to head table.

If the caterer is to handle the table decorations, proper charges should
be made to cover time and any additional help needed. Decorations used
should be billed separately from the cost of the meal, to prevent a distorted
picture of the cost of the food itself.

Informal table decorations may be anything which suggests the theme
of the occasion. When in doubt, the "fern-and-flower-line" down the center
of each table is perfectly acceptable.

Fund-raising chairmen are always searching for themes for their annual
or semi-annual affairs. Current events can always suggest new themes. Some
of the perennial themes, if used with imagination, are always good:

1. Trip around the world.
2. Trip around the country.
3. Trip around town. "Before you head for the moon, take a trip around
town!" (Local organizations and merchants can sponsor display tables and
booths. This is an excellent theme for building local interest.)

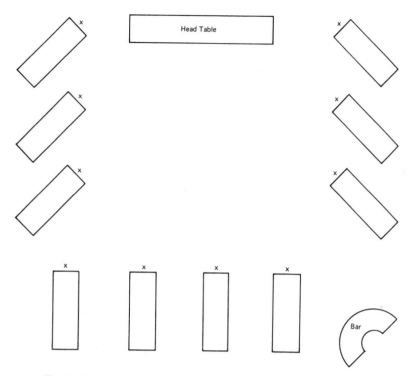

Fig. 9–2. Basic floor plan to seat 100 guests. Bar and room for dancing. 10 tables of 9, plus 12 at head table (102 actual seats). No seating where marked X so that no guest sits with his back to head table.

E. Utility Tables

Utility tables are tables placed around the room for additional service and convenience. They are not used for seating guests.

All utility tables should be covered with a white cloth. Whenever possible, these tables should be placed against a wall and out of the general path of traffic. The size of the room and the method of service will determine what utility tables are needed and where they should be placed.

Guest Register Table: This should be a bridge table covered with a cloth and set close to the entrance door, or fairly close to the reception line. Guest register book and pens should be on the table. A member of the host's family, or of the committee, should be at the table.

Gift Tables: These may be bridge, or larger tables set close to the entry door, possibly opposite the guest register table. Most hostesses prefer that all gifts remain on the table for the full length of the reception, so larger receptions may require additional tables. Gifts placed on this table are left

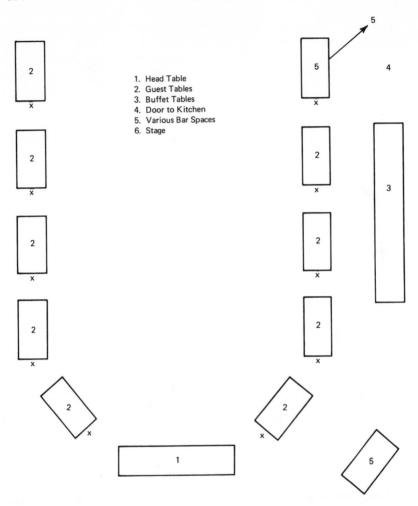

1. Head Table
2. Guest Tables
3. Buffet Tables
4. Door to Kitchen
5. Various Bar Spaces
6. Stage

Fig. 9–3. Horseshoe or U floor plan. Buffet and bar plus room for dancing or fashion show. For served meal, buffet table can be eliminated. Bar can be set up at indicated optional spaces. No place setting where marked ✕.

unopened, unlike the gift table at a bride's home where gifts are opened and displayed prior to the wedding.

Place Card Table: This table is needed only where a meal is to be served to seated guests. It should be placed reasonably close to the entry door. A 36-in. bridge table will hold approximately 300 folded place cards. All cards should be arranged alphabetically. A member of the host's family, or one of the committee members, should be assigned to distribute these cards to the incoming guests. A floor plan of the room should also be on

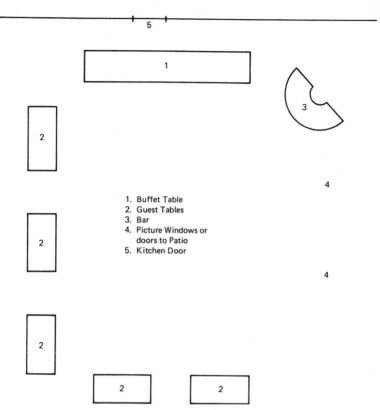

Fig. 9–4. L floor plan for smaller rooms. Buffet and bar in room. Space allowed for dancing.

1. Buffet Table
2. Guest Tables
3. Bar
4. Picture Windows or doors to Patio
5. Kitchen Door

the table for easy location of the numbered tables.

The table place card (Fig. 9–6) should always be a tent with the name of the guest written or printed very clearly. These cards are placed just above the service plate at each place setting and should be on the tables before the guests enter the room. This is the responsibility of the host or the committee in charge.

Service Table: This table is used at cocktail parties, receptions, and buffets where no place settings are made. Eight- or ten-ft tables, covered with white cloths, are placed around the room, to give the guest a convenient place to put down a used plate, cup and saucer, or glass. Waiters should clear these tables as quickly as possible.

Waiter's Stand: This is a light stand used to rest a tray of plates while serving or to place busboxes when clearing tables. These portable stands can be set up between the tables covered by each waiter during the meal. They can also be set against side walls. This may be done before the meal begins or immediately after the guests are seated.

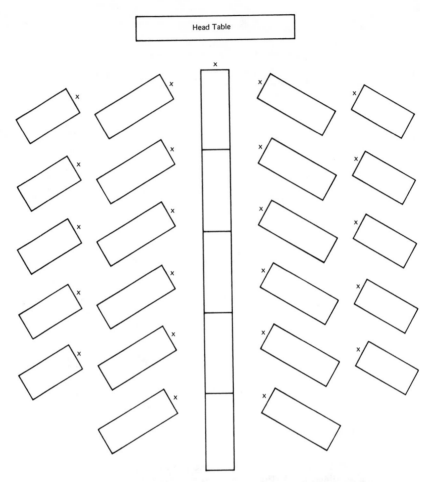

Fig. 9–5. Herringbone floor plan. Excellent for smaller rooms. 296 seats (9 at side tables, 8 at center tables); 232 seats (7 at side tables, 6 at center tables). No setting where marked X so no guest sits with his back to head table.

9–2 METHODS OF TABLE SETTING AND SERVICE

A. American

For American service, the tables will be set (Fig. 9–7) in one of the following ways:

1. with complete place setting required by the menu, plus ice cubes and water in water goblet;
2. same as 1, plus rolls, in baskets, on bread and butter plate, or on folded

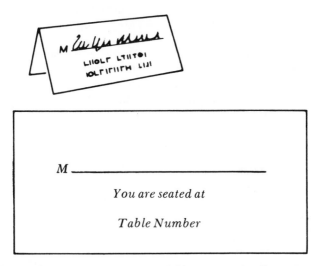

Fig. 9–6. Example of tent table place card. (Courtesy of Gillick Press.)

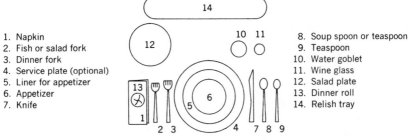

1. Napkin
2. Fish or salad fork
3. Dinner fork
4. Service plate (optional)
5. Liner for appetizer
6. Appetizer
7. Knife

8. Soup spoon or teaspoon
9. Teaspoon
10. Water goblet
11. Wine glass
12. Salad plate
13. Dinner roll
14. Relish tray

Fig. 9–7. Place setting for American, banquet, or regular service.

napkin; butter in iced butter dish or on bread and butter plate; relish trays on table;

3. same as 2, plus appetizer set at each guest place setting;
4. same as 3, plus salad placed next to each guest place setting.

Service plates may or may not be used, depending on the degree of formality and the number of guests.

General Procedure: The guest is seated and eats the appetizer. Tables are cleared of appetizer dishes and flatware. The resulting space before the guest is left empty until the next course is served.

The complete main course is placed on the dinner plate in the kitchen. The filled plate is brought in and placed directly in front of each guest in rapid succession. Waiters may carry a tray of dinner plates and serve an entire table at one time. If the salad is not already on the table, it is served immediately after the main course.

Wine is poured. The bottles are then placed on the table or in a wine cooler next to each table, in accordance with the host's instructions.

When the guest has finished eating the main course, all used plates and flatware are removed. The entire room should be cleared before the next course is served. No trays of food or "seconds" are passed.

B. Buffet

A buffet is any meal served from a large table, where all the food is attractively displayed. The food served should always make up a complete meal.

Since the elements of every catered affair are different, every buffet setup must be individually planned.

The number of guests, the menu, and also the size and shape of the room, will determine the placement of buffet tables. Allow one ten-ft buffet table to serve each 60–75 guests. For a served buffet, allow just enough space behind the tables for serving personnel. For self-service, allow space for guests to walk completely around the table. For very small groups, the table may be set against the wall.

When arranging the buffet tables, allow sufficient space in front of the tables for guests to move freely with plates of food. For more than 50 guests, it is advisable to set up two stations. When long tables are used, waiters should work at opposite sides of the same table, so that guests in the same area will be able to eat at the same time. (See Figs. 9–8 through 9–10.)

A separate table may be used for the occasion cake, additional sweets, and coffee service. Using this "sweet table" facilitates service of coffee and cake without interfering with the service from the main table, particularly if it is a large party. The sweet table may be used with all forms of buffets.

Setting the Buffet Table: Cover the buffet tables with a cloth. Linen or paper may be used. Buffet cloths should reach the floor on all sides of the table that will be seen by the guests. Linen for the sweet table must match or harmonize with that of the main table. Overskirts, leaves, flowers, rib-

---

Fig. 9–8. Front view is most commonly used table arrangement whether oblong, semi-circle, or U-shaped for buffets. All these arrangements have space behind or inside for serving personnel. Guest does not go behind tables. Centerpiece should have a flat back. (A) Front view of oblong buffet table. Guests approach from front. (B) Front view of semi-circle buffet table. It is made up of quarter-rounds. Guests approach from front and sides. (C) U-shaped (or horseshoe) buffet table. Front and side views. It is made up 2 quarter-rounds with 2 regular oblong tables behind it. Guests approach from front and along extended sides.

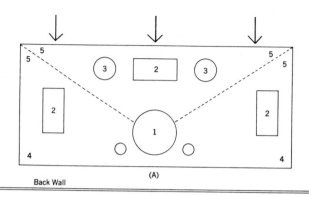

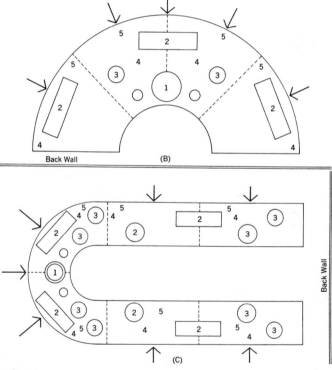

1. Centerpiece.
2. Main food item. For hot food, use chafing dishes.
3. Secondary foods: salads, relishes, bread, butter, etc.
4. Plates. If served buffet, all plates should be at back of table, within easy reach of serving personnel. If self-service, plates should be placed where guests can reach them easily.
5. Flatware and napkins. If guests are seated, then these do not appear on buffet.
   Note: Solid lines indicate individual tables; dotted lines indicate suggested sections. Arrows indicate direction from which guests will approach the table.

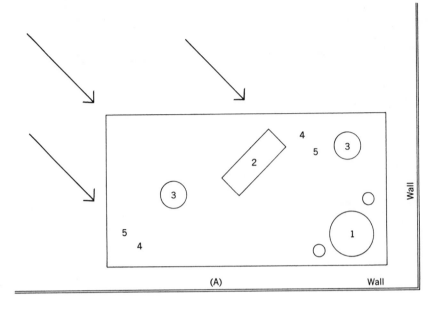

(A)   Wall

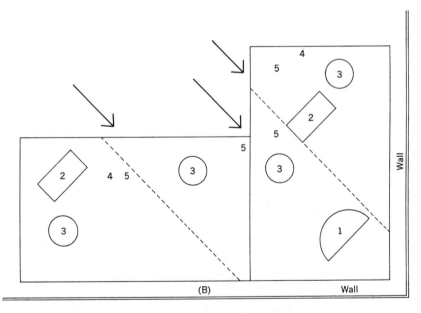

(B)   Wall

1. Centerpiece.
2. Main food item. For hot food, use chafing dishes.
3. Secondary foods: salads, relishes, bread, butter, etc.
4. Plates. If served buffet, all plates should be at back of table, within easy reach of serving personnel. If self-service, plates should be placed where guests can reach them easily.
5. Flatware and napkins. If guests are seated, then these do not appear on buffet.
   Note: Solid lines indicate individual tables; dotted lines indicate suggested sections.
Arrows indicate direction from which guests will approach the table.

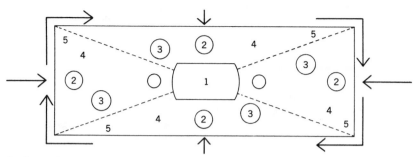

1. Centerpiece.
2. Main food item. For hot food, use chafing dishes.
3. Secondary foods: salads, relishes, bread, butter, etc.
4. Plates. If served buffet, all plates should be at back of table, within easy reach of serving personnel. If self-service, plates should be placed where guests can reach them easily.
5. Flatware and napkins. If guests are seated, then these do not appear on buffet.
   Note: Solid lines indicate individual tables; dotted lines indicate suggested sections. Arrows indicate direction from which guests will approach the table.

Fig. 9–10. Oblong buffet table set in center of room. Guests may approach table from all sides. The center table may be oblong, oval, or round, but it is set in center of room. If service is provided, then serving personnel must stand in front of table. Guests can go completely around table. Centerpiece should be round, as it will be seen from all sides.

bons, or other simple decorations may be pinned to the front and sides of the buffet cloth.

Focal Point: The focal point is that point on the table which is first seen as the guest enters the room. The tallest table item (tiered wedding cake, floral centerpiece, candelabra, melon basket) should be placed there. All the food should be set around this point in interesting and easy-to-get-to arrangements.

The focal point need not be the center of the table. The guest does not always approach the table from the front, and is not always limited to a front view of the table.

A *section* is any area of the buffet table that is complete with an assortment of all the foods being served, plus plates, flatware, napkins, and serving personnel. When a long table is used, whether it is straight or U-shaped, it should be divided into several sections so guests can be served from several lines.

When the trays are placed on the buffet table, the necessary serving

Fig. 9–9. When using a smaller room or in a home where there is no large dining room, tables may be placed close to or against a back or corner wall. If service is provided, then space must be left between table and wall. Guest does not go behind tables. Centerpiece should have flat back. (A) Oblong buffet table set in corner. Guests approach from front and one exposed side. (B) L-shaped buffet table set in corner. Guests approach from front and exposed sides if desired.

pieces—salad forks, spoons, knives, and spreaders—should be directly in front of the trays for which they are intended. If the table is rather crowded, the serving pieces may be placed on the edge of each tray.

Additional serving pieces should be held in reserve, placed conveniently behind the floral arrangement or behind some other trays at the back of the table. Even if the buffet is served, there will always be a few guests who inadvertently pick up serving pieces and walk off with them. If additional serving pieces are on the buffet, it will not be necessary for any of the serving personnel to leave their stations to replace the needed equipment.

General Procedure:

1. *Self-service:* No serving personnel are assigned to this buffet. Usually self-service buffets are limited to a small number of guests, up to 25. All food, precut and sliced as required, should be set out attractively on platters and in bowls for easy service. Serving pieces should be on the table or resting on the sides of the trays. Additional serving pieces should be placed as above.

All extra food should be placed in bowls and on trays. Those should be garnished in the same manner as those on the table. When a tray on the table is emptied, it should be removed and a full tray brought out to replace it.

Coffee, in an easy to use urn, with cups and saucers close by, may be placed on the cake table or at one end of the buffet, if space permits. Dessert should be precut and set on plates.

As there is no control over portion sizes, ten percent more food per guest is needed on a self-service buffet.

2. *Partially served:*

(a) All food and serving pieces should be on the table.

(b) The meat (or the main dish) is served by a sous-chef or waiter.

(c) The sous-chef places a portion of meat on the plate and hands the plate to a second waiter.

(d) The second waiter serves the vegetable or other hot food, and then hands the plate to the guest.

(e) The guest then serves himself the remainder of the food, salads, etc.

(f) Waiters serve cake and coffee to the guests when they are seated.

3. *Served:*

(a) Tables, chairs, and place settings without plates should be provided for the guests to be seated for the meal.

(b) All plates are placed at the back of the buffet table.

(c) The procedure is the same as the partially served buffet except that all food is served onto the guest's plate. (The guest may serve himself, if he so desires.)

(d) If a special cake is part of the menu, it should be cut as desired by the host, then served, with coffee, to the seated guests.

For this type of buffet, it is essential to have sufficient serving personnel.

C. French (Formal) Service

This is the most elegant of the various forms of service and requires the largest number of waiters in relation to the number of guests.

In making place settings, at least 28–30 in. should be left between covers (from the center of one place setting to the next), since the food will be passed and served from trays to the seated guest.

The table is set, but no food is placed on the table before the guest is seated. (See Fig. 9–11.) This table also calls for an attractive centerpiece of floral decoration and candelabra.

All food service is from the left. Beverage service is from the right. Clearing is done from the right.

General Procedure: The complete place setting is made, with an attractive service plate at each setting. This service plate is never used for food. The bread and butter plate with the butter spreader is placed directly above the service plate. The water goblet is filled and the candles are lit immediately before the guests enter and are seated.

After the guests are seated, the appetizer is brought in. Waiters bring in one serving at a time. Immediately following the service of the appetizer, the bread tray or basket is passed to each guest, and the butter rosette

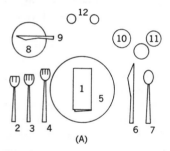 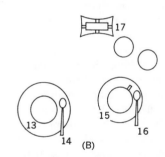

(A)   (B)

1. Napkin
2. Fish or oyster fork
3. Salad fork
4. Meat fork
5. Service plate
6. Dinner knife
7. Soup spoon
8. Bread and butter plate
9. Butter spreader
10. Water tumbler

11. Champagne glass; additional glasses needed if separate wine to be served with each course
12. Individual salt and pepper
13. Dessert plate with dessert
14. Dessert spoon or fork as needed
15. Demi-tasse cup and saucer
16. Spoon
17. Cigarettes in individual ash tray; small packets of matches should also be placed close to the ash trays

Fig. 9–11. (A) French service place setting before guest is seated. (B) French service place setting for dessert course. All used dishes and silverware are removed after main course, including bread and butter plate, and salt and pepper. Ash trays with two cigarettes and matches may be brought in at discretion of hostess. Water glass and champagne glass may also be left if desired. Proper wine glass for dessert course would be left on table. All silverware needed for dessert course is brought in with the course.

is placed on the bread and butter dish. The appetizer, liner, and flatware used for it are removed. The service plate remains in front of each guest.

The soup course is next. (Many hostesses eliminate this course.)

The fish course is served next, on its own plate, set on a liner, and placed on the service plate. Again each guest is served individually, with the waiter carrying one serving at a time.

After the fish plate and used flatware are removed, the empty dinner plate is brought. The waiter removes the service plate and places the dinner plate in front of the guest. A second waiter follows with a tray of sliced meat attractively arranged and decorated with one of the vegetables, usually the potato. He serves each guest in turn or holds the tray down at table level so that each guest may serve himself. A third waiter follows immediately with the second vegetable.

After each waiter serves two or three guests, he should return to the kitchen to replenish his supply in order to ensure that the meat and vegetables will be served hot. At larger parties, the waiter can have enough meat on his tray to serve everyone at a table, possibly six to eight guests. However, he should always make sure that the last serving of food is not cold.

Wine is poured by the waiter. Wine glasses should be refilled if necessary during the main course. Wine bottles are never placed on the table during formal service. They may be placed in a wine bucket in a stand close to each table. If champagne is poured instead of wine, glasses should be refilled as desired by the guests.

A sherbet or, frequently, a salad, follows the main course. If a salad is served, it should have a mild dressing.

The only time there is no plate in front of the guest is from the time the the salad plates are removed until the dessert is served.

A flaming dessert such as *cherries jubilee* or *crêpes suzette* may be served in the dining room. All dessert equipment—the silver chafing dish, plates, flatware, and serving pieces—can be brought in on a tea or service wagon. The dessert is passed to each guest in turn, while waiters pour the coffee. Cigarettes, matches, and individual ash trays may be brought to the table at this time.

The table is never completely cleared until the guests have left the room. Dessert plates and flatware may be removed, but the coffee cup should remain. It is polite to offer a second cup of coffee, although it is not absolutely correct for formal French service.

D. Tea

A formal tea uses a very light menu and a minimum service staff. The services of the professional caterer may, however, still be required.

Club members, friends, relatives, and guests may be honorary hostesses and may pour. The caterer's staff, however, will be needed to do the work beforehand. They will prepare the food, arrange it on trays, set the table, and then refill the trays as needed during the tea. They will also clean up and do the dishes.

The table should not be as large as the one used for a buffet that served the same number of guests. The table should have adequate space at each end for the presiding honorary hostess to be seated comfortably. (See Fig. 9–12.)

The type of food served at a tea is somewhat limited, but it should be attractive and tasty. Tea, finger, and party sandwiches, as well as assorted open-face decorated canapés, may be used. Assorted cookies, petits fours, miniature sweet rolls, and precut cake set on trays should also be on the table.

No flatware is needed except for a teaspoon. The guest serves himself sandwiches and sweets after having been served the tea. Service tables and sideboards are provided for used dishes.

Attractive trays of tea sandwiches are excellent delivery only items for the off-premise caterer.

E. Family Style

Family style is the most informal service of all. It is used frequently for community meals, such as church and school dinners, where family units are expected to attend, and is rarely used for fund-raising dinners.

When working on a family style affair, the caterer is concerned exclusively with the preparation and dishing up of the food. The committee in charge of arrangements takes care of setting up the room and the tables,

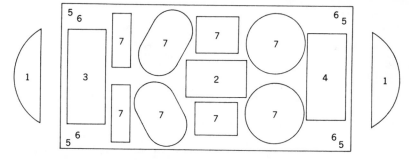

1. Chairs for honorary hostess
2. Centerpiece
3. Coffee service tray should include coffee server, cream, sugar, some cups and saucers
4. Tea service tray should include tea essence, boiling water, cream, sugar, sliced lemon, some cups and saucers
5. Napkins
6. Teaspoons
7. Trays of tea sandwiches, cookies, petits fours, etc.

Fig. 9–12. Table setup for tea for large group. *Note:* A supply of cups and saucers should be set close to each honorary hostess. When additional cups and saucers are needed, they are brought to table by waitress.

and the younger members of the community group usually act as waiters.

These dinners are not big money-makers for the caterer, but they pay expenses, help with public relations, and bring the caterer's services to the attention of more potential customers.

General Procedure: Tables are set (Fig. 9–13). For this service the coffee cup and saucer is included in the cover. Bread or rolls in baskets, butter in iced butter dishes, relish trays, salad bowls, and appetizer are all placed on the table before the guests enter the room.

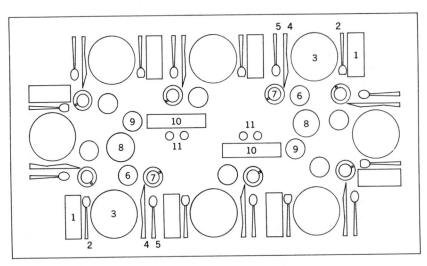

1. Napkin	7. Cup and saucer
2. Dinner fork	8. Bread basket
3. Dinner plate	9. Iced butter dish
4. Dinner knife	10. Relish tray
5. Teaspoon	11. Salt and pepper
6. Water glass	

Fig. 9–13. Table set for family-style service. *Note:* Dessert spoon or fork may be placed on table if needed. Wine glasses may also be placed on table if needed.

After the guests are seated, the main dish and accompanying vegetables are brought in on large serving platters or bowls. One large platter or bowl for each table should have sufficient portions for everyone seated at that table. Serving pieces should accompany each platter or bowl. Guests may serve themselves or appoint a "head" for each table to do the actual serving. Serving platters may be refilled according to the arrangements made with the committee. Dessert is served in the same manner. Coffee pitchers are then placed on each table.

Clearing may be done after the main course or at the end of the meal. Everyone can help by stacking the dishes at one end of the table. Then the kitchen crew removes all dishes and flatware to busboxes on serving wagons.

This method clears the room very quickly and allows the scheduled program to proceed without interruption.

The caterer should be finished when the dessert is served. The various committees in charge of cleanup should then take over.

F. Smorgasbord (Smorrebord)

This word actually means an open-face hearty sandwich. However, in catering it has come to mean a light buffet featuring fish items. This might be part of a cocktail hour preceding a dinner or it might mean a complete buffet featuring smorgasbord sandwiches. Some restaurant operations use this word to indicate a complete buffet from appetizer to dessert.

G. The Cocktail Hour

Whether in a banquet hall, private home, or elsewhere, the time for the cocktail hour and the dinner should be arranged well in advance. Despite late guests, guests who want "just one more drink," and the hostess who is not too punctual herself, no cocktail hour should be prolonged beyond the agreed dinner time. A long wait can ruin even the best meal.

For the cocktail hour, waiters may pass assorted hors d'oeuvres or set up and replenish a small buffet table. Waiters for the cocktail hour will also serve the meal.

The bartender should remain at his post until all the guests are seated for dinner. He should pour the wine and/or the champagne for dinner, and then return to the bar after the meal if the host wishes to serve again later in the evening.

H. Additional Notes on Serving

When a large number of guests must be served at the same time, all possible time-saving methods should be utilized. The preplating of salads, desserts, etc., is one of the most important of these. In general, follow this procedure:

1. Count the plates and take out only the number needed.

2. Place the plates on serving trays. If waiters are assigned specific tables with the number of guests known, each tray should have exactly the number of plates needed to serve one full table at a time.

3. Place salads on the plates. If salads or any perishable foods are preplated, the loaded trays should be kept refrigerated until serving time. Then the waiters can remove the trays from the refrigerator and go directly to the dining room.

4. Preplated desserts or nonperishable items may be left on a work table for a short time rather than placed on trays, so as not to tie up all service trays. To serve these, the waiters merely load the tray with the num-

ber of plates needed for each table. A cook's helper can assist in loading the waiters' trays to speed up service.

5. Dinner plates for the main course, which cannot be preplated, should be stacked in a warming area before the start of the meal. At serving time the counted stacks of plates are moved to the serving area and additional stacks are brought out before the last of the previous stack is gone, so that no time is lost in waiting.

All serving should be done with professional serving pieces such as ladles, measured spoons, and scoops. Using proper serving pieces will speed up the service, guarantee uniform portions, and eliminate excess handling of food.

CHAPTER 10

Arranging the Affair—III

10-1 ALLOCATION OF TIME FOR THE CATERED AFFAIR

A. Banquet Hall

The time for the end of the function as well as its start should be clearly stated between the host and caterer. It should also be clearly understood by all parties that the time of the affair means from start to finish. The rental agreement for the room should state the exact time for which the room is available. The hours should be on the contract. The estimated time to do a catered job breaks down as follows:

1. *Preparation time:* Time to prepare all the food (either the day before or the morning of the affair).

2. *Setup time:* Time to set up the room, arrange buffet tables, arrange other tables and chairs, and make place settings if needed.

3. *Serving time:* Actual time for serving. This should include the cocktail hour through the entire meal, including the second cup of coffee.

4. *Cleanup time:* Time to remove dishes, etc., from dining room, remove all buffet equipment, and move tables for guest dancing.

5. *Kitchen cleanup time:* Cleaning includes doing all the dishes used during the meal, and then cleaning the kitchen, leaving it ready for the next day's work.

If a decorations committee wishes to put up elaborate decorations, additional setup time might be needed. This would only mean that the room had to be available to the committee, which should also make arrangements for the removal of large decorations. It would not involve any of the caterer's staff.

B. Off Premises

1. *Preparation time:* Time to prepare the food (the day before or the morning of the affair) and packing the food for transportation.

2. *Travel time:* Loading the food into the trucks and going from the kitchen to the location. Unloading the food at location.

119

3. *Setup time:* Time to set up the room or rooms if in a private home. Time to arrange buffet tables and make place settings if needed. In private homes some of this work may be done the day prior to the affair.

4. *Second cooking time:* Time to reheat and arrange food on trays or in chafing dishes, or prepare food for serving.

5. *Serving time:* The actual time of serving food, from canapés and hors d'oeuvres through the entire meal including the second cup of coffee. (See Sec. 9–2H.)

6. *Cleanup time:* Removing dishes, etc., from the dining room. This includes all the equipment used on the buffet table and linen on guest tables. In private homes this means replacing any furniture that has been moved and removing all extra chairs and tables. All caterer's equipment should be loaded into the truck immediately.

7. *Kitchen cleanup time:* To cleanup the kitchen includes doing the dishes used during the meal and leaving the kitchen clean, as well as replacing any house equipment used.

8. *Return travel time:* Traveling back from the location to the commissary.

9. *Unloading time:* Replacing all used equipment and leaving the kitchen clean and in order for work the next morning.

C. Keeping Record of Time Allocation

Careful records should be kept of the time each room will be used. It would be disastrous to have the decorations committee for the evening affair arrive before the afternoon luncheon was finished.

To keep these records simply and accurately, the caterer should have a *Function Reservation* book. This book should have adequate space for each function room in the caterer's establishment (Fig. 10–1). The larger the caterer, the larger the book and the greater the number of function rooms.

The off-premise caterer might use a similar book with space for four, five, or more function rooms. If no room name is printed in the book, he can write in the location of his various jobs. The book should be set up for as many jobs as he can handle on any given day. (See Fig. 10–2.)

All function books should have dates and notations of important national and religious holidays printed at the top of each page.

10–2 TRANSPORTATION OF EQUIPMENT AND FOOD

This is a consideration for the off-premise caterer. To pack and move sufficient equipment to serve any given meal requires time and muscle. In scheduling an affair in a private home, the hostess might suggest that the caterer use various pieces of household equipment. He should weigh this carefully, however, as the cost of replacing such equipment if it is broken, bent, cracked, or damaged might be a good deal more than the saving he

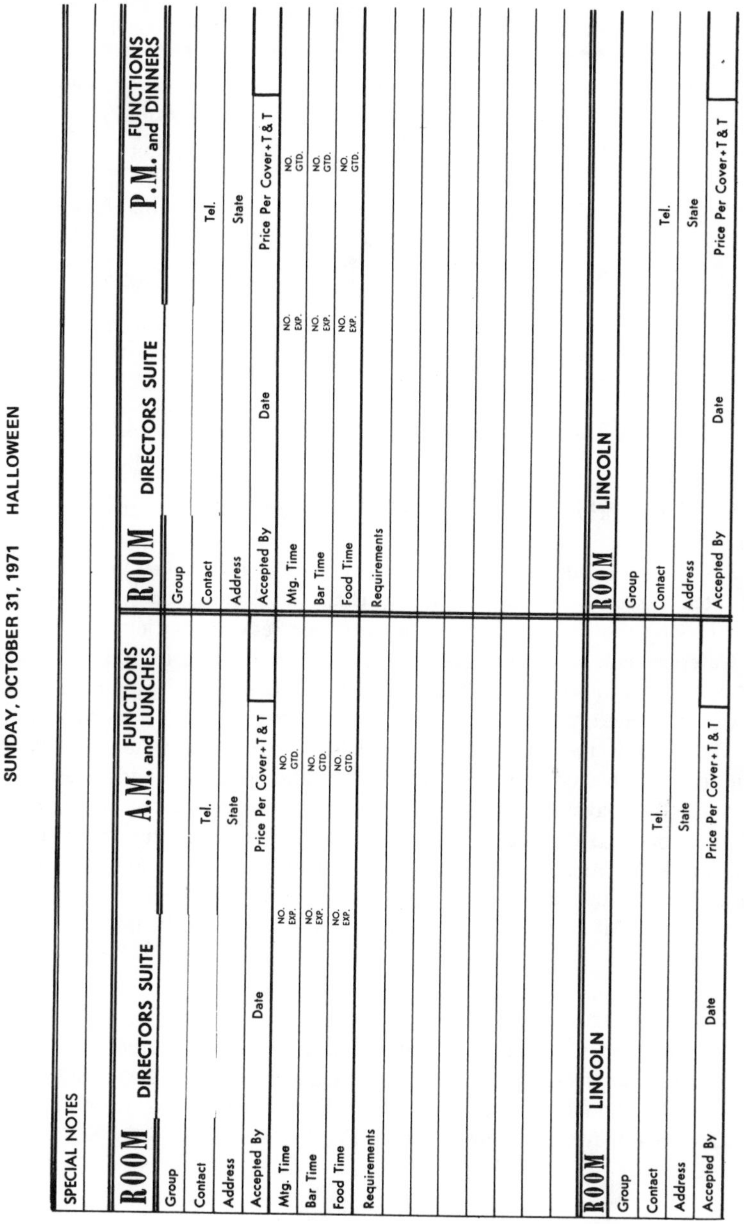

Fig. 10–1. Banquet hall caterer's appointment book.

SUNDAY, OCTOBER 31, 1971   HALLOWEEN

A.M. MEETINGS and LUNCHEONS			P.M. MEETING
ROOM			**ROOM**
Group			Group
In Charge	Tel.		In Charge
Function	NO. EXP	NO. GUAR	Function
Mtg. Time	Meal Time		Mtg. Time
Bar Time			Bar Time

Fig. 10–2.   Off-premise caterer's appointment book.

makes by not bringing his own. Specific insurance to cover breakage of house equipment is very costly.

All caterer's equipment that travels should be packed in individual, well-fitted cases. These can be moved easily and allow for quick inventory when leaving the commissary and again when leaving the job.

Caterer's equipment may be cleaned at the location or returned to the kitchen to be cleaned before being stored. All household equipment including stoves, ranges, and work tables must be left clean and in good order.

The food is the last thing to be loaded for shipment to the location. Insulated portable containers of every size and description to fit every catering need are available (Fig. 10–3). Food to be cooked on location may be left in original containers. Meat may be delivered by the meat supplier directly to the location. Schedule such deliveries very carefully so that adequate space will have been prepared for their receipt and storage until cooking time. All dairy items must be refrigerated while in transit.

10–3   FRINGE SERVICES

It is a good idea for the caterer not to get too involved with the so-called fringe services, which include musicians, photographers, and florists. However, he should know enough about them to be able to work with them in order to achieve a smoothly run affair.

A. Music

Dancing often accompanies weddings, dinners, anniversary parties, formal or informal dinners at home, school dances, or proms, whether with or without a served meal. While the caterer has nothing to do with the

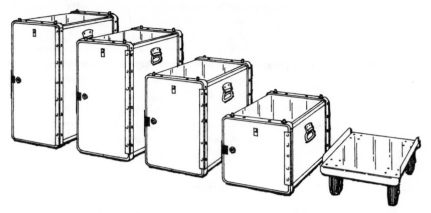

Fig. 10–3. Individual cases for food storage.

music, he should be able to recommend several groups or local orchestras. It is the responsibility of the host to make the final selection.

When union musicians are to be used in a public hall, the number of men to be hired is set by the musician's union local. All public meeting halls, banquet halls, hotels, and civic auditoriums have been classified by the local musicians union as to "number of men." This classification indicates the minimum number of union musicians that can be hired to play in any given hall and is calculated according to the footage of the hall. The number of musicians required is what the union local feels is necessary to give the best sound results. In different areas of the country the rules may differ, and one should check with the local musician's union.

The length of time that the musicians are to play is determined by the host. If the host wishes to audition the musicians, he should make arrangements directly with the leader of the group. He can attend an affair where they will be playing, preferably in the same size hall that he plans to use.

Once the musicians have been hired, the caterer should arrange to meet with the leader for a brief discussion. The host should also be present.

For a smoothly run affair it is necessary to establish:

1. time for start of the music (the musicians should be prepared to start playing exactly at the time indicated);
2. selection of music to be played for dancing and music to be played during the serving of the meal;
3. selection of special music to be played for the entrance of the honored guests, entrance of the bride and groom, cutting of the occasion cake, etc.;
4. any special requests made by the host.

Unless specifically indicated by the host, the musicians will not be served dinner. Most of the union contracts specify rest or intermission periods, but do not indicate dinner or drinks.

Experience will show that musicians usually manage to have something to eat and drink, whether or not the host has specifically ordered it. If the caterer wishes to feed the musicians, he can arrange for them to have a snack during one of their break periods. (However, for the starting caterer, who is usually operating on a very small margin of profit, this would be an additional unnecessary expense.)

School functions will use school musicians. Fraternal groups can usually supply musicians from within their own organization, in which case they will be served a dinner or whatever food is served to the membership.

The caterer and the musicians will find it mutually advantageous to cooperate in their efforts to guarantee a successful affair.

B. Photographs

The caterer should be able to recommend a few different photographers. As with the other fringe services, he should never push anyone in particular, but should allow the host to make his own choice.

When the photographer has been selected, whether he is a professional or member of the family, a meeting with the host, caterer, and photographer should be arranged. Here the various details of the function should be worked out to avoid holding up the entire party while pictures are being taken.

For example, when a wedding reception is not held in the same place where the marriage was performed, some of the guests will arrive for the reception before the bride and groom. Under these conditions, the photographer should take the pictures of the group at the altar, outside the church, and getting into the car as quickly as possible so as not to hold up the entire reception.

The photographer should supply the caterer with some clear shots of the affair. These may be of the buffet tables, the bride and groom, or some other outstanding person or event. They should be kept in the caterer's sales album. It is to the advantage of both photographer and caterer for the caterer to be able to say to a potential customer: "This is an excellent picture of the bride and groom cutting the cake. This is our special four-tiered cake. Notice how clearly the couple can be seen. This was taken by the P and F Photographers who are right here in town and who do excellent work."

C. Flowers

Flowers for a wedding are the responsibility of the parties concerned. At all other affairs, the flowers are at the discretion of the host or decorations committee.

Since this as another of the fringe services, the caterer should be able to recommend a few florists with varying price ranges. The banquet hall caterer might include the floral decorations as part of any prospectus submitted to the client, and then "farm out" that part of the work to a florist with whom he frequently works.

When the off-premise caterer wishes to include a floral centerpiece for the buffet table or flowers for the head table, he should discuss this with the host or the committee. What he has in mind should not conflict with or duplicate the decorations planned for the room.

The following sentence at the bottom of the contract might help clarify the matter: "Caterer to supply one floral centerpiece for buffet table. White flowers only to be used. Caterer's choice."

When the host or committee is to supply flowers for the buffet table, the caterer should indicate the type and size appropriate for the buffet table that is to be used. This matter should be discussed and an agreement reached as to the responsibility for the floral decorations well in advance of the affair.

D. Printing

While the caterer has no responsibility in the matter of invitations, he should stress to the host or the committee in charge that if food is to be served, an RSVP is almost mandatory. Without that response from the invited list, it is impossible to know how many guests will attend, and therefore the amount of food that is to be prepared.

As with the other fringe services, the caterer should be able to recommend a few social stationers. Beyond that, he should refrain from involvement with the wording, layout, or design of any printed matter for the catered affair. (For the one exception see *Menus* in this section.) He should receive a copy of the invitation for his file, and should verify the actual time of service indicated on the invitation.

Each catered affair will require different printed material such as tickets for prepaid reservations, place cards with table numbers, table place cards, cocktail and/or luncheon napkins with name of honoree and date of party, and menus. The caterer might suggest these to his host or the committee in charge, and allow them to choose what applies to the affair in question. These forms concern only the catered meal or the reception and do not cover any other social obligations.

Invitations: The social stationer will know the correct forms for all invitations. The invitation shown in Fig. 10–4 calls for a response. Upon receiving all the responses, the host should have food to serve the number attending. Even when the lightest menu is planned, a count of the number of guests expected will help make the affair a success.

Menus: Wedding dinners and most formal dinners, except small private parties, call for a printed menu. The caterer specializing in this form of service should be able to supply the host with the menu written out clearly and correctly for the printer. The printer should be able to set it up in proper form.

The face of the menu might have the initials of the person, persons, or organization being honored, the emblem of the organization, or some other appropriate design [Fig. 10–5(A)].

The menu itself is printed on a folded insert sheet held in place by a silk twine of matching color. The first page of the insert sheet indicates the

Mr. and Mrs. Peter Ahrens

request the honor of your presence

at the marriage of their daughter

Alison

to

Mr. Mark Park

Sunday, the tenth of October

Nineteen hundred and seventy-one

at seven-thirty o'clock in the evening

Church

Address

The favor of a reply is requested

by September 29

Name

Number of persons

Will   attend

Dinner Dance Reception

immediately following the ceremony

Room

Hotel or Reception Hall

Address

Fig. 10–4. Wedding invitation with separate reception and RSVP card.

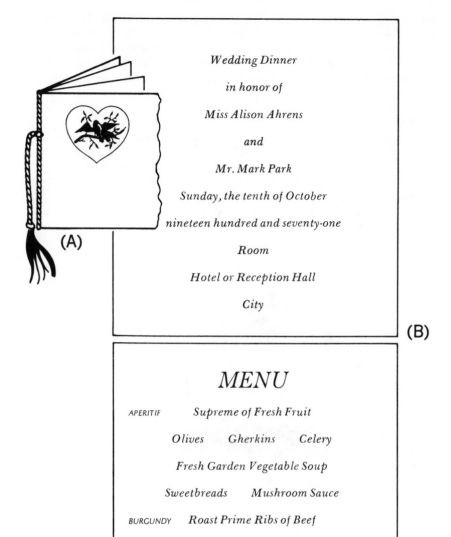

(A)

Wedding Dinner

in honor of

Miss Alison Ahrens

and

Mr. Mark Park

Sunday, the tenth of October

nineteen hundred and seventy-one

Room

Hotel or Reception Hall

City

(B)

MENU

APERITIF   *Supreme of Fresh Fruit*

Olives   Gherkins   Celery

Fresh Garden Vegetable Soup

Sweetbreads   Mushroom Sauce

BURGUNDY   *Roast Prime Ribs of Beef*

Carrots and Peas   French Fried Potatoes

Mixed Green Salad

CHAMPAGNE   *Wedding Cake*

Tea   Ginger Ale   Coffee

(C)

Fig. 10–5. (A) Face of formal menu. (B) First page of menu showing name, place, date, and occasion. (C) Menu page printed in English; wine list to left of course with which it is served. (Courtesy of Gillick Press.)

occasion for the affair, the date, and the place [Fig. 10–5(B)]. The second page or left side of the center of the menu sheet can be left blank or it might have some notation about the occasion or might list the wines to be served. If it is to be left blank, the wines should be listed to the left of the course with which each wine is to be served on the right page [Fig. 10–5 (C)]. The menu itself should be in French in a script type. However, many hosts prefer that the menu be in English in deference to guests who may not know any French [Fig. 10–5(C)].

The caterer's name should not appear on the menu and never does at private formal dinners. However, this is a choice place for a discreet line of advertising, and many caterers will make arrangements with the host or the committee whereby a line such as: "Arrangements by the P and F Caterers, This City" can be printed neatly at the bottom of the menu. At larger public affairs, particularly fund-raising dinners, this has become an accepted practice.

Alison and Mark

October 10, 1971

Fig. 10–6. Printed wedding matchbook cover. Decorated matches inside.

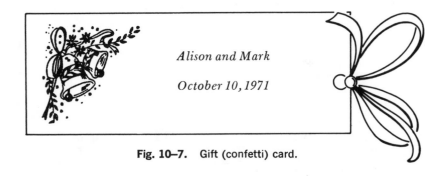

Alison and Mark

October 10, 1971

Fig. 10–7. Gift (confetti) card.

Printed Programs: This is the responsibility of the host of the committee in charge. When the program is part of the yearbook or the ad book, it might be an excellent place for the caterer to advertise. A small ad stating: "Your host for this evening is the P and F Caterers, This City. It is our pleasure to serve you." or a similar sentence, is appropriate here.

Matchbooks: Matchbooks may be used by the caterer for two purposes: 1. advertising his own service, and 2. imprinting the name of honoree and date of the party (Fig. 10–6). If the caterer uses printed matchbooks for his advertising, they should be prominently displayed in his office. They can be given to all staff members, but should be distributed only when a guest asks for a match. Unless the host or the committee in charge has given permission, the caterer's matchbooks should not be placed on display at any affair. Only matchbooks printed with the name, date, and occasion, should be used. This is not a major issue, but it can be a point of annoyance for the host or committee. It is not worth the possible customer antagonism.

Drink Stirrers: Printed plastic swizzle sticks are used only if a bar is planned. If champagne only is served, there is no need for this souvenir.

Gift Cards (Confetti Cards): Small cards (Fig. 10–7) with the name of the bride and groom are attached with ribbon to small packages of rice, or jordan almonds in predominantly Italian neighborhoods to the groom's cake. (See Secs. 2–3E and 12–2D.)

CHAPTER 11

The Bar

For any liquor service, it is necessary to have a liquor license, except when the liquor is served in a private home to guests of the host. This liquor must belong to the host and can only be given (not sold) to the guest. No liquor may be served, given, or sold to minors.

For banquet hall catering, once a liquor license is granted, a regular bar may be set up. If no liquor license is granted, a special beer and wine license may be issued. Then, only beer, wine, and champagne may be served in accordance with local licensing laws.

When a banquet hall caterer has a regular liquor license, he may also get a caterer's license. This permits him to operate a bar in connection with any affair that he is catering, regardless of the location. However, he is limited to the number of times that he may cater and use a bar in the same location other than his own banquet hall. He must file every temporary location with the local Alcoholic Beverage Control Board.

Every state has its own rules and regulations regarding the sale of liquor. For the most accurate and up-to-date information, check with the local Alcoholic Beverage Control Board. This should be done before purchasing any wine, liquor, beer, or champagne for resale.

11-1 THE BAR IN A PRIVATE HOME

In a private home, the host will supply all alcoholic beverages to be served to his guests. The caterer's staff should include a bartender. The caterer's equipment might include a portable bar, though a long table can serve adequately. The caterer should be prepared to supply all the glasses needed for the bar, as well as the mixes and ice (Fig. 11–1).

When estimating the number of glasses needed, the type of occasion, length of time the bar is to be open, and the average age of the guests

130

Item	Description and Use	Item	Description and Use	Item	Description and Use
	Line Whiskey Jigger — 1 oz. Capacity Line For "good measure" . . . or serving straight.		**10 oz. Heat Treated Beer Hour Glass** An appropriate glass for all beers, ales, porter and stout or sake.		**Lined Brandy — 1 oz. Line** Specially for brandy . . . can be used with liquers, cordials, etc.
	8 oz. Hi-Ball For all liquor highballs mixed with water, soda or ginger ale—good, too, for fizzes, daises, rickeys, sangarees, spritzers and swizzles.		**Lined Cocktail Glass — 3 oz. Line** This is the glass for a multitude of cocktails—from ever-popular manhattans and martinis to side cars and stingers.		**2 oz. Sherry** Try this also with "sipping" liquers, cordials, etc.
	11 oz. Collins Made for Tom or John Collins, plus many soft drinks.		**1 oz. Whiskey Sour** For all sours, whether made with whiskey, rum, brandy, vodka or gin.		**4 oz. Claret Wine** Proper for serving a wide variety of red and white table wines or fortified wines, such as port or muscatel.
	6-1/2 oz. Old Fashioned Besides Old Fashioneds, this is fine for aperitifs, crustas, on-the-rocks, smashes and toddies.		**1 oz. Cordial** That special service for all the delightful sips called cordials (liqueurs) —from Benedictine to Drambuie and Anisette to Triple Sec.		**5-1/2 oz. Champagne** Whether imported or domestic, white or pink, champagne and all sparkling wines belong in a champagne glass. Fine also for a frozen daiquiri.

Fig. 11-1. Different bar glassware.

should all be considered. When bringing glasses for a bar in a private home, the caterer should plan on 10 percent over the number of guests, so that the staff and the kitchen will not be tied up during the party with washing and replacing clean glasses.

The professional bartender will know how to mix and pour any drinks that are required, as well as the proper method for popping the cork of a champagne bottle. A good bartender's guide or other basic book concerning mixed drinks should be part of every caterer's library.

Local bartender's unions, as well as bartender's schools, are sources for part-time and temporary bartenders for catered affairs. Often, bartenders may be volunteers from within the organization sponsoring the affair or members of the host's family.

11-2 BOTTLE COUNT

When the host supplies the wine or liquor, he has the right to inspect the bar at any time. The caterer may assure him that the liquor is used exclusively by his guests by giving him a bottle count. When the host brings or has the liquor delivered, he and the caterer or the bartender will do an actual count of the number of bottles that are to be placed on the bar. A notation of this number is made. At the end of the affair the host with the bartender will again count the bottles. Unopened bottles, empties, and any bottles that have been broken are all taken into the count. This number should coincide exactly with the original number of bottles placed on the bar.

11-3 WINE

Wine is a festive beverage and the mark of a special occasion, and it is to the caterer's advantage to suggest wines whenever possible. Standard combinations are white wine with fish, rosé with poultry, and red wine with meat. (See Fig. 11-2.) The host's choice however, will always be the deciding factor.

Serving wine at banquets or large functions is very simple and adds much to the enjoyment of the dinner. White wine, rosé, and all champagnes should be properly chilled by placing the cases in the refrigerator several hours before serving time. When white wine or champagne is to be left at the table for the guest to pour, it may be placed directly on the table or in an ice bucket. The white cardboard tubs used for mixing paint, make excellent, easy to carry, disposable ice buckets.

When pouring wine, if the glass is generous in size, half full is enough. If the glass is small, leave at least a ½ in. at the top for safety's sake. The bottle should be close at hand, should the guest desire more wine during the meal.

According to the Wine Institute: "It is not mandatory for the waiter to pour the wine. If the waiter has no time to pour, he may uncork the bottle and place it on the table for the guests to help themselves. If the waiter pours the first serving, the bottle should be left on the table or in a table cooler easily accessible, so that the guests may refill their glasses." (See Figs. 11–3 and 11–4.)

APPETIZER WINES *SUCH AS:* Sherry Vermouth Flavored Wines	Serve chilled, without food or with HORS d'OEUVRE NUTS, CHEESES
RED DINNER WINES *SUCH AS:* Burgundy Claret Rosé (Pink)	Serve at cool room temperature, with HEARTY DISHES: STEAKS, CHOPS, ROASTS, GAME, CHEESE DISHES, SPAGHETTI *(Serve Rosé chilled, with any food.)*
WHITE DINNER WINES *SUCH AS:* Chablis Rhine Wine Sauterne	Serve well chilled, with LIGHTER DISHES: CHICKEN, FISH, SHELLFISH, OMELETS, ANY WHITE MEATS
DESSERT WINES *SUCH AS:* Port Muscatel Tokay Cream (Sweet) Sherry	Serve chilled or at cool room temperature, with FRUITS, COOKIES, NUTS, CHEESES, FRUIT CAKES, POUND CAKES
SPARKLING WINES *SUCH AS:* Champagne Sparkling Burgundy	Serve well chilled, with any food: APPETIZERS, THE MAIN COURSE, OR DESSERTS *(And especially good in festive party punches)*

Fig. 11–2. Most popular wine and food combinations. (Courtesy of Wine institute.)

11–4 CHAMPAGNE

Champagne is traditionally used for a special occasion toast. Champagne may be served directly from the bottle or in various punches. When served straight, it is never decanted and is always served in a coupe or champagne glass.

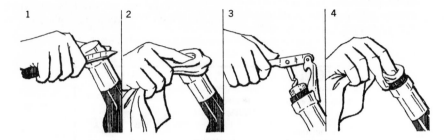

Fig. 11–3. Opening the wine bottle. Step 1: cut foil. Step 2: wipe mouth. Step 3: draw cork. Step 4: wipe again. (Courtesy of Wine Institute.)

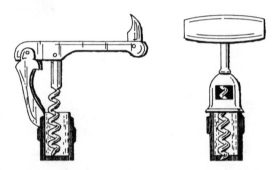

Fig. 11–4. Two popular types of corkscrews. Corkscrews with levers and knife blades preferred by waiters and T-type automatic pullers by waitresses. Cork should be penetrated fully before pull is begun. (Courtesy of Wine Institute.)

A. Amount of Champagne

Under ordinary circumstances, one case of champagne will serve approximately 90–100 drinks. The host will decide just how much champagne he wishes to be served. It is then for the caterer to suggest how many cases will be needed. Using the average of 2½ drinks per guest for a reception or dinner, three cases would be more than ample to serve 100 guests.

B. Opening the Champagne Bottle (see Fig. 11–3)

The following explains the correct way to open a bottle of champagne (courtesy of the Wine Institute):

"To open a bottle of sparkling wine, first loosen the wire hood by untwisting the loop of wire which is there for that purpose. The wire and top of the foil capsule can be removed in a single motion, holding a thumb on top of the cork to keep it from popping out unexpectedly. Normally, all that is needed to remove the cork is to twist it slightly and let the inside pressure force it out. If it is stubborn, however, upward pressure may be applied simultaneously with the two thumbs to loosen the mushroom part of the cork from the neck of the bottle. While the cork is being removed, the bottle should be held at a 45-degree angle, which reduces the likelihood of the wine overflowing. The cork is held tightly as it leaves the bottle, to prevent it from flying out and striking someone.

"Pouring is done in two motions: the first, filling the glass with foam, and the second, completing the pouring.

"Fill the glass only about ⅔ full. A napkin is not desirable in pouring champagne (except to wipe the bottle when it is removed from the cooler) because it hides the label. The bottle is returned to the cooler after each pouring to keep the wine cold and thus preserve the effervescence."

When champagne is served from the bar, the glasses are set on the bar, coupe up, and filled as the guest approaches. Champagne should never be poured ahead of time and allowed to stand.

Traditional champagne coupes come in 4-, 4½-, 5-, and 5½-oz sizes. There are also many novelty shapes and sizes that may be used in the private home. The caterer should limit his selection to the traditional coupe in one of the first three sizes listed. The 4½-oz is generally preferred. The 5½-oz is rather large for the catered affair and is more often used in bars and lounges.

C. Champagne Toast

Champagne to be passed to the guests at a wedding buffet for a toast to the bride calls for some advance preparation.

1. All champagne glasses should be set, coupe up, on serving trays.

2. All serving staff for passing champagne should be ready to serve at the same time.

Fig. 11–5. This large champagne or punch fountain holds approximately 6 gal, has concealed lights, and offers a constant flow from four attractive spouts. It is approximately 32½ in. high with 21-in. bowl diameter and therefore would only fit on a rather large buffet table.

Fig. 11–6. Chased silver punch bowl holds 2–3–4 gal and has matching ladle. Glass punch bowls usually hold 1–2 gal. (Courtesy of Abbey Rents.)

3. Waiters may assist the bartender in popping the corks and pouring as rapidly as possible.

4. Champagne is passed as soon as each tray of glasses is filled so that every guest has a glass at the same time and the toast may be proposed while the champagne is still effervescent.

D. Champagne Poured at the Table

Immediately after the main course is served, the champagne is poured. All waiters should assist in the pouring so that all glasses are filled at approximately the same time and the champagne may be enjoyed with dinner.

Champagne glasses are refilled as often as the host, by previous arrangement, has indicated. After the first round is poured, a full bottle may be placed on each table or in a cooler, allowing the guests to help themselves. In a crowded dining room or banquet hall, the floor stand cooler might present a hazard.

In all but the most formal French service, an extra bottle of champagne placed on the table is an acceptable practice. It assures the guest as much champagne as desired and does not require additional staff to pour.

E. Champagne from the Fountain

At a buffet, the champagne fountain makes a very elegant display (Fig. 11–5). It is easy to keep filled and easy for the guest to serve himself. However, when straight champagne is used, the fountain should never be filled to capacity. It should be refilled frequently with newly opened bottles, as the circulating of the champagne through the fountain tends to reduce its effervescence. A better choice for the flowing fountain is champagne punch, which is fortified with sauterne and sparkling water. When this punch is served, the fountain may be filled to capacity. Regardless of what drink is served, however, the fountain should be refilled before it is empty.

11–5 PUNCH BOWLS

Champagne punch or fruit punch may be served from punch bowls (Fig. 11–6). Straight champagne is never served in this manner. An ice piece decorated with plastic flowers in keeping with the occasion may be floated in the punch.

The traditional punch bowl of silver or glass on a base and set on a tray with its matching ladle is never decorated. However, a metal or plastic bowl might have plastic flowers or ribbons secured to its sides, in keeping with the other table decorations.

Punch cups should be used for fruit, wine, and champagne punch. Whatever the mixture, there should be adequate cups or glasses to serve all guests.

CHAPTER 12

Special Cakes for Special Occasions

12–1 TYPES OF CAKES

The special cake is the highlight of the catered affair; it may be a wedding cake, an anniversary cake, or a number cake.

1. The wedding cake (Fig. 12–1) is traditionally arranged in tiers separated by dividers. Dividers may be white plastic columns, swan or floral columns, or inverted champagne glasses with a small sugar flower set in each glass. Cakes should be round or square for the best effect. Heart-shaped tiered cakes do not show up very well and unless well made and decorated, they tend to look out of shape. (For information concerning tiered cake sizes, see Table 12–1.)

2. The anniversary cake may be round, square, or oblong, tiered only for very special occasions. Wedding anniversary cakes are often single-layer, heart-shaped. Birthday cakes may also be any desired shape.

3. The number cake is most often used for significant birthdays and numbered anniversaries—Sweet 16 or 25, 50, or 75. The numbers are cut from sheet cakes piled two or three high, then iced and decorated.

For most catering operations it is practical and economical to buy all baked goods from a professional bakery. This includes occasion cakes, cookies, petits fours, tarts, pies, rolls, and breads. Quantity baking requires specially trained workers, specialized equipment, and large and expensive ovens.

Most bake shops will gladly cooperate with the caterer in the matter of supplying exactly the type, size, and shape of cake desired and will deliver it to the place of the affair at the stated time. The latter is very important because of the difficulty in transporting fancy tiered cakes. Furthermore, many of the large tiered cakes have to be assembled where they will be served and once assembled cannot be moved.

Careful consideration should be given to the decoration of the occasion cake. In order to avoid mistakes in wording and spelling of names, the caterer should ask the host to write or print exactly what is to be written on the cake (Fig. 12–2).

Fig. 12–1. Tiered wedding cake with champagne glass dividers.

TABLE 12–1. TIERED CAKE SIZES

No. of Tiers	Size (in in.) of Tiers Starting from Bottom	Serves
2	9, 6	20
2	10, 7	25
2	11, 8	30
2	12, 9	40
3	12, 9, 6	50
3	13, 10, 7	65
3	14, 11, 8	80
3	15, 12, 8	100
3	16, 12, 8	125
4	16, 13, 9, 6	150
4	17, 13, 10, 7	175
4	18, 14, 10, 7	200
4	20, 16, 12, 8	235
4	22, 16, 12, 8	275
5	22, 17, 14, 11, 8	325
5	24, 18, 14, 11, 8	400

(Happy Birthday Hal)

In the middle of the cake

Then - all over the surface of the cake in no special order, like signatures, all the following names :

Joe	Fran
Jules	Dorothy M.
Dan	Lynne
Archie	Dorothy
Chuck	Antonia
Rose	Eadie

Jules Dorothy Rose Archie Joe
Chuck HAPPY BIRTHDAY HAL Eadie
Antonia Dan
Fran Dorothy M. Lynne

Please space the names out a little better.

Sheet cake- pineapple filling use all colors for names.

Fig. 12-2. Customer's order for occasion cake.

12-2 CUTTING THE OCCASION CAKE

A. The Wedding Cake

Since the cutting of the occasion cake is the high point of the catered affair, it is usually photographed. The caterer, host, and photographer should work out the details to avoid any last-minute confusion that might mar the ceremony.

When the cake is to be cut, the bride and groom should stand at the cake table. Both holding the specially decorated cake knife, they make the first cut in the cake from the bottom tier. They may then share this piece of cake. A cake plate, two cake forks, and napkins should be close at hand for their convenience.

After the photographs have been taken, the caterer's staff takes over the cutting and serving of the cake. The top tier with the ornament is removed and placed on a small tray. This can be left on the buffet table or removed to the kitchen. This top tier and the ornament are usually taken home by the parents of the bride and saved (frozen) for the first anniversary celebration. The second tier, which is now exposed, is cut and served completely before cutting into the next lower tier. On all tiered cakes with dividers, each layer is completely cut and served so that the dividers may be removed and sent back to the kitchen, leaving the next lower layer exposed (Fig. 12–3).

Special care should be exercised when champagne glasses are used as dividers, so as not to dislodge the tiers. The glasses are removed carefully and sent back to the kitchen, washed, packed, and sent home with the top tier of the cake.

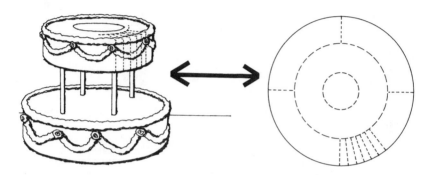

Fig. 12–3. Top tier is removed with ornament. Cut second tier as any round cake.

The individual tiers of the cake may be cut in different ways to obtain the correct number of portions (Fig. 12–4).

The tiered cake without dividers is cut in a different manner completely (Fig. 12–5).

When the occasion cake is square or oblong, as a sheet cake, it is best to cut straight lines and divide each section evenly (Fig. 12–6). For children's portions, simply cut any of the regular portions in half.

Sherbet or ice cream should be served as follows with the cake:

1. Scoops of sherbet or ice cream may be placed on the cake plates in the kitchen and trays of these plates brought to the cake table. A portion of cake is then added to each plate before serving.

2. The cake may be removed to the kitchen for cutting, but only if it is small enough to be lifted and placed on a tea wagon easily.

3. Sherbet or ice cream may be brought out in a covered container and served on the cake plate with the cake from the buffet or cake table. (The ice cream container should be covered with aluminum foil and placed on a tray which is then set on the table.)

B. Special Occasions Other Than Weddings

The person (or persons) being honored steps to the cake table. When there is a candle lighting ceremony, he blows out the candles and makes the first cut in the cake. The honored guest should never be expected to cut

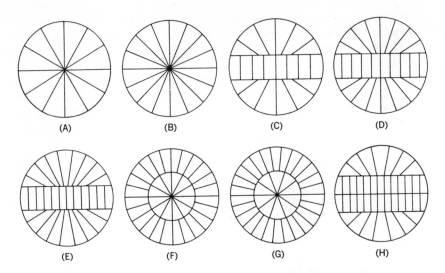

Fig. 12–4. Cutting guide for tiered wedding cake. (A) 8-in., 2-layer cake; yield: 12 servings. (B) 9-in., 2-layer cake; yield: 16 servings. (C) 10-in., 2-layer cake; yield: 20 servings. (D) 11-in., 2-layer cake; yield: 26 servings. (E) 12-in., 2-layer cake; yield: 30 servings. (F) 12-in., 2-layer cake; yield: 36 servings. (G) 13-in., 2-layer cake; yield: 36 servings. (H) 14-in., 2-layer cake; yield: 40 servings. (Courtesy of American Institute of Baking.)

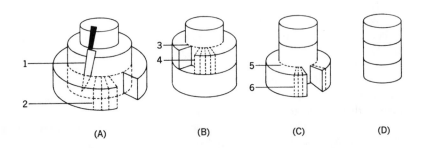

Fig. 12–5. Cutting tiered cakes. (A) Cut vertically through bottom layer at edge of 2nd layer as indicated by dotted line no. 1; then cut out wedges as shown by 2. (B) Follow same procedure with middle layer: cut vertically through 2nd layer at edge of top layer as indicated by dotted line no. 3; then cut wedges as shown by 4. (C) When entire 2nd layer has been served, cut along dotted line 5; cut another row of wedges as shown by 6. (D) Remaining tiers may be cut as desired. (Courtesy of American Institute of Baking.)

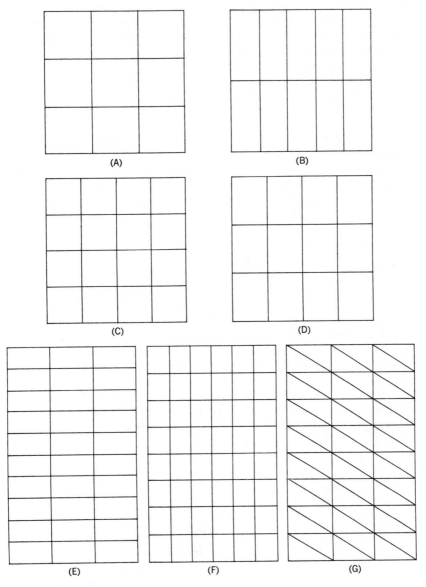

Fig. 12–6. Cutting square or sheet cake. (A) 8 × 8 in.; yield: 9 servings:. (B) 8 × 8 in.; yield: 10 servings. (C) 9 × 9 in.; yield: 16 servings. (D) 9 × 9 in.; yield: 12 servings. (E) 9 × 13 in.; yield: 30 servings. (F) 18 × 25 in.; yield: 48 servings. (G) 18 × 25 in.; yield: 48 servings. (Courtesy of American Institute of Baking.)

the cake for serving. After the first cut is made, he rejoins the guests, and the caterer's staff takes over.

Candle Lighting Ceremony: This simple ceremony of having various guests come forward to light a candle on the occasion cake is an extremely effective method of allowing many honored guests to be recognized at one time. (This is not done at weddings.)

Candles should be placed on the occasion cake before the meal. At the start of the ceremony, usually after the main course, the master of ceremonies will light a long taper and hand it to the honoree. Then as each honored guest is called forward, the honoree hands him the taper. Each honored guest then lights one candle in turn and returns the taper to the honoree.

When all candles are thus lit, the honoree will blow them out, and the orchestra will play "Happy Birthday" or any other appropriate tune. The honored guests may then have their picture taken around the cake as one specially honored guest makes the first cut in the cake. The guests then return to their seats. The cake is cut and served by the caterer's staff. Coffee and tea are served at the same time.

There are no definite rules about this procedure, but the above has become somewhat traditional at anniversaries and similar occasions.

C. Number Cakes

The caterer will give the baker a set of paper patterns which he will use to cut and assemble the number cake. An extra set of these should be made, to be marked off to show exactly how the cake should be cut. (See Fig. 12–7.)

When a small number cake is used, one or two small round cakes decorated in the same manner as the number cake can be cut and served as needed. Extremely large number cakes are very difficult to transport.

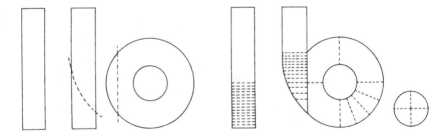

Fig. 12–7. Number cake "16." The 1 and straight side of the 6 will be 10 in. long and 3 in. across. Round bottom of the 6 will be 9-in. round cake. Cut center out. Lower part of column and round cake can be cut so they will fit together to make figure 6. The 1 will be cut into 20 ½-in slices. Column of the 6 will be cut into 18 or 20 ½-in. slices. 9-in. round will be cut into 18 slices. Center of 9-in. round will be cut into 4 pieces. The 16 can be cut into approximately 78 portions.

D. Groom's Cake

Traditionally, this is a heavy fruit and rum cake with small favors—toy wedding rings, coins, thimbles, etc.—foil-wrapped inside the cake. It is cut into small squares, wrapped, and put in small white cake boxes (1½ x 2 in.). The box may be tied with ribbon, and a gift card attached.

Since the cost of individually boxed pieces of cake makes this tradition quite expensive, hostesses now wrap the squares of cake in plastic covered with aluminum foil. These are then secured with a ribbon and a gift card attached. (See Sec. 10–3D.) These small gifts can be placed on a large tray on the buffet or passed around by a member of the caterer's staff, who will inform the guests that this is the groom's cake.

A few pieces of the groom's cake should be put aside to go home with the top tier of the bride's cake.

E. Cake for the Absent Guest

The host may indicate that he wishes to have slices of the bride's cake for friends and relatives who could not attend. The caterer should be prepared for this with a supply of plastic wrap, waxed paper, and foil or glassine bags. A gift card, supplied by the host, should be included with each wrapped slice.

CHAPTER 13

Centerpieces

The most attractive centerpiece for a buffet table is one that is edible, either completely or in part. Edible centerpieces must be designed individually for each catered affair. Such work requires extra time and thought in planning.

The occasion cake is frequently used, when there is no separate sweet table. If no other specialty item is on the menu and a separate sweet table is desired, then salads, decorated attractively, can be used as a table centerpiece. A floral centerpiece can be placed behind the edible centerpiece.

Edible centerpieces may also be used on the buffet table as part of the regular menu. Except for their placement on the buffet table, these decorative pieces are treated in the same manner as all other food. When planning a buffet that includes a decorative piece, whether a centerpiece or not, be sure to have enough of the food item to serve all guests. In most cases, the centerpiece by itself (fruit basket, for example) will not hold sufficient food to serve all guests. Therefore, additional amounts of the food, not necessarily decorated but sliced and cut as required, should be kept in reserve in the kitchen. The centerpiece tray should be replenished as needed.

13-1 ICE PIECES

Ice pieces of unusual design or of large size are available only where there is an ice house. They can be made on the premises only if the caterer has a large walk-in freezer and someone trained in this art. Because of the expense and difficulty involved in making and moving these ice pieces, they are used mostly by large hotels and banquet halls for very special occasions. However, smaller ice pieces may be made very simply (Fig.13-1). Any medium sized gelatine mold that will fit into the freezer may be used. The procedure is as follows.

1. Choose a simple design or floral decoration.
2. Use plastic flowers and figures (bells, swans, etc).
3. Place a small amount of water in the bottom of the mold. Place the design in this water and allow it to freeze. This is to prevent the decorations from moving. Then add water to fill the mold and allow that to freeze.

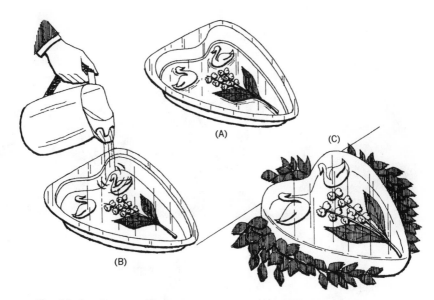

Fig. 13–1. Heart-shaped ice piece. (A) Decoration with small amount of water in mold. (B) Completing freezing with balance of water. (C) Finished ice mold.

4. To unmold, simply invert the mold and wipe it with a hot wet cloth. Be sure that the ice is supported on the underside so it will not crack when it comes loose from the form.

When placing the ice piece on the table be sure it is in a deep tray or there is a pan below to catch the melting water. A medium-sized ice piece should last for quite some time on an ordinary buffet table. Of course, if the room is very warm it will melt sooner. Ice pieces may also be floated in the punch bowl.

13–2 EDIBLE MAIN-DISH CENTERPIECES

Eggplant Penguin

The eggplant penguin, (Fig. 13–2) while not edible, is a delightful centerpiece, used on a tray of deviled eggs, or on a relish tray, or at a children's party. It may also be placed on a small tray with no food, and used strictly as a decorative piece.

Eggplant, fat, round, solid	1
Eggs, hard-cooked	1
Shortening, white	1 cup
Cloves or sliced stuffed olives	for eyes
Carrot or raw beet	1 slice, ½ in. thick
Parsley	1 sprig

Fig. 13–2.   Steps in making eggplant penguin.

1. Cut a thin slice from the bottom so that eggplant will stand upright.
2. Peel only front area. Do not disturb collar.
3. Cover peeled area thickly with softened white shortening.
4. Slice two thin strips of the purple skin from the sides, cutting from the bottom to the top, but do not cut them off. These are the flippers.
5. Place the peeled, hard-cooked egg on top of the eggplant and secure it with toothpicks.
6. Using cloves as picks, attach sliced stuffed olives to the egg for eyes.
7. Make a small hole in the slice of carrot or beet, and pull the stem of the parsley through. Put a pick through the carrot and secure this to the top of the egg as a hat (or use a small paper hat).

Galantine of Chicken

This dish is made of chicken and various other meats, vegetables, and seasonings. The finished galantine is actually a large roll of meat. It should be sliced in advance with the slices laid out on the serving tray, so that the colorful filling shows.

Capon or stewing Chickens	1–5 lb
Pork	1 lb
Veal	1 lb
Beef tongue	1–2 lb
Pâté de fois gras	1 can, 1½ or 2 oz
Salt pork or bacon, sliced thin	½ lb
Egg whites	6
Pistachio nuts	¼ cup
Stuffed (Spanish) olives, drained	½ cup

Truffles, whole	2 or 3
12–15 pitted black olives may be used instead of truffles	
Mushrooms, whole fresh	½ lb
Sherry	1 pt
Cream	1 pt
Salt and white pepper	1 tsp salt
	½ tbs pepper
Onions, carrots, celery	for stock
Water	for stock

1. Bone raw chicken. Use bones in stock. Remove half of the meat from chicken. Reserve skin to wrap around galantine.
2. Boil beef tongue. Cook, peel, and slice in ½-in. square strips. Wrap strips in the thin strips of salt pork or bacon. Reserve.
3. Cut pâté into strips same size as tongue strips. Wrap in salt pork or bacon. Reserve.
4. Grind pork, veal, and chicken meat very fine. Mix thoroughly with egg whites, seasoning, nuts, olives, truffles, whole mushrooms, wine, and cream.
5. Spread half of meat mixture over chicken skin.
6. Lay strips of tongue and pâté on meat. Cover with the additional ground meat mixture.
7. Roll up as a jelly roll. Press gently and then roll tightly.
8. Wrap tightly in clean dish towel. Tie ends to hold shape and around the middle [Fig. 13–3(A)].
9. Place roll in simmering stock. Boil for about 1 hr. Lower heat and allow galantine to simmer for 1½ to 2 hr longer. If galantine is very large, allow to simmer an additional ½ hr.
10. When galantine is cooked and if towel has come loose, remove galantine very carefully from stock, rewrap, retie, and replace it in hot stock. Allow galantine to cool in stock from 4 to 6 hr or overnight.
11. When galantine is thoroughly cooled, remove from stock. Unwrap carefully and wipe surface with a clean cloth to remove any excess fat. Place on work rack and tray, and refrigerate.
12. Prepare a *chaud-froid* and vegetables from which the decoration will be made. (See recipe for *salmon glâcé* in this section.)
13. When galantine is thoroughly cool, coat with *chaud-froid* [Fig. 13–3(B)]. Lay design on *chaud-froid* [Fig. 13–3(C)]. Dip each piece of cut vegetable into clear glaze before placing it on *chaud-froid*. When design is completed, coat entire surface wih clear glaze.
14. Slice part of galantine and place on serving tray [Fig. 13–3(D)].

Ham Peacock

This is a fancy display made from basic foods. The tail of the peacock should be made up of various relishes from which the guests will help themselves. (See Fig. 13–4.)

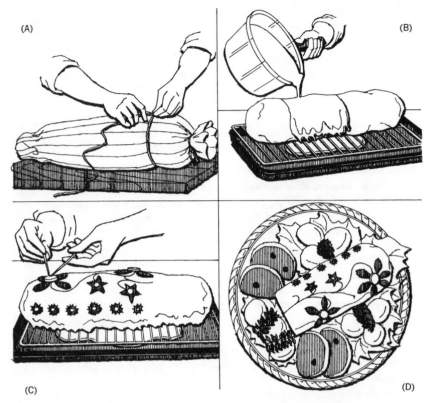

Fig. 13–3. Preparing galantine of chicken. (A) Galantine roll being tied before cooking. (B) Cooked galantine receiving first coat of *chaud-froid*. (C) Completing design on galantine. Undecorated area will be sliced for tray display, so no design is necessary. (D) Part of galantine sliced and placed on tray. Note that design ends at cut edge.

Canned ham	any size
Sweet potato or yam	1 for head of peacock
Black olives	2 slices, for eyes
Long metal skewers	for tail
Frilled picks	4 or 5, for comb
Metal skewers	2, for securing head to body
Paper doilies	for ruff

1. Bake ham in usual manner, but stand it on its side instead of laying it down.
2. Cut slice from bottom, so it will stand. Slice front from short end so head can be attached.
3. Fill skewers with various relishes.
4. Place ham on tray. Place skewers in position for tail.

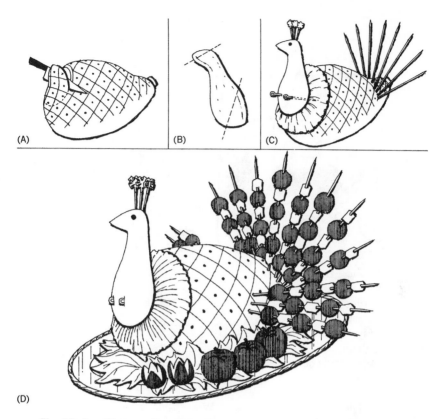

Fig. 13–4. Diagram for assembling ham peacock. (A) Ham on its side with dotted line indicating slice to be made. (B) Shape for head. Dotted lines indicate where to cut yam. (C) Skewers inserted for tail and attaching head to ham. (D) Completed peacock with relish tail. Tray garnished with radish roses and crab apples.

5. Carve sweet potato into shape to resemble peacock head. Attach securely to body with two skewers. Place black olive slices for eyes at each side of head. Place four or five frilled picks at top of head for comb. Fold doilies and secure around area where head is attached to body.
6. Place on serving tray. Garnish with parsley and additional relishes such as used on tail.
7. To serve, remove head and slice the ham.

Lobster Fantasy with Shrimp Salad

The lobster shell is used as a bright display background for quantities of lobster and shrimp salad. (See Fig. 13–5.)

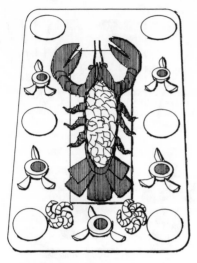

Fig. 13–5. Assembling tray for lobster fantasy with shrimp salad.

Lobster, fresh	1, 2½ lb
Lobster tails	4
Shrimp	2–3 lb
Celery	1–2 lb
Mayonnaise	as needed
Gelatin	2 tbs
Eggs, hard-cooked	6–8
Bread	1 unsliced loaf, day-old

1. Boil lobster and lobster tails. When done, cool and remove all meat. Reserve lobster shell. (To remove meat, cut underside with sharp knife. Remove meat without breaking shell.)
2. Cook shrimp and peel. Reserve 12 whole shrimp. Make salad from balance of shrimp.
3. Cut eggs in halves or thirds and make deviled eggs. Stuff whites and refrigerate until needed.
4. Cut lobster meat in ½-in. slices. Make salad from pieces that fall off.
5. Trim crusts from an unsliced loaf of bread and cut in shape of a base for lobster.
6. Place bread on serving tray. Place lobster shell on bread, tail up. Secure it with picks.
7. Make thick clear glaze from gelatin and 2 cups of water.
8. Coat lobster shell with glaze. Place slices of lobster meat in a row down the lobster shell. The gelatin should hold them.
9. Make shrimp rosettes at the bottom of the loaf of bread. Place large black olive or radish rose at center of each rosette.
10. Place shrimp and lobster salad in lettuce cups on tray alongside the bread.
11. Cover exposed parts of bread with parsley or watercress.
12. Place frilled picks at top of loaf between sections of lobster tail.

13. Use deviled egg halves as garnish. Lemon wedges and tomato wedges may also be used.
14. Extra salad may be kept in lettuce cups on a reserve tray, and the salad replaced as this tray is emptied.

Note: The number of servings from this tray will depend on the amount of salad that is prepared.

Salmon Glâcé

Salmon, fresh	size desired
Court bouillon*	sufficient to poach salmon
Chaud-froid sauce*	sufficient to coat salmon (2 or 3 coats)
Clear glaze	sufficient to coat salmon lightly after design is completed
Raw vegetables	carrots, green pepper, pimiento, leeks, black olives, Spanish olives, according to the design

1. Clean salmon. Remove head. Do not remove tail.
2. Wrap salmon in clean cloth to preserve shape and prevent breaking upon removal from stock. Poach in court bouillon until done.
3. When fish is done, remove pot from fire and allow fish to cool in bouillon.
4. Make *chaud-froid* sauce.
5. When fish is cool, remove carefully and place on rack or in work tray in which approximately ¼-in. clear glaze has been placed. Fish will set in this glaze. This coats and protects the bottom of the fish. Refrigerate until fish is cold to the touch.
6. Cut vegetables and plan design to be worked on exposed side of fish.
7. Coat fish with one thin coat of *chaud-froid*. Return it to refrigerator and allow to set. Apply second and third coat, returning fish to refrigerator between each coating.
8. When final coat is set and fish is completely covered and cold, set design on *chaud-froid* as follows:

   (a) Slice red radishes as thin as possible.
   (b) Cut tiny circles of beets, carrots, green pepper, and black olives.
   (c) Place spring onion greens or leek greens in boiling water until they are limp, about ½ min.
   (d) Cut long thin strips and long ovals of the greens.
   (e) To assemble: Each piece of design should be dipped into a clear glaze before being applied to *chaud-froid* surface. (See. Fig. 13–6.)

---

* Recipes appear after *salmon glâcé* instructions.

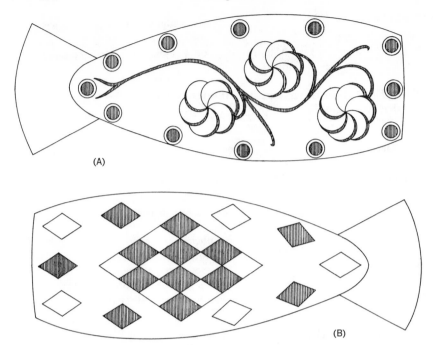

Fig. 13–6. Designs for salmon glâcé must be worked on *chaud-froid*. (A) Stem and leaves are thin strips of green of leeks. Flowers are thin slices of red radishes. Edge is sliced Spanish olives. (B) Harlequin design made up of interlocking diamonds—pimiento, green pepper, and carrots make an interesting color display.

    i. Place center where center of flower is to be.

   ii. Arrange slices of radishes, overlapping, around it.

  iii. Add leek stem and leaves.

  iv. Use thin strips of carrots, green pepper, or green leeks for marking fish tail.

9. When the design is complete, sprinkle lightly with cool clear glaze, and refrigerate until serving time.

10. To place fish on serving tray, lift fish very carefully with two wide spatulas to prevent breaking, and place it on lettuce-lined serving tray. If fish is about 9 lb or more, help will be needed to move the fish intact.

11. Garnish tray with lemon wedges, radish roses, black and green olives, and parsley, or just place a ring of small crackers around edge of tray.

12. When serving, cut through to the bone, making slices of approximately ½ in. When half the fish is served, turn it over and serve remaining half.

Court Bouillon

The quantities will be determined by the size of the fish to be poached. For each 2 qt of water add the following:

Wine, white	2 cups
Salt	2 tbs
Carrots, sliced	2
Onions, medium	2
Bay leaves	4
Peppercorn	6–8
Lemons, sliced	½

1. Place all ingredients in pot. Add fish. Place on medium heat.
2. When bouillon starts to simmer, lower heat.
3. Do not let fish boil, but simmer gently until done.

White Chaud-Froid Sauce

The sauce is made hot but served cold. It is a rich creamed gelatin sauce used to give an even coating to cooked, boiled, or poached fish or fowl. Brown *chaud-froid* sauce is used for meats. *Chaud-froid* sauce is usually decorated. 1½ qt is sufficient to coat a 10–12-lb poached salmon.

Butter	½ cup
Flour	½ cup
Milk	2 cups
Stock	2 cups
Salt	½ tsp
Gelatin, unflavored	4 tbs
Cold water	½ cup, to dissolve gelatin
Cream	½ cup
Mayonnaise	½ cup

1. Make white sauce from butter, flour, milk, and stock.
2. Soften gelatin and mix into hot white sauce. Mix thoroughly and cool. When completely cool, add mayonnaise. Stir well.
3. Add cream, stirring constantly.
4. Spoon over fish, making two or three thin coats rather than one thick coat. Allow *chaud-froid* to set between each application. If *chaud-froid* gets too thick, place in a pan of hot water, and as it heats it will get thinner.
5. *Chaud-froid* should be applied only to *cold* food. It will not adhere to anything warm. *Chaud-froid* may be kept in refrigerator for several days and reheated to be used when needed.

Gilded Turkey

The gilded turkey makes a striking edible centerpiece. The gold leaf is available at most paint and sign stores along with the application brush. One book of 24 sheets will cover an area of approximately 1½ sq ft, or the breast and legs of one large turkey. Grade XX Deep Signboard Gold Leaf is most effective. Choose a type that has no alloy mix. Use the following method to gild the turkey:

1. Roast turkey in usual manner, taking special care that skin on breast remains whole.
2. When turkey is done, remove from pan and allow to cool.
3. Place bird on its back on work table. Slit skin from back of thigh around drumstick along the side and up to joint of wing.
4. Lift skin from back end of breast bone and roll it gently forward toward neck. Do not cut skin off.
5. When white meat is exposed, slide knife point along one side of keel bone and remove white meat in one large piece. Remove white meat from other side.
6. Slice meat, either by hand or machine, but keep slices in order. Replace meat against keel bone as close to original position and shape as possible.
7. Draw skin back over sliced meat.
8. Prepare a clear glaze as follows:

Gelatin, unflavored	2 tbs
Cold water	½ cup
Boiling water	1¾ cups

   (a) Dissolve gelatin in cold water.
   (b) Add mixture to boiling water, lower heat.
   (c) Cook until clear, 2 or 3 min. Allow to cool.

9. Wipe turkey skin with warm damp cloth to remove as much grease as possible. Allow turkey to cool.
10. Wash turkey skin lightly with about one fourth of clear glaze. Allow it to cool thoroughly and coat it with remainder of glaze. This step is most important as gold leaf will not cling to any fatty or greasy surface. It will adhere to a gelatin base.

The actual application of the gold leaf is not difficult, but requires a steady hand and a room with absolutely no air current. The slightest breeze, even someone passing by quickly, is sufficient to dislodge the gold leaf from the page and cause it to crumble.

A sheet of gold leaf is approximately 3⅜ sq in. It must be picked up on the edge of the application brush by static electricity. (See Fig. 13–7.) Rub the brush against a clean cloth until it picks up the necessary static electricity. Then, touch the flat side of the brush to one edge of the sheet

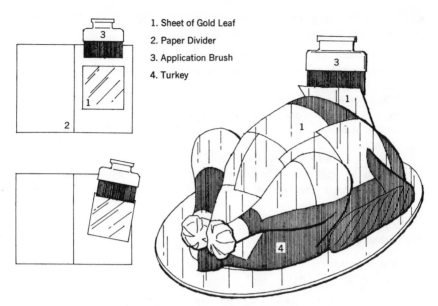

1. Sheet of Gold Leaf
2. Paper Divider
3. Application Brush
4. Turkey

Fig. 13–7. Application of gold leaf.

of gold leaf lifting it quickly but gently from the paper page on which it is resting. The gold leaf will cling to the brush and swing free of the paper. Move it into the position desired and let it touch the gelatin-coated turkey. It will immediately adhere to the gelatin surface. Lift the brush away gently. Continue in this manner, laying the sheets next to one another, overlapping as necessary. Once the gold leaf is on the turkey, it will not blow off, though it will probably come off if touched.

Fill the back opening and the area around the legs with parsley or mustard greens.

Gold paper doilies should be wrapped around the exposed bone at the end of the drumstick.

To serve, place the turkey on a lettuce-lined tray and garnish with half peaches filled with cranberry sauce or spiced crab apples. To serve the turkey, just lift the skin from the back of the breast bone and fold it forward to expose the already sliced meat. Serve as needed. The skin may be pulled back to cover the bone after serving.

13–3 MELON BASKETS

Melons in season make attractive centerpieces and have the added feature of always being fresh. The basket will have the initial or motif for the specific affair, a personalized touch that adds much to the overall effect of the table decoration.

Watermelons allow the largest area for working out designs; however, smaller melons may also be used successfully (Fig. 13–8). The general procedure for carving all melons is the same.

1. Score melon with complete design or initial. Keep it simple.
2. Cut design deeply into skin, using a ball point pen that has run dry or or a lemon peeler.
3. When all markings are complete, cut melon into shape desired. (It is much easier to work design on a whole melon than to try to cut a design after melon has been cut into shape and scooped.)
4. Scoop out as much of melon as desired for cutting into serving pieces. Refrigerate until serving time.
5. To serve, refill melon basket with meat and any additional cut fruit that is needed. Prepare sufficient extra fruit to refill basket as needed to serve all guests.

Old-Fashioned Sailing Ship

The watermelon carved in this shape allows more space for serving fruit than do the taller baskets.

1. Score melon lengthwise, leaving front and back higher than center. Scoop portholes with a small ball scoop, going only through the green and allowing the white to show through.
2. Cut melon as indicated in Fig. 13–9. Scoop all meat from both halves

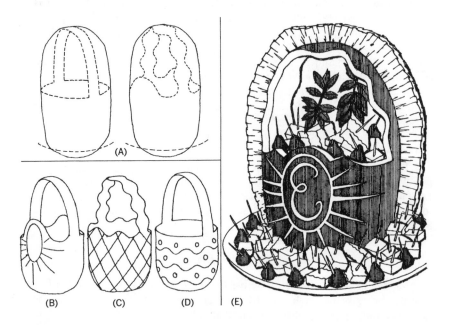

Fig. 13–8. (A) Side view. Cut on dotted line for simple tall basket. (B) Front view of sunburst. Initial may be placed within sunburst. (C) Traditional woven basket. (D) Circles may be cut with small ball scoop. (E) Completed melon basket.

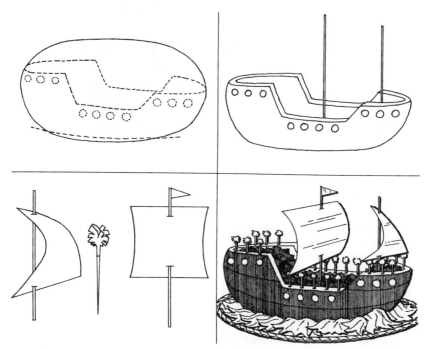

Fig. 13–9. Old-fashioned sailing ship. This can be carved from watermelon or any other large well-shaped melon.

and cut into serving pieces. Other fruit may be added. Refrigerate.

3. Two or three sails may be used, depending on size of the melon. Cut oblong and triangular sails from aluminum foil. Place them on dowel sticks and set dowels in hull of ship at positions desired. Do not pierce outer (bottom) shell with these sticks.

4. Guard rails around bridge and edges of ship can be made from frilled picks or maraschino cherries and mandarin orange sections on plastic picks.

5. Set completed ship on serving tray. Fill with fruit and set on buffet.

Church Altar

Unlike the melon basket, there is no space in this display for the cut fruit. Thus, an additional tray will be needed for the fruit to be served. This basket may be placed in the center of a large tray filled with cut fruit or on a small silver tray surrounded by flowers and somewhat apart from the other fruit.

1. Select large squat melon rather than tall one.

2. Score as shown in Fig. 13–10.

3. Cut out approximately one fourth of melon, leaving solid base and small shell-like top.

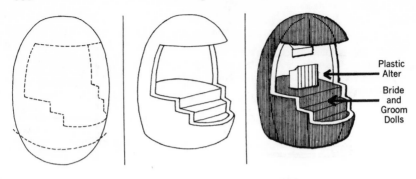

Fig. 13–10.   Church altar carved from watermelon.

4. Scoop out sufficient meat to allow space to put small altar in shell.
5. Carve steps.
6. Use small plastic altar and whatever back wall decoration that is in keeping with occasion.

Baby Carriage

This is an ideal centerpiece for a baby shower (Fig. 13–11).

1. Use any small round melon. Score and remove approximately one fourth of melon.
2. Scoop out sufficient meat from top, back, and sides to allow room for plastic doll and blanket.
3. Handle can be made from aluminum-covered dowel sticks, tied together to hold shape.
4. Wheels may be plastic, or slices of orange or grapefruit.
5. Decorate carriage with tiny pink or blue bows.
6. Place on silver tray at center of table. Place fruit on separate tray.

13–4   FRUIT BASKETS

Individual fruit baskets are lovely, but require a great deal of work. When needed in large quantities, they also require a great deal of refrigeration space. However, if time and space permit, they can be made hours in advance of serving time.

Grapefruit Basket

1. Cut grapefruit in half.
2. Remove all meat as carefully as possible to retain shape of segment halves. Place in large bowl.
3. Remove remaining segment skins from shell.
4. Refill grapefruit basket with segments to which other fruit (in season) has been added:

Fig. 13–11. Baby carriage carved from melon.

(a) melon pieces,
(b) apple chunks dipped in lemon juice,
(c) grapes,
(d) orange or mandarin orange segments.
5. Top with maraschino cherry, large strawberry, or sprig of fresh mint.
6. Refrigerate until serving time.

Orange Basket

There are many uses for these small baskets on the buffet table, foremost of which is to hold cranberry sauce for turkey trays. These baskets should be made without handles, as the handles impede service, particularly when guests are serving themselves. Orange baskets are made in the same manner as grapefruit baskets.

Pineapple Basket

These are probably more costly than any of the other individual baskets, but there is no way to imitate the taste of fresh pineapple.

1. Cut pineapple in half lengthwise through the top greens, taking care not to break greens off. If pineapples are particularly large, they may be cut lengthwise in thirds or quarters.
2. Using a serrated grapefruit knife, cut out meat in one large piece. This may be cut into thin slices or wedges and mixed with other cut fruit, or just piled back into pineapple skin. Maraschino cherries or mandarin orange sections make attractive garnishes.
3. Refrigerate before serving.
4. When serving, place pineapple baskets on table so all green leaves point in same direction.

Pineapple baskets may also be made by removing the green top and cutting in half, similar to the grapefruit cut. The pineapple meat is then scooped. This fruit is then cut into chunks and replaced in the shell with the other cut fruit. This method makes for a higher basket, but it is not as colorful as the long cut with the green tops still attached.

Melon Carnival

For the best effect the melon carnival should be brought out whole, then sliced and served from the buffet. It should be prepared at least one full day in advance.

Melon, canteloupe or honey-dew	1, 10 in. in length
Fruit flavored gelatin	2 packages
Cocktail fruit salad	1, 1-lb drained can

1. Peel melon. Cut heavy slice from bottom so it will stand. Do not cut through to core.
2. Cut hole in top and remove all seeds. Rinse inside with cold water. Set upside down to drain.
3. Prepare gelatin according to package instructions, but decrease total of water for both packages by about ½ cup.
4. When gelatin is cool, add drained fruit. Allow gelatin to start to set, then pour it quickly into melon. Stir inside melon once or twice to be sure fruit is evenly distributed.
5. Set melon in refrigerator. Do not move or disturb for at least 6 hr or until gelatin is firmly set.
6. To serve, turn melon on its side and set on lettuce-lined serving tray. Slice melon through with sharp knife dipped in hot water. One slice is a portion.

CHAPTER 14

Food Decoration

Creative ability in catering means the talent of designing and decorating food. A caterer should remember that simple decorations on salads and attractively arranged buffet tables will add considerably to the appearance of a room.

14-1 TRAY GARNISH AND DESIGN

Even the tastiest food will usually call for some garnish or decoration to improve its appearance when served. Most hot food requires a simple garnish, such as parsley, watercress, or something similar that can be added quickly. This will not hold up the service nor will it allow the food to cool unnecessarily.

Cold food, which has more standing time, allows for more garnish and decoration, although no food should be kept on the work table any longer than necessary. When planning a buffet, plan in advance exactly how each tray of food is to be set out and decorated. Cut the decorations in advance.

All cold food on trays should generally have some decoration or garnish, and the food, as placed on the tray, should form a design. (See Fig. 14-1.) If the cold food is colorful, such as decorated petits fours or fancy cookies, additional decorations may not be required. Such food should be set out in a manner which displays its decorative shape and color. If the cold food is dry, such as cookies, canapés, or hors d'oeuvres, a paper doily should be placed under the food. Cold sliced meat or cheese should be placed on a bed of lettuce.

Cold salad with dressing (cole slaw, shrimp salad, potato salad, etc.) should be served in a bowl or deep tray. A simple design or initial cut from other solid foods makes an attractive decoration. Radish roses or other vegetable flowers may also be used as salad garnish. Lettuce, parsley, or mustard greens can be placed around the edge of the salad.

The cost and time required for the decoration of individual canapés and

163

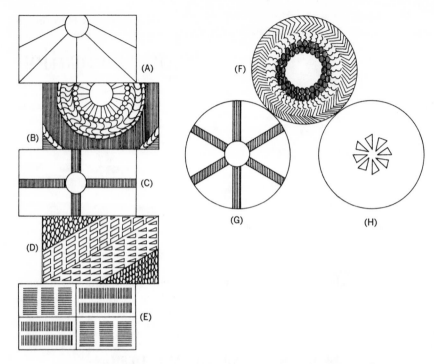

Fig. 14–1. Patterns for setting food on trays. Square or oblong designs: (A) sunburst; (B) semi-circle; (C) quartered with centerpiece; (D) oblique, no centerpiece; (E) quartered, no centerpiece. Round or oval designs: (F) circle; (G) spokes; (H) sardine center for canapé.

sandwiches, regardless of the quantity to be made, should be planned in advance. (See Sec. 14–3.)

In each of the basic tray designs in Fig. 14–1, the lines indicate divisions between various types of foods. The lines suggested are simple allowing large areas for food, yet still keeping an attractive pattern. The semicircle and the sunburst should be used only on a table that will be set against the wall, or on a served buffet. All other designs can be used as space and menu permits.

A variety of shapes of trays—round, oval, oblong, and square—will add to the appearance of the table, although a great number of small trays will clutter the table and need constant refilling. Use the largest trays, within reason, for the number of guests to be served. If two or more trays of the same food are to be served—for two stations—the shape of the tray and the design should remain the same, if possible.

Trays should not be refilled at the table. Empty trays should be removed to the kitchen and fresh trays brought out. Guests will wait while a tray of food is being replaced. Particular care should be taken to see that no empty tray remains on the table.

14–2 CARVING FLOWERS AND DESIGNS FROM RAW VEGETABLES

There are many flowers and designs that can be carved by hand from various raw vegetables. This is a highly specialized skill requiring practice and patience. While the finished decorations are lovely, flower carving is time-consuming and expensive, and therefore, most caterers restrict their carving to radish roses and carved initials.

The flowers and designs shown here can be done simply and quickly. Any initial can be fashioned from strips of pimiento, green pepper, or carrots.

Radish Roses

Radish roses can be used as decoration on a salad bowl, in the center of meat and cheese trays, and on relish trays. The procedure is as follows:

1. Remove top. Cut greens, leaving approximately ½ in. of green at bottom.
2. Score along dotted lines (Fig. 14–2). Slide point of knife under red skin and loosen it from body of radish. Do not cut it off. Peel off only red areas marked × in figure.
3. Place radishes in cold water and refrigerate for several hours before use.

Note: Commerical radish rose cutters are available in all restaurant supply houses. These make only one style of rose, but are excellent for quantity use.

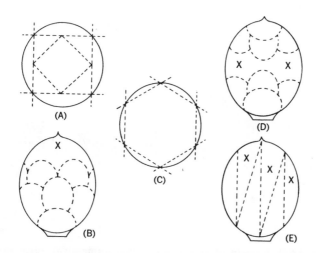

Fig. 14–2. Various designs of radish roses. (A) Diamond; (B) rose; (C) simple rose; (D) Japanese lantern; (E) poinsetter.

Shield (Fig. 14–3)

1. Slice carrots, beets, and white turnips, ⅛ in. thick.
2. Trim so all slices are same size, either round, triangular, or square.
3. Cut design from center of each, using sharp knife, or truffle, or chocolate cutters.
4. Remove centers, but do not destroy remainder of slices.
5. Reverse centers. Place beet center in turnip, carrot in beet, and turnip center in carrot slice.
6. To use, place on top of potato salad, or on *chaud-froid* coated food, or impale on toothpicks and insert in party triangles, or on top of closed sandwiches.

Black-Eyed Susan

1. Pare and slice carrots and white turnips ⅛ in. thick. (Turnip slice should be approximately one third larger than carrot.)
2. Cut series of triangles from carrot as shown in Fig. 14–4(A). Cut in the order numbered to guarantee evenly spaced leaves.
3. To assemble, place cut carrot on top of turnip slice. Place a small circle of green pepper or black olive in center. Place on toothpick and add to centerpiece or salad (Fig. 14–4B).

14–3 DECORATION OF CANAPES

All canapés are open face and should be decorated. Decorations may be made from any combination of food that is compatible with the food used on the canapé, such as

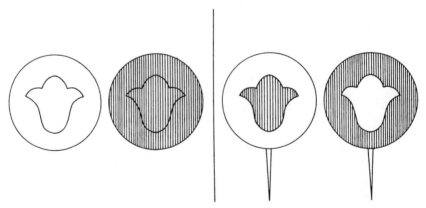

Fig. 14–3. Shield of sliced carrots and turnips with reversed cutout center designs.

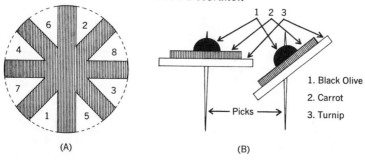

(A)   (B)

1. Black Olive
2. Carrot
← Picks →   3. Turnip

Fig. 14–4. Black-eyed Susan. (A) Cutting carrot slice; (B) 2 methods of assembling.

Sliced stuffed olives   Pimientos
Green peppers   Carrots
Black olives   Pickles, gherkins
Anchovies   Cocktail onions

All of these may be cut into various shapes with a sharp knife or with tiny truffle cutters, or cut into thin strips.

Lightly colored mayonnaise with cream cheese pressed through a small star tube makes an attractive decoration for canapés. However, this type of decoration is extremely fragile. It is best used when the canapés will not have to be boxed or transported.

One or two decorations should be placed on top of each canapé, but the entire surface should not be covered with the decoration. A sliced stuffed olive and a strip of pimiento or green pepper repeated on many canapés will make a lovely flower garden. (See Fig. 14–5.)

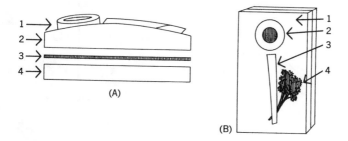

(A)

(B)

(A)
1. Sliced olive and pimiento strip
2. Salad (meat or cheese)
3. Spread, mayonnaise, butter, or margarine
4. Bread

(B)
1. Tea sandwich, or canape
2. Slice of stuffed olive
3. Strip of pimiento or green pepper
4. Sprig of parsley

Fig. 14–5. Canapé decoration. (A) Side view; (B) top view.

When sandwich-size bread is used, the design can be laid out once on the entire surface, then cut into four sections. (See Fig. 14–6.) This will require a sharp, thin knife. In this manner, four decorated canapés can be made in the time usually required to decorate one. This method may also be used for the lengthwise slice of bread, repeating the whole pattern three times over the surface, and then cutting the bread into 12 small squares.

Sardines can be laid out to form an attractive design. [See Fig. 14–7(A).] They should be placed at even intervals on the bread which has been spread with mayonnaise. Each sardine is then decorated with a thin strip of pimiento or green pepper. When the bread is cut, the individual canapés can be set in a straight line or in a circle, points in, to make a center for a large tray of canapés. Any solid pieces of meat, fish, or cheese, may be used in much the same manner as the sardines.

The lengthwise slice of bread may also be spread with various salads, then decorated with three strips of pimiento, green pepper, and cheese, or any other small designs cut from these vegetables. [See Fig. 14–7(B).] The bread can be cut and placed on the tray of the sardine canapés.

Canapés are usually needed in large quantities. It is especially valuable to be able to make designs that can be applied quickly and simply, yet appear quite intricate when set out, as those described above.

14–4 DECORATING COLD MEAT

Large pieces of meat, whether sliced, partially sliced, or left whole, may be decorated for the buffet. They may be sliced at the table or in the kitchen, with additional trays of the cold sliced meat held in reserve to speed up service.

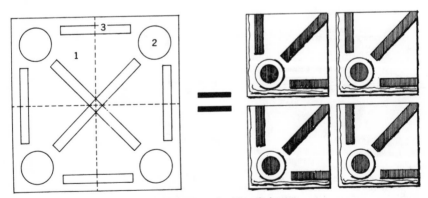

1. Bread covered with salad
2. Stuffed olive slice
3. Strips of pimiento or green pepper

Fig. 14–6. Canapé decoration using sandwich slice of bread. (A) Whole slice decorated. (B) Slice cut into 4 pieces.

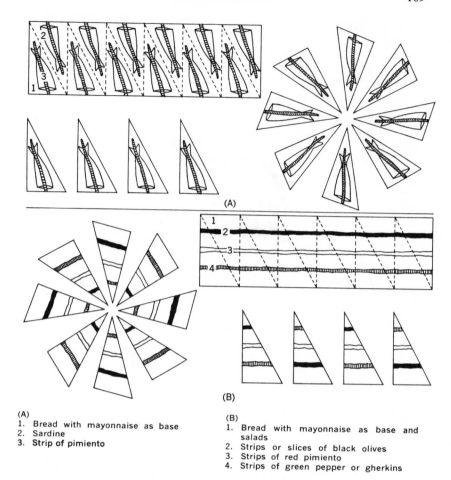

(A)

(B)

(A)
1. Bread with mayonnaise as base
2. Sardine
3. Strip of pimiento

(B)
1. Bread with mayonnaise as base and salads
2. Strips or slices of black olives
3. Strips of red pimiento
4. Strips of green pepper or gherkins

Fig. 14–7. (A) Canapé decoration using long slice of bread with sardines. (B) Canapé decoration on long slice of bread using various spreads.

The most popular of these cold meats for buffet service are top sirloin, roast beef, ham, and tongue.

For an interesting presentation or an edible centerpiece, the meat should be decorated. (See Fig. 14–8.) It may be coated with a glaze or a *chaud-froid,* and decorated in a manner similar to the *salmon glâcé.* The *chaud-froid* medallion is an efficient and effective method of decorating any cold meat, fish, or poultry. The general procedure for decorating meat is as follows:

1. Roast or cook meat in usual manner.
2. Allow meat to cool thoroughly.
3. Decide upon method of presentation:

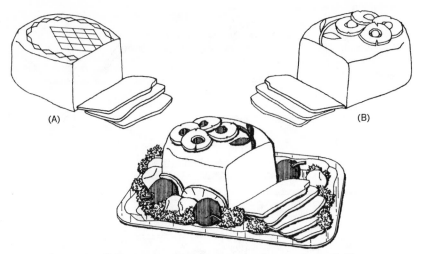

(A)   (B)

Fig. 14–8. Decoration of cold meat. (A) Harlequin medallion design. (B) Pineapple flower ham, partially sliced.

(a) Slice meat completely and stack it as close to original shape as possible.
(b) Make a "waterfall" by slicing approximately one fourth of meat. Stack slices against remaining section as in Fig. 14–8. Leave meat unsliced.

4. Decorate meat.
5. Set on serving trays. Decorate trays and serve.

To coat meat with a clear brown glaze, be sure meat is thoroughly cold. Place in refrigerator before coating. Wipe off excess fat.

Clear Brown Glaze

Gelatin, unflavored	2 tbs
Cold water	½ cup
Brown stock	2 cups

1. Add dissolved gelatin to cold stock. Bring to boil. Stir.
2. Lower heat, cook until liquid is clear.
3. Remove from heat and cool. If glaze should set in the work pan, place pan in hot water for a few minutes.

To make a brown *chaud-froid* (see *salmon glâcé* recipe in Sec. 13–2), substitute browned butter for the butter and beef bouillon or brown stock for the plain stock.

Medallion

A medallion is a decorated *chaud-froid* (either white or brown) made separately from the item it is to cover. Just before serving time the medallion may be placed on the meat, fish, or poultry and brought to the table. A medallion made in advance may be kept in the refrigerator for a day or two. When colored *chaud-froid* is kept too long, the colors fade into one another and blur the design. Cut vegetables should be used if the medallion will have to stand for any length of time.

1. Prepare one half of *chaud-froid* recipe in Sec. 13–2.
2. Prepare 2 cups of clear (not brown) glaze.
3. Pour about half of finished *chaud-froid* to ½-in. deep into two dinner plates or large oval platters. (One is extra in case the first breaks when being moved.) Refrigerate.
4. Divide remainder of *chaud-froid* into three or four small bowls. While *chaud-froid* is still in liquid state, color these in red, yellow, green, or black. Pour these into individual plates to thickness of ¼ in., refrigerate, and let set hard. These will be cut to form design. Raw vegetables may also be used to form designs.
5. To decorate, remove hardened base *chaud-froid* and turn it out. *Do not use heat.* Lift one side of *chaud-froid* from plate, using a paring knife or spatula to get in under it. Lift it off or turn it over onto another plate or tray, into which a thin layer of clear glaze has been placed and allowed to set. Turning the *chaud-froid* upside down will leave a shiny surface on which to place the design.
6. Cut colored *chaud-froid* or raw vegetables into the desired shapes. Dip each piece of design into cool clear glaze before placing it on base medallion. Allow it to set in place. When the design is completed, coat entire surface lightly with clear glaze. This may be sprayed on, if small sprayer is available.
7. Replace completed medallion [Fig. 14–8(A)] in refrigerator until needed. When needed, lift medallion from tray and place gently on top of meat, fish, or poultry. Meat must be cold or *chaud-froid* will melt. Additional clear glaze may be sprayed around edge of medallion to secure it to meat. Parsley placed around edges will outline design.

The main advantage of making a medallion is that it can be prepared well in advance, when there is no rush to complete the actual food items. Simple drawings, as well as more complicated designs, may be worked out very effectively in the *chaud-froid*. Some other designs besides the harlequin that are extremely effective are floral designs (see *salmon glâcé* recipe in Sec. 13–2), initials set in a heart, and flower basket (see Sec. 14–5).

Pineapple Flower on Ham

This is a simple flower and can be done in a few minutes. Work directly on the meat. [See Fig. 14–8(B).]

1. Place four slices of canned pineapple so that they overlap slightly.
2. Place red maraschino cherries in center of each slice.
3. Cut thin strips of green pepper for stems and leaves. Place on ham.
4. Garnish tray with crab apples, tiny Irish potatoes, and parsley.

14–5 SALAD DECORATION FOR BUFFET SERVICE

Any large salad except the tossed green variety may be decorated for buffet service. The decoration may be a simple design or an initial cut from vegetables. The salad should be egg, potato, shrimp, macaroni, or any salad that can be smoothed over so that the design will show up. The procedure is as follows:

1. Place salad in bowl, platter, or deep tray from which it will be served.
2. Lay out design on board or plate, and then transfer it to salad. This design should be placed on top of salad and left there. No gelatin coating is necessary.
3. Use parsley, watercress, or mustard greens as garnish around edge of bowl or around edge of design.

CHAPTER 15

Menu File

General and everyday menus and recipes (which can be found in any good cook book) are not covered here. Unless otherwise indicated, the menus are prepared for regular, American service to the seated guest. Buffet menus will indicate whether served, partially served, or completely self-service. Special notations will be listed on the various menus where they are needed.

Where a variety of appetizers, main dishes, or desserts are shown, they will be listed together. It is for the caterer to make the selection. In choosing, the caterer should keep in mind the budget and the facilities available. He should offer as wide a selection as possible. He should also offer something different, perhaps his own specialties, as long as he is sure they can be prepared and served properly under the existing conditions.

Many general cook books offer special menus for the minor holidays. However, these are generally small at home affairs with friends and family doing the food preparation and serving. For the caterer it is best therefore to ignore these minor holidays unless there is a large public affair scheduled in conjunction with the day, or the day has special local interest.

For example, most president's birthdays tend to be ignored except in their native state. Holidays such as May Day and Halloween are for the most part "no caterer's day."

"Local days," on the other hand, may be very good catering days. Check with the chamber of commerce for special local day celebrations— annual openings of civic events such as art exhibits, musicals, festivals, county fairs, sports events, school proms, and class dances. These are all excellent opportunities for catered parties.

Flexibility is the keynote in all menu planning. The menu should fit the occasion. Practically any menu can be adapted to suit any occasion with the addition of a theme for table decorations and perhaps a minor change or two in the basic menu. For example, a small rolled scroll tied with school color ribbons will turn an ordinary luncheon into a "Graduation Day Lunch." Antipasto instead of an ordinary salad as the appetizer will give an Italian flavor to the dinner.

15–1 SERVING FOREIGN FOODS

The universality of certain foods is such that they are perfectly acceptable on any table. An excellent example of this is French bread. This item is generally accepted as the substitute for local bread with any foreign foods. However, a catered dinner party is not the place to try to break in new food tastes. Therefore, coffee is usually served at the end of a meal in the United States, regardless of the beverage that would be served with the meal in its native country.

The recipes in this book for all foreign dishes have been adjusted so that they can be prepared in any well-stocked commissary or kitchen. When a foreign dish would be particularly difficult to prepare and serve in large quantities, or might not be accepted because of its very unusual flavor, a substitute has been offered which is similar to the original, but easier to prepare and more acceptable to the guests.

15–2 SERVING CHILDREN'S PORTIONS

In preparing the menu and price, discuss with the hostess the matter of children. Youngsters from 11 or 12 years of age are served as adults. Under that age, they may be served smaller portions with charges made accordingly.

15–3 SIDE-DISH SALADS

The selection of side-dish salads in Chap. 16 may seem somewhat limited in view of the hundreds of different salads offered in various cook books. However, fancy, involved, and difficult-to-serve side-dish salads are fine for home or small group entertaining, but they are not acceptable for the large catered affair.

Over a period of years, experience has shown that the salads listed below were the most frequently used for side-dish salads. They met with the most success from the standpoint of guest acceptance, as well as ease in preparation and serving:

1. tossed green salad with chef's dressing,
2. mixed salad (tossed green with tomato added),
3. vinaigrette (mixed assorted vegetables with French dressing),
4. hearts of lettuce with dressing,
5. avocado and tomato slices or wedges with dressing.

15–4 HOW TO USE THE MENU FILE

In the following pages, sample menus are given for different occasions. In general, a full dinner consists of an appetizer, the main course, and dessert.

For a dinner of approximately 25–50 guests, offer a choice of one appetizer from three. However, be sure that it will not duplicate or conflict with the main dish or salad. Have a relish tray on each table.

For the main dish, again offer three choices. If the vegetables are the same for all three dishes, list them separately on the menu, below the main dishes, together with the salad. Specify the salad dressing offered.

Main dish
Main dish
Main dish
  Potato and green vegetable
  Salad with dressing

On the other hand, if each main dish calls for different vegetables, they should be listed together with the main dish. The salad is listed separately.

Main dish, boiled potato, green beans
Main dish, rice, tomato slice
Main dish, broccoli, broiled tomato
  Salad with dressing

The type of bread offered should fit with the meal and should always be served with a plate of butter. For dessert, a choice should also be offered. It could either be the occasion cake, or fruit, or gelatin, etc. Suggested beverages should be listed in general classifications such as wine, champagne, beer, coffee, tea, soft drinks, or punch. The sample menus in this chapter are prepared for American service, unless otherwise specified. The asterisks indicate that the recipes are listed in Chap. 16.

A. Anniversary Dinner

DINNER   25–30 guests

No cocktail hour. Champagne to be poured at table immediately after main course is served.

Choice of 1   Fruit cup (fresh fruit in season)
                     Half grapefruit—strawberry garnish or
                         anniversary garnish, silver leaf, etc.
                     Vichyssoise (hot or cold)*

Choice of 1   Roast duck with orange sauce*
                         Hunter wild rice*
                         Creamed mixed vegetables
                     Prime ribs of beef au jus*
                         Browned potato*
                         Green beans
                     Filet of Sole Florentine*
                     Broiled white fish or halibut, with butter
                         sauce

                     Tomato slices on bed of lettuce
                     Small dinner rolls, with butter

Dessert   Anniversary cake

Beverage	Coffee, tea
	Champagne as indicated
Service	Formal French

B. Bar Mitzvah

1. DINNER, MEAT MEAL   **50–200 guests, adults and children**

Cocktail hour   Assorted hot and cold hors d'oeuvres to be passed. Bar setup or champagne. Champagne to be poured at table immediately after main course is served.

Choice of 1   Gefilte fish in natural juice*
Viennese sweet and sour rolled cabbage*
Chopped liver (pâté)* rosette, garnished
Relish tray*

Choice of 1   Roast prime ribs of beef au jus*
Roast half chicken, with spiced peaches
Pot Roast*
     Oven browned potato*
     Fresh garden peas

Tossed green salad, with chef's dressing
Traditional challah (large braided egg bread)

Dessert   Traditional bar mitzvah (open book) cake

Beverage   Espresso, tea, punch

2. DINNER, DAIRY MEAL

Note: At a dairy meal no meat of any form may be served.

Cocktail hour   Assorted hot and cold canapés and hors d'oeuvres to be passed. These are to be made of fish, egg, cheese, and vegetables only. Bar setup. Wine or champagne to be served with main course.

Choice of 1   Gefilte fish in natural juice*
Chopped egg and browned onions*
Herring bits in wine
Relish tray*

Choice of 1   Baked fresh fish (no shellfish may be
used)
Parsley new potatoes
Fresh garden peas with mushrooms
Cheese blintzes* with sour cream†
Asparagus spears, with pimiento gar-
nish
Mixed salad (with tomato, chef's dress-
ing
Traditional challah (large braided egg
bread)

Dessert   Traditional bar mitzvah book cake
Beverage   Coffee, tea, punch

Note: The candle lighting ceremony may occur after the main course
is served. (See Chap. 11.)

C. Bachelor or Stag Party

DINNER   **20–35 guests**

Cocktails are served before dinner. The etiquette books, to the contrary,
state that drinks are usually served during and after this meal as well.

Cocktail Hour   Bar opened. Hors d'oeuvres (cocktail
franks, miniature meatballs, cheese
tray, and crackers). Relish trays on
tables.

Choice of 1   Steak (New York cut, minute, cube)
Salisbury steak
Baked potato, with sour cream and
chives
Green vegetable (not creamed)
Lettuce and tomato salad, Roquefort
dressing
Dinner roll, with butter

Dessert   Plain
Beverage   Lots of coffee

If no cheese is served for hors d'oeuvres, then trays of solid cheese with
fruit and nuts may be served as dessert.

The bartender may be one of the guests. The host or a member of the
party often takes complete charge of the bar and liquor service.

---

† Wine instead of champagne served with this.

If entertainment is scheduled, the meal should be served quickly. The tables should be cleared, except for the coffee, cheese, and fruit trays, before the program is scheduled to begin.

D. Barbecue

All meat should be cooked on outdoor grills, open pits, fireplaces, or barbecues, in full view of the guests. However, very large cuts of beef may have to be cooked before the guests arrive, then removed to the serving table to be sliced. Adequate cooking space and sufficient personnel to cook the quantity of food needed are absolutely necessary. The number of waiters and busboys will be determined by the amount of serving that guests are to do themselves. Even for a self-service buffet, waiters are needed to refill the trays, to keep the buffet table attractive, to serve beverages, and to clean up.

Choice of 2 meats	Steaks (precut): New York, minute, sandwich, cube
	Kabobs (beef, lamb, or chicken pieces en brochette, alternating with various vegetables; suggested for smaller groups)
	Burgers: Beef and chili*
	Fish: whole, steaks, or fillets
	Turkey, barbecued whole then sliced to order
	Ham, whole or precut steaks
	Lamb rack, leg or precut lamb chops
Sauces	Texas barbecue sauce*
	Chef's own sauce
	Chili barbecue sauce
Choice of 1	Fresh corn broiled in aluminum foil
	Idaho potato baked in aluminum foil
	Sweet potato or yam baked in aluminum foil
	Assorted relishes
	Cole slaw
	Tossed green salad with assorted dressings
	Hot biscuits, with butter
Dessert	Fruit pie
Beverage	Coffee, tea, soft drinks
	Beer
Service	Buffet, informal

E. Bazaar

Bazaars can be either buffet, barbecue, or cafeteria style. They are usually held in conjunction with fund-raising operations. Schools, and religious and fraternal organizations use this method of fund-raising and social activity as an annual event. If various committees contribute part of the food and services, the caterer may supply some of the food and also act as coordinator.

1. BUFFET

Hot dishes	Spaghetti, with meat or mushroom sauce Spaghetti and meat balls in tomato sauce Fried chicken: halves, quarters, or bits* Frankfurters with baked beans Spanish rice Casseroles: meat and vegetables or stews*
Cold dishes	Cold sliced meat trays (ham and cheese, turkey, salami, tongue, picnic meats) Sliced cheese trays (avoid cheese spreads) Sandwiches, with any of meats listed above Relish tray*

Salads	Platters or sandwiches
	  Egg salads assorted*
	  Fruit and cottage cheese
	  Crunchy tuna fish salad*
	  Chicken salad*
	  Elegant shrimp salad*
	
	Side-Dish Salads
	  Potato*
	  Cole slaw
	  Macaroni*
	  Bean*
	  Mixed green
	
	Molded salads
	  Perfection salad*
	  Lime and pear*
	  Assorted fruit gelatin salad

Desserts	Cakes, cookies, pies
Beverage	Coffee, tea, milk, soft drinks
Service	Buffet, informal

2. BARBECUE (See Sec. 15–4D)

The menu will be determined by the budget as well as by the number of volunteer workers available to man the grills and to serve.

3. CAFETERIA STYLE

A kitchen and counter setup is needed here. Many county and local fair buildings as well as churches have this physical setup which is utilized during fairs and bazaars. The operation is the same as any cafeteria operation. The guest takes what he wishes and pays for it at the end of the line.

In warm weather, a choice of one or two salads such as egg salad, tuna fish salad, shrimp salad, diced ham salad, or cottage cheese and fruit salad (depending on the price) can be offered plus a bed of lettuce, scoop of potato salad, or cole slaw, carrot sticks, radish rose, and tomato slice.

Hot dish selections might include beef stew, fried chicken (half, quarter, or bits), franks and beans with sauerkraut, or spaghetti (in any of its many forms).

In winter, hot soups and vegetables such as mashed potatoes, baked beans, and green vegetables can be added to the menu. All sandwiches should be made to order from any of the salads offered on the salad plate.

For dessert, offer cakes, cookies, and pies (usually donated by the committee). Beverages can include hot or iced coffee, tea, soft drinks, and beer (if permit is available).

F. Bon Voyage

Space is usually extremely limited, and serving facilities are practically nonexistent aboard a ship for the outside caterer. At airports, except for the use of the airport dining rooms, catered parties are discouraged.

Plan bon voyage or farewell parties at home, or in a public hall close to the point of departure. Bon voyage parties are often held in an office. They are of short duration, so service should be fast.

G. Breakfast

1. COMMUNION   20–30 guests

First Communion is generally held in the spring of the year with breakfast about 10:30–11:00 a. m. at home. Everything at home should be ready to serve at least 15 min. before the scheduled time for the guests to arrive.

	Fruit juice
Choice of 1	French toast wedges* and individual sausage
	Pancakes or waffles
	Minced ham omelet

Bacon and eggs

Rolls and butter

Beverage   Milk or chocolate milk for youngsters

Coffee for adults

2. WEDDING   25–200 guests

Breakfast is served at about 11:30 a.m.

Champagne cocktail

Fresh fruit cup with melon balls

Choice of 1   Mushroom omelet with mashed potatoes

Creamed chicken* in patty shell

Sliced tomato on bed of lettuce

Casserole dishes (not spaghetti)

Eggs Benedict* with cheese sauce

English muffins or biscuits

Marmalade, butter

Beverage   Coffee served wih traditional tiered wedding cake

3. FUND-RAISING   25–150 guests

Chilled fruit juice

Choice of 1   *Group A*

(from group A   Cheese omelet

or group B)   Bacon, ham, or sausage and eggs

Pancakes or waffles with bacon

Group B

Platters of assorted cheeses on each table

Fish platters: sardines, tuna, anchovy, smoked salmon

Rolls, biscuits, bread, miniature sweet rolls

Beverage   Coffee

This may be a solicitation for funds or a pep rally for volunteer workers. There will certainly be short speeches. Waiters should not pour coffee or clear tables during the speeches. Arrange with the chairman in advance for serving. Find out whether tables are to be cleared, or if a pitcher of coffee is to be placed on each table so guests may pour a second cup themselves during the speeches. For serving, group A will require one waiter per 25–30 guests, and group B one waiter per 35–40 guests. Group B has all the food on the table, so the waiter only pours coffee.

H. Buffet

Any type of food may be served. Assorted hot or cold hors d'oeuvres, open-face decorated canapés, and party triangles may be passed or placed on the table. Hot hors d'oeuvres should be kept warm in chafing dishes or on hot trays. For originality you can make various miniatures.

Potato pancakes*
Breakfast pancakes with crumbled bacon
Chinese egg roll*
Mexican tacos
Italian pizzas*
Grilled cheese squares
Hamburgers on half of a tiny bun*

Shrimp bowl with cocktail sauce*
Cold sliced meats and cheeses on trays (see Sec. 14–1)
Salads
  Main dish
    Chicken, liver paté, egg, shrimp (but not if shrimp bowl is on the menu)

  Side dish
    Potato, macaroni*
    Cole slaw, tossed green
    Fruit in season
    Carrots and raisins

  Molded
    Perfection*
    Pear in lime gelatin*
  Relish tray*

  Hot Meat
    Roast beef
    Corned beef
    Ham
    Leg of lamb

Note: Meat may be sliced in the kitchen and sent out to the buffet table on a tray, a dozen or so slices at a time, if the party is small (under 60 guests), and the guests will not all eat at the same time. If all guests will eat at the same time, then the meat can be sliced at the buffet table.

Hot meats	Coq au vin*, with Parisian potatoes
	Beef Stroganoff, with buttered noodles
	Curry of chicken*, beef, or shrimp, with rice
Vegetables	Any green vegetable, buttered, served from chafing dish
	Any side-dish salads

Bread	Rolls, bread sticks, sliced assorted breads, with butter
Dessert	Occasion cake
Beverage	Coffee, tea, punch, soft drinks Open bar, or champagne

Menu for 100 guests should have the following for a cold buffet

Assorted hot and cold hors d'oeuvres
Miniature specialty
Choice of two cold sliced meats (or one cold meat and two main-dish salads)
Choice of two side-dish salads
Choice of gelatin molded salad or fruit tray
Relish trays
Bread and butter
Condiments (as needed by main dishes)
Dessert (may be the occasion cake served plain or with sherbet)
Beverage

For hot buffet

Assorted hot and cold hors d'oeuvres
Specialty or shrimp bowl
One hot meat carved at buffet or one hot meat dish served from chafing dish
One cold sliced meat and cheese tray
One casserole dish (starch)
Choice of two side-dish salads or tossed green salad
Relish tray
Bread and butter
Condiments (as required by main dish)
Dessert (may be the occasion cake served with sherbet or plain)

I. Children's Parties

1. BIRTHDAY LUNCH (up to ten years of age)   **10–12 guests**

Chilled fruit juice

Choice of 1   Small hamburger on miniature bun
        French fried potatoes
        Sliced tomato
    Pancakes or waffles
        Bacon or ham

    Party triangle* trays
        Peanut butter and jelly
        American cheese
        Chicken salad

Dessert	Birthday cake and ice cream
Beverage	Milk, chocolate milk, fruit punch
Service	Informal

Children's parties should have a theme, if possible. Children do not like to spend too much time at the table. Be prepared for spills. Fancy paper bibs should be supplied along with paper hats and other table decorations.

2. FROM TEN TO MID-TEENS   15–18 guests

Choice of 1   Fruit cup
                     Fruit juice on the rocks

Choice of 1   Curley frank sandwiches*
                     Pizza party* (guests make their own
                         pizza from choice of toppings)
                     Southern fried chicken bits*
                     Teen's barbecue (franks or chicken with
                         fresh corn or potato wrapped in foil
                         and cooked on outdoor grill)

                     Potato salad
                     Coleslaw
                     Relishes, with lots of pickles
                     Mustard
                     Rolls, with butter

Dessert   Individual fruit tarts or doughnuts
Beverage   Soft drinks
Service   Informal

3. SWEET 16   24–30 guests

Choice of 1   Fruit cup
                     Fruit juice on the rocks
                     Shrimp cocktail

Choice of 1   Salisbury steak
                     Hot turkey sandwich supreme*
                         Duchess or mashed potatoes
                         Fresh garden peas with mushrooms

                     Relish trays
                     Dinner rolls, with butter

Dessert   Sweet 16 cake with sherbet
Beverage   Coffee, fruit punch, soft drinks

J. Graduations or Commencements

1. For public or grade school, see Sec. 15–4I.
2. For high school, see Secs. 15–4D and 15–4I.
3. For college, see Sec. 15–4K.

K. Cocktail Reception

25–100 guests

This is a most popular method of entertaining large groups; perfect for graduations, engagements, anniversaries, open house, office parties, wedding receptions, farewell and welcome home, etc. The usual time for a cocktail party is from 3:00 to 5:00 p.m., although it may be scheduled to start earlier and last longer, depending on the occasion. The buffet table should be decorated according to the theme of the party.

Assorted open-face decorated canapés*
Assorted hot hors d'oeuvres*
Assorted finger sandwiches* (pinwheels, ribbons, checkerboards, party triangles)
Occasion cake* (optional)
Coffee (optional)
Bar—host's choice of liquor or champagne

L. Fund-Raising Dinner

100–200 guests

Cocktail hour	Assorted hot and cold hors d'oeuvres* to be passed
Choice of 1	Shrimp cocktail
	Tomato aspic ring with shellfish garnish*
	Relish tray on table
Choice of 1	Roast beef*
	Steak
	London broil
	Sliced ham or ham steak
	Foil-wrapped baked potato with sour cream and chives
	Green vegetable
	Dinner roll, with butter
Dessert	Individual fruit tart with whipped cream
Beverage	Coffee, tea
	Bar setup for cocktail hour

M. Luncheon

75–150 guests, women only

Choice of 1   Fruit juice
Fresh fruit cup (in season)
Shrimp cocktail

Choice of 1   Salad plate
    Crab or shrimp Louis*
    Cottage cheese and fruit
Hot dishes
    Creole, with rice
    Chicken à la king*, with toast points
    Turkey Tetrazzini*, with broad noodles
    Hot turkey sandwich supreme*
    Hawaiian meat loaf*
      Green vegetable as required
      Small side-dish salad

    Rolls, biscuits, crackers, with butter

Dessert   Fruit shortcake with whipped cream
Individual pastries

Beverage   Coffee, tea
No bar setup, but cocktail may be served
    as guests are seated

BUDGET SALAD LUNCHEON

Here are five budget salad luncheons for ladies' luncheons(though they can also be used for men's clubs). Appetizers, bread and butter, and desserts are the same for all, unless otherwise indicated.

Choice of 1   Tomato juice cocktail
Assorted fruit juices

Luncheon   1. Chicken–mushroom soufflé sandwich
       Sliced tomato and cucumber
    2. Cheese blintzes with sour cream
       Mixed salad
    3. Cottage cheese with fruit on bed of
       lettuce
    4.† Mushroom chow mein, with crisp
       noodles
       Buttered rice

---

† This is not a salad meal, but is often considered on the list of salad or light ladies' type luncheons.

5. Salad plate featuring any meat or
fish salad, with potato salad or
cole slaw, garnished with tomato
slice, carrot sticks, olives, and
celery fingers

Luncheon rolls, bread, or assorted biscuits and muffins, with butter

Choice of 1	Individual fruit tart or pastry Slices of occasion cake
Beverage	Coffee, tea

N. Dinner, Formal, Small

12–24 (possibly 30) guests

Cocktail Hour	Assorted hot and cold hors d'oeuvres
Choice of 1	Tomato aspic supreme* Molded shellfish extraordinaire* Quiche Lorraine*
Choice of 1	Vichyssoise* French onion soup* with croutons

Choice of 1	Chateaubriand*
	Veal scallopini Marsala*
	Roast cornish hen
	   Noodle squares Florentine* or Hun-
	   ter wild rice
	Fresh tomato filled with green beans
	   amandine

	Tossed green salad with chef's dressing Dinner rolls, with butter
Choice of 1	Cherries jubilee* (from chafing dish) Lemon ice box cake with mandarin fruit sauce* Creme de cocoa royale* Profiterole with chocolate sauce*
Beverage	Bar open for cocktail hour Sherry with appetizer Champagne or zinfandel with dinner Tokay or creme sherry with dessert Coffee, tea
Service	Formal

O. Showers

These are ladies' activities and call for a light menu. (See Secs. 15–4G and 15–4M.) It is most important that the table be decorated to indicate the theme of the shower.

TEA

Assorted canapés (cold only)
Assorted finger sandwiches
Assorted party triangles
Petits fours, fancy cookies
Occasion cake (optional)
Tea, coffee

DESSERT

Usually late in the afternoon or evening, after dinner.

Champagne cocktails*
Lemon ice box cake with mandarin fruit sauce or
Individual fruit and custard tarts with whipped cream or
Any rich dessert
Occasion cake
Coffee, tea

BABY SHOWER

Sweet table with assorted fancy cookies, petits fours
Occasion cake
Coffee, tea

Cigars for the men and chocolates for the ladies are passed by the proud father. If the shower is held in an office or father's place of employment, or if at home with mother and new baby in attendance, the reception should be of short duration. The service is self-service buffet (honored guests may be asked to pour tea). Champagne cocktails are passed by a waitress.

P. Budget Dinners

The following are five budget dinners for men's clubs or similar organizations: (Appetizer, bread and butter, and desserts are the same for all, unless otherwise indicated.)

Choice of 1   Tomato juice
                    Lettuce and tomato salad

Dinner   1. Roast half chicken
                    Roast potato
                    Green vegetable (not creamed)

2. Chicken mushroom chow mein,*
   with crisp noodles
   Fried rice*
   Egg roll*

3. Sauerbraten (spicy pot roast)*
   Potato pancakes
   Green vegetable

4. Baked fresh salmon steak, with
   lemon garnish
   Parsley potato
   Green vegetable

5. Eggplant Parmesan
   Baked spaghetti
   Green vegetable

Choice of 1   Individual fruit tart
                    Fruit pie
                    Ice cream
Beverage   Coffee, tea

Q. Dinner–Dance, Midnight Supper

Bar will be open all evening from 9:30 p.m. and one or two trays of decorated open-face canapés will be placed on the bar and refilled as needed. Dinner will be served at 12:15.

BUFFET

8-oz sirloin steak† on large onion roll,
   with pickle slice
Vinaigrette salad
Relish tray

Dessert   Fruit pie or assorted cookie trays
Beverage   Coffee, tea
                 Bar remains open throughout evening
Service   Buffet, partial service

15–5 FOREIGN DINNER MENUS

A. Chinese

10–50 guests

Choice of 1   Tomato juice
                 Egg foo yung*

---

† Steaks are placed on rolls and then on a serving tray and brought to the buffet table. Guests help themselves, or are served. Dessert is preplated and brought to buffet table.

Choice of 2	Chinese barbecue spare ribs
	Mushroom chow mein, with crisp noodles*
	Beef or chicken chop suey*
	Sweet and sour chicken (beef or shrimp*)
	Lobster Cantonese*
	Egg roll*
	Rice, steamed or fried
Choice of 1	Almond cookies
	Pineapple chunks
	Kumquats
	Sherbet
Beverage	Tea, coffee
Service	American or family style

B. English

1. DINNER   **15–100 guests**

	Small individual salads
Choice of 1	Steak and kidney pie*
	Roast beef and Yorkshire pudding
	Boiled beef, with horseradish sauce*
	Roast leg of lamb or mutton
	Boiled potato
	Green peas, with mint*
	Rolls, with butter
Choice of 1	English rice pudding
	Cheese wedges with fresh fruit
Beverage	Tea, coffee

2. LUNCH

Choice of 1	Baked finnan haddie
	Mashed potatoes
	Fried filet of sole (fish 'n chips)
	French fried potatoes
	Rolls, with butter
Dessert	English pound fruit cake
Beverage	Tea, coffee

C. French

1. DINNER   **20–150** guests

Cocktail hour   Assorted open-face decorated canapés
Spicy stuffed mushroom caps (mock snails)
Blini,* with caviar and sour cream
Relish tray

Choice of 1   Quiche Lorraine* (individual tartlets)
Vichyssoise*
French onion soup, with croutons

Choice of 1   Coq au vin*
   Buttered fine noodles
   French cut green beans
Blanquette de veau
   Parsley potatoes
   French cut green beans

French green salad, with chef's dressing
French bread or French rolls, with butter

Choice of 1   Crepes suzette,* from chafing dish (for small groups only)
Cherries jubilee* (from chafing dish)
Peach Melba*
Pear Helene*
Profiterole*

Beverage   Bar for cocktail hour, host's choice
Champagne with main course
Creme sherry with dessert
Service   Formal French

2. LUNCH   **10–30** guests

Hearts of lettuce, with French or Roquefort dressing
French onion soup, with croutons*

Choice of 1   Quiche Lorraine*
Cheese soufflé

French bread, with butter

Beverage   Sherry or white wine, served before salad
Coffee

D. German

25–50 guests

Chicken soup with dumplings
Tongue in sweet and sour raisin sauce*

Choice of 1

Spare ribs, with sauerkraut
Knockwurst (large franks), with sauer-
    kraut
Roast veal, with beer
Sauerbraten with potato pancakes*
    Boiled potato, with butter, or hot
        potato salad*
    Green vegetable, with butter
Lettuce and leek salad*
Rye and pumpernickel breads

Dessert   Apple cake squares (Dutch)
Beverage   Beer
              Coffee
Service   Family style

E. Greek

10–30 guests

Choice of 1

Rice in cabbage leaves, with lemon
Baked eggplant, with tomato

Choice of 1

Stuffed cabbage, with meat and rice
Pilaf of lamb
Roast leg of lamb, with garlic seasoning
    Rice

Mixed green salad with tomatoes
Dark bread with cottage cheese (butter)

Dessert   Fruit-filled puff pastry
Beverage   Light wine
              Black coffee
Service   Family style

F. Hawaiian (Luau)

10–500 guests

Large trays of raw vegetables, with as-
    sorted spicy dips
Pineapple baskets, with mandarin orange
    garnish
Shrimp bowl on ice with cocktail sauce

Choice of 2†	Barbecued spare ribs, with pineapple sauce
	Pineapple glazed chicken*
	Kabobs: chicken, meat, or fish, alternating with wedges of tomato, pineapple, and peach
	Hawaiian meat loaf*
	Rice, white or carnival*
	Gold and green salad*, with French dressing
	Perfection salad mold* (gelatin)
	Muffins, popovers, bread sticks, with butter or cottage cheese
Dessert	Ambrosia* or fresh fruit pie
Beverage	Hawaiian fruit punch, champagne punch
	Coffee
Service	Buffet, self-service

G. Indian

10–150 guests

Choice of 1	Pomegranate juice
	Cranberry juice
Main course	Eight-boy curry,* (shrimp, beef, or chicken curry with rice and eight condiments from which the guest makes his choice)
	1. Hard-cooked eggs, chopped
	2. Chutney
	3. Fresh grated cocoanut
	4. Green peppers, diced
	5. Bacon, crisp, crumbled
	6. Currant jelly
	7. Pickles, chopped
	8. Salted peanuts, chopped
	Rice, steamed
	Mixed vegetable salad, with French dressing
	French bread and butter (optional)
Dessert	Fruit sherbet
Beverage	Iced beer with dinner

---

† Number of meat dishes may be increased as number of guests increases.

	Coffee, tea
Service	Family style

H. Italian

15–50 guests

Choice of 1	Antipasto* Individual pizzas* Melon with prosciutto (Italian ham sliced paper thin) Minestrone soup
Choice of 1	Chicken tetrazzini* or eggplant Parmesan Spaghetti with tomato sauce Veal scallopini Marsala* Hunter wild rice* Old fashioned lasagne Pasta atiano (Sicilian)* Green salad or sliced tomato, with Italian dressing French bread or bread sticks, with butter
Choice of 1	Strawberries in wine* Biscuit tortoni Ice cream with cookies
Beverage	Red, rose, or white wine, host's choice Black coffee

I. Mexican

10–50 guests

Choice of 1	Deviled eggs with guacamole salad Avocado and tomato sections on bed of lettuce, with chef's dressing
Choice of 1	Chicken fricassee Arroz con pollo (chicken with rice) Chili con carne Tamales Veal or pork chops à la Encinada* Rice, plain or with beans Buttered carrots Baked yellow squash French bread, with cottage cheese spiced with onion salt

Dessert	Fruit compote
Beverage	Tequila
	Coffee
Service	American or family style

J. Russian

10–50 guests

Borscht with sour cream (hot or cold)
Blini,* with caviar and sour cream

Choice of 1   Beef stroganoff*
Shashlik (lamb, onions, tomatoes on skewers, broiled)
Buttered noodles
Green beans

Vinaigrette salad
Dark rye or Polish dark corn bread, with cottage cheese, butter

Beverage   Vodka from water tumblers
Strong tea, coffee

Service   Family style

K. Scandinavian

10–50 guests

Make large open-face sandwiches (not to be confused with bite-size canapés or finger sandwiches). Each of these sandwiches is sufficient as a main course. Chafing dishes with various hot foods and a very rich dessert along with solid cheese wedges and fruit set on the buffet will complete this smorgasbord. For example, offer a choice of 2 of the following served from the chafing dish:

Swedish meatballs*
Stuffed cabbage*
Seafood casserole

Make several of each variety of sandwich, adding to the variety as the number of guests increases.

1. Sliced ham and cheese on rye bread, sliced pickle garnish.
2. Rye bread spread with tartar sauce, covered with whole shrimp.
3. Four whole sardines on white bread, sliced egg, mayonnaise trim.
4. Cold sliced roast beef on lettuce with tomato slices.

5. Sliced ham rolled with cole slaw on wheat bread.
6. Shrimp salad on dark bread, four whole white asparagus garnish.
7. Meat salad spread thick with tomato wedges and olive garnish.
8. Cold sliced meat balls on dark bread, mustard garnish.

For dessert offer chocolate or lemon cream pie, or individual fruit tarts, or fruit in season on a cheese tray. Beverages include an open bar, host's choice, rose wine with the smorgasbord, and coffee and tea. The service is self-service buffet.

CHAPTER 16

Recipe File

Every caterer should have a secret recipe file. It should be a file of recipes* that have proven successful—easy to prepare, easy to serve for uniformity of portion, tasty, and generally well accepted by the guests.

Every caterer's reference library should contain at least one good general cook book, a quantity cook book, a card file, and collected recipes from newpapers, magazines, friends, and relatives. (See Appendix D.) Recipes should be added to the secret recipe file only after they have been tested and notations made about preparation, serving, acceptability, and costs. A separate file for foreign foods should be kept.

The recipes in this chapter are for all dishes marked with an asterisk in Chap. 15 as well as a few caterer's specials not found in most general cook books. All recipes are for quantity servings ranging in portions from 10 to 100. The quantity served from the recipe given is always indicated. Using larger or smaller servings will vary the total number of portions.

On canapés, hors d'oeuvres, and fancy decorated items, it is very difficult to give exact quantities, since the ability of the cook will determine the amount of some food items used. For example, the amount of *chaud-froid* needed to coat a poached salmon will vary depending on the size of the salmon, the thickness of the *chaud-froid,* the temperature of the ice box, how much of the *chaud-froid* adheres to the fish each time, and whether three coats are sufficient or a fourth is needed. Also, the amount of food used to make the decoration is completely dependent on the design chosen by the chef.

Careful notations of all changes from the original recipe should be made on secret recipe file cards.

---

* See also Chap. 13.

The sandwiches for the mobile units must be uniform. Great care should be taken to achieve such uniformity. The use of graded scoops will help keep the size of the portion of filling exact on each sandwich (see Sec. (16–1). Most meat, fish, and egg salads can be adapted to the mobile unit sandwich.

The following outline shows the method of presentation of the recipes in this chapter.

NAME OF RECIPE

Yield

Description of the dish, if necessary.

Ingredients	Quantities
Listed here with descriptions as needed	Listed here with descriptions as needed

1. Method of preparation is shown in simple sentences.
2. Each operation will have a new line if possible.
3. All descriptions of method are complete.

Below preparation instructions, will appear any additional pertinent material, as well as all variations of an original recipe.

16–1 MEASUREMENTS

The following are measurement and weight equivalents:

3 tsp = 1 tbs
4 tbs = ¼ cup
5 tbs and 1 tsp = ⅓ cup
2 cups = 1 pt
2 tbs liquid = 1 oz
4 qt = 1 gal
2 tbs liquid = 1 oz
16 oz = 1 lb
2 cups fat, shortening, butter, or margarine = 1 lb
4 cups all-purpose flour = 1 lb (approximately)
3 medium potatoes = 1 lb (approximately)
4 medium tomatoes = 1 lb (approximately)
3 medium onions = 1 lb (approximately)
2¼ cups granulated sugar = 1 lb
2¼ cups brown sugar firmly packed = 1 lb
3½ cups confectioner's sugar = 1 lb
2 cups raw rice* = 1 lb
3 cups raisins = 1 lb

---

* 2 cups raw rice increases to 6–8 cups when cooked.

A. Standard Serving Utensils

1. *Scoops:* The number on the scoop indicates the number of scoopfuls to make 1 qt. Use level measures at all times.

Scoop	Level Measure
6	⅔ cup
8	½ cup
10	⅖ cup
12	⅓ cup
16	¼ cup
20	3⅕ tbs
24	2⅔ tbs
30	2⅕ tbs
40	1⅗ tbs

2. *Ladles:* Ladle sizes are usually indicated by cup measure.

¼ cup = 2 oz
½ cup = 4 oz
¾ cup = 6 oz
1 cup = 8 oz

3. *Serving Spoons:* Serving spoons, whether solid or perforated (slotted), are not usually identified by number to indicate the capacity. It is therefore necessary to weigh or measure the quantity of food from the spoon to know the number of spoonfuls for the size of portion desired.

Note: Although in most recipes the cooking time for meats is usually given, Tables 16–1, 16–2, and 16–3 for roasting meats are included here for reference.

TABLE 16–1. TIMETABLE FOR ROASTING RIBS OF BEEF

Oven-Ready Weight, (lb)	Oven Temperature, (°F)	Roasting Time, (hr)	Meat Thermometer Reading, (°F)
6	325	2¼	140, rare
	325	2½	160, medium
	325	3⅓	170, well done
8	325	3	140, rare
	325	3½	160, medium
	325	4½	170, well done
10–11 (4 ribs)	325	4½	140, rare
	325	5	150, medium
13–14 (5 ribs)	300	5	140, rare
	300	5½	150, medium
20–22 (7 ribs)	300	4¼	130, rare
	300	5	140, medium

TABLE 16–2. TIMETABLE FOR ROASTING UNSTUFFED TURKEYS

Oven-Ready Weight, (lb)	Oven Tempera- ture, (°F)	Approximate Cook- ing Time, (hr)
5–9	325	2½–3
9–12	325	3–3½
12–16	325	3½–4½
16–21	300	4½–6
21–26	300	6–7½

TABLE 16–3. TIMETABLE FOR ROASTING MEATS

Variety and Cut of Meat	Oven-Ready Weight, (lb)	Meat Thermometer Reading, (°F)*	Cooking Time 325°F
Lamb			
Leg	6–7	180	3–3¾
Shoulder	5	180	3
Pork, fresh			
Leg (fresh ham)	14	185	6
Loin	5	185	3
Shoulder	5	185	3½
Pork, cured			
Ham, whole	16	170	4¼
Ham, piece	6	160	2½
Veal			
Leg	8	170	3½
Loin	5	170	3
Shoulder	6	170	3½

* 160°F, medium; 170–185°F, well done.

16–2 RECIPES

AMBROSIA (FRESH FRUIT BOWL)

Yield: 1 serving

Fruit sherbet	1 large scoop
Fruit	
Fresh pineapple	1 wedge
Canned pineapple	½ slice
Melon balls	
Sliced fresh peaches	
Strawberries	
Maraschino cherries	
Grated cocoanut	Generous sprinkling

1. Place scoop of sherbet in bottom of sherbet glass.
2. Arrange all cut fruit attractively over sherbet.
3. Sprinkle grated cocoanut generously over top.
4. Top with maraschino cherries.

Variations

Add any fruit in season. For buffet:

1. Prepare large quantities of cut fruit.
2. Fill large serving tray, melon basket, or glass punch bowl.
3. Place fruit in layers with generous sprinkling of grated cocoanut between each layer of fruit.
4. Cover top with grated cocoanut and maraschino cherries sprinkled over cocoanut.

BOILED BEEF IN HORSERADISH SAUCE

Yield: 10 8-oz servings

Brisket of beef, fresh	5 lb (2 pieces)
Water	To cover meat in pot
Salt, pepper	To taste
Celery	6 stalks
Carrots, large, quartered	3
Onions, large, quartered	2

1. Place all ingredients in large pot.
2. Bring water to boil. Lower heat and allow to simmer for 3–3½ hr or until meat is fork tender.
3. Remove meat. Reserve 2 cups strained stock for sauce.
4. Slice meat for serving. Horseradish sauce is passed with meat, not placed on plate.
5. White horseradish or horseradish sauce may be served.

Horseradish Sauce

1. Prepare medium-thick white sauce using 2 cups of strained stock.
2. Add 2 tbs white horseradish for each cup of sauce. Add more horseradish for stronger sauce.

BEEF POT ROAST

Yield: 25 4-oz servings

Boned rolled rump*	15 lb
Shortening or margarine	1 cup
Onions, large, diced	4
Celery, diced	4 stalks
Salt	1 tsp
Pepper	½ tsp
Garlic powder	Optional
Stock and/or water	2–3 cups

---

* Chuck though an economical cut of meat, has the round bone or the blade bone. It is therefore difficult to slice uniformly for quantity servings.

1. Brown meat on all sides in shortening.
2. Add seasoning, vegetables, and stock. Liquid should reach about 2–3 in. in pot.
3. Cover and cook over low heat on top of range for 3 hr or until fork tender. Add more liquid if needed.
4. Remove meat to cutting board, slice in portions (two slices per portion.)
5. Strain gravy. Spoon gravy over each portion.

PRIME RIBS OF BEEF AU JUS

Yield: 30–40 medium 10⅔-oz raw weight servings

Beef rib, oven-ready	25 lb
Carrots, diced	4
Onions, large, diced	2
Celery, diced	6
Salt, pepper, celery salt	To taste
Garlic powder	Sprinkling (optional)

1. Preheat oven to 375°F.
2. Lay diced vegetables in bottom of roasting pan. *Do not* add water.
3. Add seasoning to vegetables, sprinkle some over meat.
4. Place meat *bone down* in pan. Insert meat thermometer in meat.
5. Roast for length of time indicated in Table 16–1.
6. When meat is done, place it on cutting board and cover with clean cloth. Allow to "set" for approximately 15 minutes before slicing.
7. While meat is "setting," strain vegetables. *Do not* mash them through strainer, but when liquid has drained off discard vegetables. Add stock or water, if needed, to increase quantity of gravy. Adjust seasoning. Keep gravy very hot.
8. Slice meat and serve. Spoon *au jus* gravy over each slice.

Special Notes on Roast Beef au Jus

1. Meat should be ordered "oven-ready."
2. Use meat thermometer. Check temperature of oven often.
3. Check time of serving to allow time for roast to "set" before slicing.
4. Season vegetables generously.
5. *Do not* cover meat while it is cooking. *Do not* baste or turn meat.
6. *Do not* flour a roast.
7. *Do not* guess when it is done. Use a meat thermometer.

BEEF STROGANOFF

Yield: 20 1-cup servings

Beef, round	3½ lb cut in thin strips
Seasoned flour	2 cups (approx.)
Oil	For browning meat

Gravy

Flour	½ cup
Shortening	½ cup
Meat stock	1 qt
Tomato sauce	1 cup
Celery, cut in chunks	2 cups
Mushrooms, stems and caps	1 cup
Sour cream	1 pt

1. Roll cut beef lightly in seasoned flour.
2. Brown in oil or shortening.
3. Make gravy from flour, shortening, stock, and tomato sauce.
4. Add meat, celery chunks, and mushrooms.
5. Bake at 350°F for 1 hr or until meat is tender. Stir occasionally.
6. Just before serving, remove pan from oven and stir in 1 pt of sour cream. Serve immediately. May be served over broad noodles.

The Hunt–Wesson People

BAKED TOMATO BEEFBURGERS
Yield: 48 2½-oz servings

Beef, ground	8 lb
Bread crumbs	1 lb
Eggs, well beaten*	8
Onions, diced	1 cup
Water	1 pt
Salt	2⅓ tbs
Pepper	1 tsp

Sauce

Tomato paste	1 qt
Sugar	2 tbs
Onions, finely chopped	1 cup
Water	1 qt
Salt	1 tsp
Thyme	1 tsp
Bay leaves	4
Sandwich buns	48

1. Combine beef, dry bread crumbs, eggs, diced onions, water, salt, and pepper.
2. Place equal amounts of meat mixture in two ungreased steam-table pans (12 × 20 × 2½ in.) and press it down evenly. Cut meat in each pan into 48 equal-sized servings, separating them well.

---

* If dried egg solids are used, use 1 pt.

3. For sauce, combine tomato paste, sugar, thyme, and bay leaves. Add salt, onions, and water. Pour one half of tomato sauce evenly over portioned hamburger mixture in each pan. This sauce is not precooked.
4. Bake in moderate oven (350°F) for 45 minutes.
5. To serve, place one meat portion plus sauce on each sandwich bun.

BISQUE, SHRIMP

Yield: 16 ⅔-cup servings

Shrimp, raw, peeled	2½ lb
Butter	½ cup
Onions, large, diced	1
Celery, diced	5–6 stalks
Carrots, medium, diced	1
Tomatoes, medium	1
Water	2¼ qt + 1 cup
Whitewash	¾ cup flour dissolved in 1 cup cold water
Bay leaves	2
Lemon slices	2–3
Salt	1 tsp
Pepper	⅛ tsp
Sherry	1 cup or more if desired
Cream	1 pt
Parsley, diced	For garnish

1. Melt butter. Sauté cut vegetables until onions are clear but *not* brown. Add water, seasoning. Boil 15–20 minutes.
2. Add shrimp and ½ cup sherry. Simmer for 30 minutes.
3. Add whitewash. Stir. Simmer 10 minutes more. Add ½ cup sherry.
4. Remove from fire. Discard bay leaves and lemon slices.
5. Remove 8 whole shrimp. Cut in half lengthwise. Reserve.
6. When bisque is cool, put through blender, 2 cups at a time until all is done and very smooth.
7. To serve, heat very gently. Add more wine if desired. Adjust cream. Serve. Garnish each portion with ½ shrimp and finely diced parsley.

BLINI

Yield: 10 servings, 2 per person

Miniature Russian pancakes served with caviar and sour cream.

Yeast, dry	½ package dissolved in 2 tbs water
Milk	½ cup
Sugar	1 tsp
Salt	⅛ tsp
Flour, white	¼ cup

Flour, buckwheat	¼ cup
Eggs, separated	1
Caviar, black	One 3½- or 4-oz jar
Sour cream	½ pt

1. Dissolve yeast in water and let it stand.
2. Scald milk with sugar and salt. Cool. Add to yeast.
3. Add about one half of flour to milk. Mix. Cover with clean towel. Set in warm place for about 1 hr or until light.
4. When mixture is light, add balance of flour. Beat until smooth.
5. Add beaten egg yolk.
6. Whip egg white until it holds peaks. Fold gently into batter.
7. Cover batter again, set in warm place 15–20 minutes.
8. On a lightly greased griddle make small pancakes. Each pancake should be about 2 in. across. Cook on both sides.
9. Finished pancakes can be stacked in large pie tin and kept in warm oven until serving time. Pancakes may be refrigerated and reheated when needed.
10. To serve, place a quantity of blini on serving tray along with small dish of sour cream and caviar. Caviar may be served from original glass container. Demi-tasse spoons make excellent sour cream and caviar servers. Place small amount of each of these on blini and serve it to guest. A small pie server may be used.

BLINTZES

Yield: 25 servings, 2 per person
100 miniatures

Batter for Blintz Skins

Eggs, well beaten	8
Milk	2½ cups
Flour	2½ cups
Salt	1 tsp
Oil	¼ cup

Cheese Mixture for Filling

Cottage cheese, small curd	1 qt
Eggs, well beaten	1
Sugar	2 tbs
Flavoring, lemon or orange	1 tsp
Fruit rind, lemon or orange, grated	1 tbs
Fruit, crushed pineapple or berries, drained	1 cup

1. Mix all ingredients for filling. Refrigerate.
2. Beat eggs with milk, salt, and flour. Add oil last.

3. Heat lightly greased 6-in. frying pan for dinner-size blintzes, 3-in. pan for miniatures.
4. Pour small amount of batter into hot pan—batter should sizzle as it hits pan—cover bottom of pan with batter, and pour excess back into bowl immediately.
5. Cook until skin is set and lightly browned at edges. Cook one side only. Turn out immediately.
6. Repeat until all batter is used. Once skins are cold, they may be stacked and covered with clean damp cloth and held until ready to be filled.
7. To fill, place 1 tbs of cheese mixture in center of dinner-size blintz (1 tsp for miniatures) and fold envelope style (Fig. 16–1).
8. Folded blintzes should then be fried lightly on both sides until golden brown.
9. Blintzes may be held in warm oven until serving time. They may be refrigerated or frozen for future use.
10. Serve with sour cream on the side.

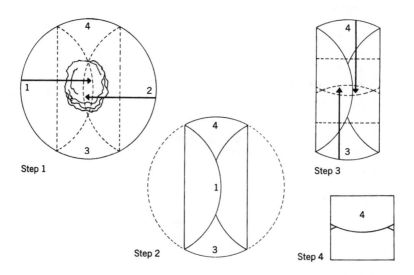

Fig. 16–1. How to fold blintzes. Skin is folded in envelope style to completely enclose filling.

OPEN-FACE DECORATED CANAPES
Yield: 250 assorted

Egg salad	6 hard-cooked eggs, celery, mayonnaise, seasoning
Caviar, black	One 3½- or 4-oz jar
Tuna fish salad	One 6½- or 7-oz can, celery, mayonnaise, seasoning

Sardines	One can brislings, used whole One can any other kind for salad, with mayonnaise and lemon juice
Shrimp	½ lb cooked, some cut lengthwise as garnish for egg salad, balance made into salad, with finely chopped celery, mayonnaise, and seasoning
Meats	Sliced ham, turkey, corned beef, salami
Cheese	½ lb or 8 slices, any variety
Spread	8 oz package
Bread	All loaves, sliced lengthwise
Pullman (sandwich) Loaf *	5 loaves (4½ will be needed for the count)
Regular loaf†	6 loaves (5¼ will be needed for the count)

1. Decoration: Cut small designs from carrot slices, green pepper, and pimiento. Slice stuffed olives, tiny pickled onions, gherkins, and pickles. (See Sec. 14–3.)
2. Prepare all salads. Refrigerate until ready to use.
3. Cut decorations. Refrigerate.
4. Trim crust from bread.
5. Spread sliced bread with butter, mayonnaise, margarine, or mustard for meat canapés.

   (a) Cover entire surface with salad. Cut as desired (Fig. 16–2).
   (b) Cover half (lengthwise) with caviar and other half with cheese spread. Cut so each canapé is two-tone.
   (c) Place 12 brislings on one slice of bread. Garnish each sardine with thin strip of pimiento or green pepper.
   (d) Cover bread with a thin layer of cheese spread and lay strips of meat lengthwise. Cut canapés crosswise or in triangles.

7. Place one decoration on each cut canapé.

The designs, shapes, spreads, and combinations are limited only by good taste, budget, and time for preparation. When large quantities of canapés are needed, limit the assortment and the method of cutting. Make all the same food combination with the same decoration, and cut the same shape and size.

Canapés can be placed directly on serving trays, but more likely would be placed in pizza boxes for refrigeration or freezing until needed.

---

* Pullman loaf = 6–7 lengthwise slices, 1 ft long. 1 slice = 10 or 12 canapés.
† Regular loaf = 6–7 lengthwise slices, 8 in. long.

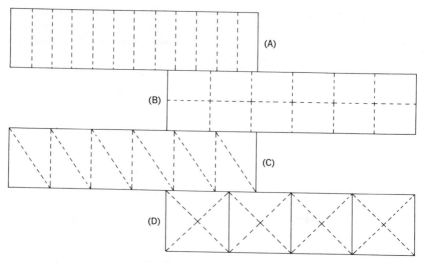

Fig. 16–2. Four basic designs that can be cut from a pullman or sandwich loaf sliced lengthwise.

Pinwheel Canapés

Pinwheels may be used as tea sandwiches or canapés. They do not need any decoration. (See Fig. 16–3.)

1. Use Pullman loaves, sliced lengthwise. Trim crusts.
2. Place slices on cloth wrung in cold water. Cover with second cloth, also wrung in cold water. Run rolling pin over bread several times to compress it slightly for easier handling. Place rolled slices next to each other on baking tin. Place sheet of waxed paper between layers of rolled bread, until ready for use.
3. When all bread is rolled, spread on work table.
4. Spread bread with mayonnaise to which a small amount of food color has been added.

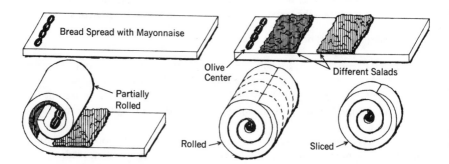

Fig. 16–3. Method of filling, rolling, and slicing pinwheels. For professional-looking pinwheels, it is important to roll bread flat before spreading any fillings.

5. Place stuffed olives, sardines, and cocktail onions or quartered gherkins at one end of bread.
6. Spread bread with two additional compatible salads, leaving spaces as shown in Fig. 16–3. Use egg salad and tuna fish salad, or ham salad with cheese spread, etc.
7. Starting at olive end, roll bread over salads.
8. Wrap in wax paper. Refrigerate overnight. May be frozen.
9. To serve, unroll from wax paper and slice approximately ½ in. thick. Place on tray. If frozen, allow roll to thaw partially, then slice.

Checkerboard Canapés
1. Spread two regular sandwich slices of white and two slices of brown bread with different salad fillings. Stack alternately, white and brown. Press together. Trim crusts. (See Fig. 16–4).
2. Using sharp knife cut stack into four sections: A, B, C, and D. Turn sections B and D upside down and press back together.
3. Wrap in wax paper and refrigerate. May be frozen.
4. To serve, slice across checkerboard 1, 2, 3, 4 and place on paper cupcake cup for easy serving.

Note: Margarine (softened), butter, or mayonnaise may be spread on each section, as it is cut and before pressing back into shape. If refrigerated before serving, this will hold parts of checkerboard together.

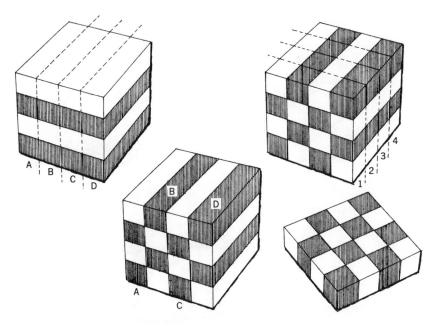

Fig. 16–4. Checkerboard canapés.

Russian Hats or Flower Pots Canapés

1. Using round cookie or biscuit cutter, cut circles from white and dark bread.
2. Spread each circle with different salad filling and stack two high. Top with unspread bread circle.
3. Spread top and sides with mayonnaise and roll completely in finely diced parsley or finely chopped nuts, whichever goes with sandwich fillings.
4. Refrigerate before serving. Do not freeze.
5. For flower pots, proceed as above but do not cover with mayonnaise. Instead ice with softened cream cheese to which a bit of food coloring has been added.
8. Top each flower pot with flower carved from fruit or vegetable, a radish rose, or large strawberry.

Heart Canapés	**Yield: 12 servings, 1 per person**
Bread	36 slices
Butter or margarine	⅓ cup softened

Dried Beef Spread

Dried beef, chopped	⅔ cup
Horseradish	2 tsp
Celery, finely chopped	¼ cup
Mayonnaise	¼ cup

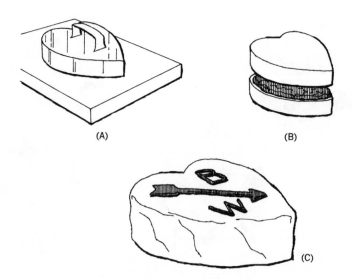

(A)   (B)   (C)

Fig. 16–5. Heart canapés.

Chicken Filling

Chicken, cooked, chopped	⅔ cup
Pimiento, chopped	2 tbs
Mayonnaise	2 tbs
Lemon juice	1 tsp

Icing

Cream cheese	One 3-oz package
Sour cream	½ cup

1. Using heart-shaped cookie cutter, cut heart shapes from each slice of bread [Fig. 16–5(A)]. Spread with butter.
2. Make dried beef spread and chicken fillings or use any other salad combinations. Spread 12 heart shapes with each of the salads.
3. To assemble sandwiches, place chicken layer on top of beef layer and top with unspread heart shape [Fig. 16–5(B)].
4. Beat cream cheese and sour cream until smooth. Spread mixture on top and sides of sandwiches.
5. Initials, arrows, or hearts may be made with piping jelly or some of softened cream cheese colored lightly with food color. Initials may also be cut from red pimiento and green pepper. [See Fig. 16–5(C).]

American Institute of Baking

CHAMPAGNE STRAWBERRY BOWL

Yield: 50 3-oz servings

Bar syrup, precooled	1½ cups
Grenadine, precooled	½ cup
California champagne, well chilled	5 large bottles
Strawberries, halved	2 qt
Orange slices	3 dozen
Lemon or pineapple sherbet	2 qt (optional)

1. Combine bar syrup and grenadine.
2. Add champagne, strawberries, and orange slices.
3. Pour over large block of ice in punch bowl. Mix gently.
4. If large block of ice is not available, ice cubes may be used to keep punch cold.
5. For extra decorative touch and taste, top punch with scoops of lemon or pineapple sherbet.

Wine Institute

CHAMPAGNE PUNCH

Yield: Approx. 24 servings

Lemon ices, softened	1 qt
Club soda	1 qt
Champagne	1 qt

Variations
1. Substitute orange or other fruit ices for lemon ices.
2. Add 1 pt of Rhine or May wine.
3. Add thinly sliced orange and/or lemon to punch bowl.
4. Add drained maraschino cherries.

Note: If large quantities of punch are to be made, place a block of ice in punch bowl to keep punch chilled.

CHATEAUBRIAND

Yield: 1 lb raw weight per serving

Filet or tenderloin	Quantity as needed
Salt, pepper	To season meat
Garlic salt	Optional
Oil	To cover meat lightly

1. Trim off excess fat and tie meat tightly. Do not roll meat.
2. Oil meat lightly and season.
3. Preheat over to 375°F. Insert a meat thermometer in thickest part of tied meat.
4. Allow approximately 1 hr roasting time for an 8-lb filet.
5. Remove meat from oven when thermometer registers *rare*.
6. Allow meat to set 10–15 minutes.
7. To serve, slice one very thick or two medium slices.
8. Broiled buttered mushroom caps can be placed on each slice.

Note: Chateaubriand does not call for any gravy or sauce. Chateaubriand should be served rare.

CHEESE BALLS

Yield: 30–35 balls

Cheddar cheese	½ lb
Worcestershire sauce	½ tsp
Prepared mustard	1 tsp
Margarine	½ cup
Flour	1 cup

1. Substitute various other cheeses for cheddar.
2. Refrigerate until firm.
3. Shape into small balls about ½ in. Refrigerate until ready to use.
4. Bake on cookie sheet at 350°F for 12–15 minutes.
5. Serve immediately.

Variations
1. Substitute various other cheeses for cheddar.
2. Add ½ package of dry onion soup mix.
3. Add crumbled crisp bacon to cheddar cheese mix.

CHERRIES JUBILEE
Yield: 24 4-oz servings

Vanilla ice cream	¾ to 1 gal
Bing cherries	Three 1-lb cans
Currant jelly	2 cups
Cornstarch	¼ cup dissolved in ¼ cup cold water
Kirsch	12 oz

1. Add cornstarch dissolved in cold water to juice from bing cherries. Add currant jelly. Mix thoroughly. Heat until cornstarch is cooked and sauce is clear.
2. Pour sauce into chafing dish. Add bing cherries. Keep warm.
3. To serve, warm kirsch. Pour gently over cherry sauce in chafing dish. Light it.
4. Spoon 3 tbs of flaming sauce over each portion of vanilla ice cream.

CHICKEN A LA KING (CREAMED CHICKEN)
Yield: 50 6-oz servings

Chicken, cooked, cubed	5 lb
Flour	1 lb
Shortening	3½ cups
Chicken stock	3½ qt
Salt	1 tbs
White pepper	½ tsp
Milk, hot	2 qt
Eggs, hard-cooked, diced	12
Mushrooms, sliced, sautéed in butter	2 lb
Pimiento, thin strips	8 oz
Green pepper, thin strips	2

1. Make white sauce from flour, shortening, chicken stock, salt, and pepper.
2. Add milk, chicken, mushrooms, eggs, pimiento, and green pepper.
3. Keep very hot, do not boil. Spoon portions into patty shells.
4. Serve immediately.

Note: For creamed chicken, the hard-cooked eggs, pimiento, and green pepper strips may be omitted.

CHICKEN TETRAZZINI
Yield: 25 servings

Chicken, cooked, diced	2½ qt
Egg noodles	1½ lb
Chicken fat, butter, or margarine	1 cup

Celery, diced	1 qt
Green pepper, chopped	1½ cups
Onions, finely chopped	½ cup
Flour	½ cup
Milk	7 cups
Cheddar cheese, sharp	1 lb
Salt	2 tbs
Pepper	1 tsp
Worcestershire sauce	3 tbs
Corn, whole kernel	One 1-lb can
Potato chips, crushed	6–8 oz

1. Cook noodles according to package directions. Keep hot.
2. Melt shortening and add celery, green pepper, and onions. Cook over low heat until vegetables are tender, but not brown. Add flour; blend thoroughly. Add milk at once. Cook until thickened, stirring constantly. Into this sauce blend cheese, salt, pepper, Worcestershire sauce, chicken, and corn. Stir until cheese is melted. Heat thoroughly, but do not boil.
3. Place hot noodles in 18 × 12 × 2 in. greased pan, then pour in sauce. Portions may also be placed in individual casseroles.
4. Sprinkle with potato chips. Bake in 350°F oven for 30 minutes or until bubbly. Serve hot.

Poultry and Egg National Board

CHICKEN IN WINE SAUCE (COQ AU VIN)

Yield: 10 ½-chicken servings

Chickens, fryers	Five 2½-lb
Onions, diced	2 large
Celery, diced	2 stalks
Margarine or butter	For frying
Chicken stock	2 cups
Salt, pepper	To taste
Sherry	2 cups (approx.)
Seasoned shortening	1 cup (approx.)

1. Coat chickens with seasoned shortening and roast until half done.
2. Make brown sauce from onions, celery browned in butter, chicken stock, and seasoning. Use sherry for one half of total liquid.
3. Cut chickens into serving pieces (Fig. 16–6). Cook in sauce until fork tender. Add additional sherry and adjust seasoning as needed.
4. To serve, place portion on plate and spoon gravy over it.

Variations

1. *Coq au vin Veronique:* Add small green seedless grapes to sauce a few minutes before serving time.
2. *Hunter style:* Add sautéed sliced mushrooms to sauce 15–20 minutes before serving time.

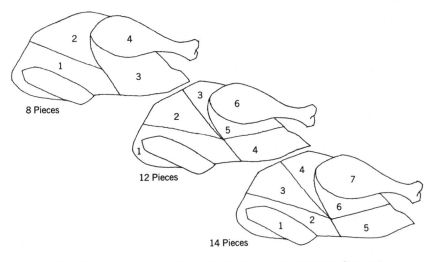

8 Pieces

12 Pieces

14 Pieces

Fig. 16–6. To cut poultry into 8, 12, or 14 servings, first cut fowl in half, then proceed as shown. A sharp knife, poultry shears, and small cleaver when used properly will cut pieces cleanly and avoid jagged edges of bone.

CHICKEN, FRIED

Yield: 40–50 pieces

Southern Fried, Batter for 4–5 Cutup Chickens

Seasoned flour	2 cups
Baking power	2 tsp
Salt	1 tsp
Milk	2 cups
Eggs, well beaten	6

1. Cut raw chicken into serving pieces.
2. Dip in batter.
3. Fry in deep fat until golden brown, but not completely cooked.
4. Remove to deep roasting. Finish in 350°F oven, 25–35 minutes.

Egg and Crumb Coating

Simplest method for large quantities. Coated chicken pieces can be refrigerated before frying.

Seasoned flour, in bowl	2 cups
Eggs, well beaten	6
Milk	2 cups
Bread crumbs, in separate bowl	1 lb

1. Cut raw chickens into serving pieces. Dredge in flour.
2. Add eggs to milk. Dip chicken in egg–milk mixture.
3. Dip in bread crumbs and coat thoroughly.
4. May be refrigerated and held for several hours before frying as above.

Alternate Methods

1. Roast whole chickens until half done. Let cool, cut into serving pieces, and proceed with either method above.
2. Parboil chickens until half done. Let cool, cut into serving pieces, and proceed with either method above.

Note: These alternate methods cut frying time by more than half; however they will not produce a final produce that tastes as good as the original method listed.

CHICKEN–MUSHROOM SOUFFLE SANDWICH
Yield: 45 sandwiches

Bread, enriched, fresh or day-old	90 slices
Butter or margarine	⅔ cup
Chicken	45 slices cooked, or 2 lb 14 oz chopped
Cream of mushroom soup, condensed	2⅛ qt
Milk	2 qt
Tarragon, crushed	1½ tsp (optional)
Parmesan cheese, grated	1 cup
Bacon	45 slices
Mushroom caps, small	14 dozen (optional)

1. Trim crusts from bread.
2. Spread bread slices with butter.
3. Using chicken slices as filling make each two slices into sandwich.
4. Arrange 15 sandwiches in bottom of three greased steam table pans (12 × 20 × 2½ in.) fitting them close together.
5. Combine soup, milk, and tarragon. Pour one third of mixture over sandwiches in each pan.
6. Sprinkle with cheese.
7. Bake in hot oven (450°F) for 20 minutes or until browned.
8. Cut bacon slices in half crosswise, fry or broil until crisp.
9. Sauté mushrooms in bacon drippings or butter.
10. When sandwiches are browned, garnish each with bacon and mushrooms. Serve immediately.

American Institute of Baking

PINEAPPLE CHRISTMAS WREATHS
Yield: 24 servings, 1 per person

Pound cake	3 lb
Butter or margarine, softened	¾ cup
Brown sugar, firmly packed	1½ cups
Cinnamon	¾ tsp
Sliced pineapple	24 slices (one no. 10 can drained)
Maraschino cherries, red, halved	12

Maraschino cherries, green, cut in   6
   slivers
Sour cream   ½ cup

1. Trim top from cake to make even surface; trim sides if needed.
2. Cut cake horizontally into three equal-sized layers; cut each layer into eight servings.
3. Arrange cake slices on bun pan (18 × 26 × 1 in.).
4. Combine butter, brown sugar, and cinnamon; spread about 1 tbs of mixture over each slice of cake.
5. Broil slowly until bubbly and shiny.*
6. Top each cake slice with pineapple slice. Trim with red cherries. Place slivers of green cherries to resemble leaves.
7. Fill center of pineapple slice with 1 tsp of sour cream.

COCKTAIL SAUCE

Yield: approx. 1 gal

Ketchup   2 qt
Chili sauce, prepared   1 qt
Horseradish   1 cup
Worcestershire sauce   ¼ cup

1. Mix all ingredients thoroughly.
2. Refrigerate until serving time.
3. Serve with wedge of lemon.

COLD CURRY SALAD DRESSING

Yield: approx. 1 qt

This is an excellent dip for relish tray or for shrimp.

Mayonnaise   1 qt
Curry powder   1 tbs
Lemon juice   2 tbs

1. Mix thoroughly.
2. Refrigerate before serving.

Note: More curry may be added for stronger flavor.

CORNED BEEF AND CABBAGE

Yield: 15–18 6-oz servings

Corned brisket of beef   12 lb
Cabbage   2–3 heads (6 or 8 wedges per head)
Potatoes   15–18

---

* At this point cake slices may be cooked, covered, and stored, to be finished to order or when needed.

1. Place corned beef in pot and cover meat with water. Bring to a boil, then lower heat and let meat simmer until fork tender.
2. Boil cabbage. For additional flavor some of stock from corned beef pot may be added to cabbage water.
3. Boil potatoes.
4. Remove meat from water, slice, and stack slices in shallow roasting pan. Pour some strained stock over meat.
5. Slice cabbage and place wedges in separate shallow pan. Drain.
6. Drain potatoes and place in shallow pan for easy serving.
7. To serve, place wedge of cabbage on plate, cover it with slices of meat, and place potato alongside.
8. Horseradish, horseradish sauce, or mustard may be passed.

Note: For quantity serving always cook corned beef, cabbage, and potatoes separately.

CORNISH HEN A L'ORANGE
Yield: 24 ½-hen servings

Cornish hens	12
Butter or margarine	1 cup
Salt, pepper, garlic powder	To taste
Lemon juice	½ cup
Orange juice	1½ cups
Orange slices, thin	24

1. Split hens down middle, and sprinkle with seasoning.
2. Melt butter in shallow roasting plan. Place cut hens skin side down in butter. Roast 20 minutes. Turn skin side up. Baste with orange juice. Roast until done.
3. Remove from roasting pan. Add remainder of fruit juice to pan juices, bring to a boil, then strain.
4. For buffet service, place hens in large shallow chafing dish, cover with sauce, or place on serving trays.
5. For dinner service, place portion on individual plates. Spoon gravy over hen, and garnish with slices of fruit.

CRAB BALLS
Yield: approx. 70 crab balls

Crab meat	1 lb
Onions, grated	1 tbs
Butter or margarine	¼ cup
Flour	½ cup
Milk	1 cup
Eggs, beaten	2
Worcestershire sauce	½ tsp

Salt	¼ tsp
Pepper	Dash
Dry bread crumbs	¾ cup

1. Remove any shell or cartilage from crab meat.
2. Cook onions in butter; then blend in flour. Add milk gradually and cook until thick, stirring constantly.
3. Beat eggs thoroughly, add some sauce, mix thoroughly, and then add egg–sauce mixture to balance of sauce, stirring constantly.
4. Add crab meat to sauce, blend into paste, and cool.
5. Portion crab mixture with teaspoon. Shape into balls.
6. Roll balls in bread crumbs. Refrigerate 1–2 hr.
7. Fry in basket in deep fat for 2 minutes or until golden brown. Drain on absorbent paper.
8. Serve on toothpicks or use thin pretzel sticks instead of toothpicks.

CREAM PUFF MINIATURES

	25–30	50–60	125–135
Boiling water	½ cup	1 cup	2 cups
Oil	¼ cup	½ cup	1 cup
Salt	¼ tsp	½ tsp	1 tsp
Flour, all-purpose sifted	½ cup	1 cup	2 cups
Eggs, unbeaten	2	4	8

1. Heat oven to 400°F.
2. Bring water to boil in large saucepan. Reduce heat to low; add oil, salt, and flour.
3. Cook stirring vigorously until mixture leaves sides of pan and forms compact ball.
4. Remove from heat, and cool slightly. Add eggs one at a time, beating hard after each addition until mixture is smooth and glossy.
5. Drop using rounded teaspoonful onto unoiled cookie sheet or using no. 7 star tube and sleeve; make puffs 1-in. across. Leave 1-in. space between each puff.
6. Bake 30–45 minutes or until puffs are light and dry. Cool.
7. Cut open and fill with the following:

Spicy cheese mix	Any cold meat salad
Thick chicken à la king	Egg salad
Thick shellfish Newburg	Tuna fish salad

8. To serve hot cheese, à la king, Newburgs, place filled puffs on cookie sheet in medium oven, cover lightly with aluminum foil. Heat about 10 minutes. To serve cold, place on tray and serve.
9. Filled puffs to be served hot may be refrigerated or frozen. Filled puffs to be served cold may be refrigerated but not frozen.

The Hunt–Wesson People

CREPES SUZETTE

Eggs	3
Milk	2 cups
Salt	1 tsp
Sugar	2 tsp
Flour	1 cup

1. Beat eggs with milk and salt.
2. Add flour and sugar. Beat until smooth.
3. Fry as blintzes.
4. To fill, use any fruit jelly. Fold crêpe in half or in thirds.
5. To flame, while crêpes are still warm pour 2 or 3 tbs warmed brandy over them in serving plate. Flame and serve while still flaming.

Variations   **Yield: 10 servings, 2 per person**

1. Spread each crêpe with Suzette butter, fold in quarters. Place under broiler for a few seconds. Serve immediately. Recipe for Suzette butter follows:

Butter, creamed	½ cup
Orange juice or curaçao	¼ cup
Confectioner's sugar	½ cup

Cream butter. Add orange juice or curaçao and sugar. Cream thoroughly. Refrigerate until needed. Should be soft for serving.

2. Spread each crêpe with blueberry or loganberry jam. Fold in thirds. Dust with powdered sugar. Broil until sugar browns. Serve immediately.

CURLY FRANKS

Yield: 12 servings

Frankfurters	2 lb
Tomato soup, condensed	Two 10-oz cans
Tomato sauce	Two 8-oz cans
Water	1 cup
Worcestershire sauce	2 tbs
Onions, large, diced	1

1. Quarter frankfurters lengthwise, make long strips.
2. Combine remaining ingredients, add frankfurter strips. Simmer 10 minutes. Frankfurters will curl while cooking in sauce.
3. Serve on hamburger buns or on small hero loaves.

Lea and Perrins Worcestershire Sauce

CURRY SAUCE

1. Proceed as for basic white sauce.
2. Add 1 tsp of curry powder for each 4 tbs of flour (for each 2 cups of sauce).

3. Mix curry powder with flour *before* adding flour to melted butter.
4. Add liquid to flour–curry–butter mixture stirring constantly. Cook over medium heat until desired thickness, and curry is throughly cooked.
5. More or less curry will be needed depending on the strength of curry powder and sharpness of sauce desired.

DUCK WITH ORANGE SAUCE (DUCK A L'ORANGE)
Yield: 12 dinner servings

Ducks	3 (3½ to 4 lb each)
Lemons	2
Oranges	3
Mandarin oranges	One 8-oz can
White wine vinegar	½ cup
Sugar	¼ cup
Cointreau or orange-flavored brandy	3–4 oz

1. Roast ducks in usual manner.
2. Slice thin slivers of rind from lemon and orange. Boil slivers in water for a few minutes, drain, and reserve rinds.
3. Cook sugar and vinegar until liquid disappears and sugar turns light brown. Add juice of lemon and orange and some liquid from mandarin orange sections. Simmer gently for a few minutes, then add slivers of peel and half of drained mandarin orange sections.
4. Remove ducks from roasting pan. Drain off fat from pan. Save brown pan sauce and add it to simmering orange sauce.
5. Cut ducks into serving portions (quarters) and place 4–6 portions on serving tray. Garnish with thin slices of orange, lemon, and a few mandarin orange sections. Spoon hot orange sauce over portions of duck. Serve immediately. Replenish tray as needed.

EGG FOO YUNG
Yield: 10 servings, 1 per person

Scallions, sliced crosswise	½ cup
Celery, sliced crosswise	½ cup
Meat	½–¾ cup
Eggs	5
Bean sprouts	½–¾ cup
Soy sauce	1 tbs
Oil	¼ cup (approx.) for frying

Sauce

Cornstarch	1½ tbs
Bouillon	2 cups
Soy sauce	2 tbs
Sugar	1½ tsp
Garlic powder	⅛ tsp (optional)

1. Brown cut scallions and celery lightly in small amount of oil.
2. Use diced roast pork, cooked chicken, or roast ham.
3. Beat eggs. Add meat, scallions, celery, bean sprouts, and soy sauce to beaten eggs.
4. Heat small amount of oil into frying pan. Stir egg mixture well. Pour about 2 tbs of mixture into pan. As soon as it sets, turn pancake over. Allow to brown slightly. Three or four pancakes may be made at one time. They should be 3½–4 in. across.
5. As pancakes are finished, remove to shallow roasting pan. Place in warm oven until serving time.
6. To make sauce, dissolve cornstarch in small amount of cold water. Add to bouillon with all other ingredients. Bring to boil. Lower heat and simmer for 5 minutes or until sauce is clear.
7. Spoon half of sauce over egg foo yung in oven. Serve with an additional spoonful of sauce over each pancake.

EGG ROLL, CHINESE
Yield: 40 dinner servings
80 miniatures

Eggs	6
Water	2½ cups
Salt	1 tsp
Flour	3 cups

1. Beat eggs thoroughly.
2. Add all other ingredients. Beat thoroughly for 10 minutes until batter is very smooth.
3. Follow instructions for blintzes. Method of frying, filling, and folding is the same.
4. Any assortment and mixture of compatible meats and vegetables can be used for fillings. Celery, onions, scallions, and chinese cabbage, all shredded and sliced finely, may be browned lightly in oil, seasoned, then spooned into egg roll skin. Thin slivers of meat, poultry, or shellfish may be added to vegetable mixture.
5. Before making last fold of egg roll, coat edges no. 3 and no. 4 in Fig. 16–1 with lightly beaten egg. This will cook the folded skin closed. If no egg coating is used, the skins may unfold when placed in hot oil.
6. Egg rolls are then deep fried until skin is golden brown, about 2 or 3 minutes. Drain.
7. Egg rolls may be served immediately, refrigerated, or frozen for future use. To reheat, place egg rolls on cookie sheet in medium-heated oven for 10–12 minutes or until hot. Time to reheat will be determined by size of egg rolls.

EGGS BENEDICT WITH CHEESE SAUCE

Yield: 24 servings

Eggs	24
English muffins	12
Butter	½ lb
Ham	12 slices
Paprika	To sprinkle

Cheese Sauce

Medium white sauce	1 pt
Cheddar cheese, diced	1 cup
Worcestershire sauce	2–3 drops

1. Prepare cheese sauce by mixing medium white sauce with cheddar cheese and Worcestershire sauce. Heat in double boiler until cheese is melted and sauce is bubbly.
2. Poach eggs. If holding is necessary here, remove cooked eggs from hot water when done and place in shallow pan of ice cold water. Poached eggs may be kept thus in refrigerator for several hours or overnight.
3. Split and butter muffins. Place buttered muffins on baking sheet and toast lightly in oven.
4. Spread ham slices on baking sheet and heat in oven.
5. To heat eggs if they were cooked earlier, place in hot water for about two minutes.
6. Remove baking sheet with muffins from oven. Place one slice of heated ham on each muffin half.
7. Place well-drained egg on ham.
8. Cover egg with 2 tbs of hot cheese sauce.
9. Sprinkle lightly with paprika. Serve immediately.
10. After eggs benedict are completed, if holding is necessary, the entire baking sheet may be kept in a medium oven for a short while. Eggs will continue to cook while being held.

Variations

1. Substitute slice of white bread, crusts trimmed, for muffin half.
2. Substitute slice of smoked salmon for slice of ham.
3. Substitute slice of Canadian bacon for slice of ham.
4. Substitute various other cheeses for cheddar in sauce.

Note: Hollandaise sauce is very fragile, does not hold up well, and is difficult for quantity servings.

EGGPLANT LOGS

Yield: 24–30 logs

Eggplant, medium	1
Flour, seasoned	1 cup

Eggs, well beaten	2
Water, cold	¼ cup
Bread crumbs	1 cup (or more)
Oil	For frying

1. Peel eggplant. Slice ¾-in. thick. Cut slices into logs.
2. Dredge logs in flour. Dip in egg–water mixture. Coat completely in bread crumbs.
3. Refrigerate coated logs 1–2 hr.
4. Deep fry until coating is golden brown and eggplant is soft to touch.
5. Drain. Serve with tartar sauce.
6. Eggplant logs may be served immediately, may be refrigerated and reheated in 350°F oven for future serving, or may be cooled, frozen, and then reheated for future serving.

EIGHT-BOY CHICKEN CURRY

Yield: 20 servings

This dish takes its name from the number of condiments served with it. The number of condiments may be varied from two up, and the name should be changed accordingly.

Stewing hens	Two 5–6 lb each
Onions, medium, diced	6
Apples, medium, diced	4
Celery, diced	8 stalks
Olive oil	½ cup
Curry powder	½ cup (approx.)
Pepper	½ tsp
Ginger	1 tsp
Tabasco sauce	1 tsp
Flour	½ cup
Cream	1 qt
Egg yolks, slightly beaten	6
Sherry	1 cup
Rice, raw	1½ lb

1. Boil chickens in usual manner until done. Reserve stock.
2. Sauté onions, apples, and celery in oil until golden brown. Add curry, simmer for another 5 minutes.
3. Add 2 qt chicken stock and seasoning, simmer 20 minutes more.
4. Blend in flour and cook until thickened, stirring constantly.
5. Bone and dice chicken, add to sauce. Let stand 2–3 hr for flavor to develop.
6. When ready to serve, add cream, egg yolks, sherry, and adjust seasoning. Heat thoroughly and serve over steamed or boiled rice.
7. Serve the following condiments in separate bowls:

Eggs, hard-cooked diced	8
Chutney	4 cups
Cocoanut, fresh, grated	2 cups
Green peppers, diced	3
Bacon, fried crumbled	1 lb
Currant jelly	1 cup
Pickles, diced	1 cup
Peanuts, salted	1 lb

Variations

Substitute shrimp or beef for the chicken. *Note:* Add some of the sauce to cream, egg yolks, and sherry. Mix thoroughly and return this mixture to the balance of the sauce as guarantee against curdling. There is not much danger of the sauce curdling, if it is cold when the sherry is added; however, this step is advisable.

FILET OF SOLE FLORENTINE
Yield: 10 servings

Filet of sole, large	10
Oil	½ cup (approx.)
Seasoned flour	1½–2 cups
Spinach, frozen	Two 10-oz packages
Almonds, slivers	1 cup
Butter or margarine	½ cup
Lemon juice	¼ cup

1. Wipe filets dry and dip lightly in oil.
2. Dip in seasoned flour. Place on flat pan. Dot with butter or margarine. Broil until done, 15–20 minutes depending on size and thickness of filets. Do not turn fish over.
3. Cook spinach according to package instructions. Drain. Season with salt, pepper, and butter.
4. Melt butter, add almond slivers, and lemon juice.
5. Place broiled fish on serving plate. Place portion of seasoned spinach in center of fish.
6. Spoon melted butter with lemon juice and almonds over fish and spinach. Serve immediately.

FRENCH DRESSING (BASIC)
Yield: approx. 3 qt

Oil	2 qt
Vinegar	1 qt
Lemon juice	¼ cup
Prepared mustard	2 tbs
Salt	1 tbs
Pepper	2 tsp

1. Mix all ingredients thoroughly.
2. Refrigerate. This dressing will separate when allowed to stand. Shake well before serving.

Variations

1. *Italian:* Add 2–3 large cloves of crushed garlic and 1 tsp of crushed oregano to dressing.
2. *Tomato:* See *French dressing supreme.*

FRENCH DRESSING SUPREME
Yield: approx. ½ gal

Oil	3½ cups
Tomato soup, condensed	3 cups
Vinegar	1 cup
Water	¼ cup
Sugar	3 tbs
Onions, grated	2 tbs
Worcestershire sauce	2 tbs
Salt	1½ tbs
Dry mustard	1½ tbs
Tabasco sauce	3–4 dashes
Garlic	1 clove

1. Place all ingredients in mixing bowl. Mix at second or medium speed until all ingredients are well blended and mixture thickens.
2. Refrigerate. May be stored in covered jar in refrigerator.

The Hunt–Wesson People

FRENCH TOAST WEDGES
Yield: 6 2-wedge servings

Bread, white, unsliced	1 loaf
Eggs, well beaten	3
Sugar	1 tbs
Vanilla	1 tsp
Milk	3 cups (approx.)
Margarine or butter	For frying

1. Trim crusts from bread. Cut into 2-in. thick slices (6–7 slices). Cut each slice diagonally to make two wedges.
2. Beat eggs; add milk, sugar, and vanilla.
3. Soak wedges of bread in egg mixture. Lift carefully and fry in medium or deep fat until golden brown, turning as needed.
4. Place on baking sheet; keep in warm oven until all are done or until serving time.
5. Serve with marmalade, jelly, or syrup.

GEFILTE FISH

**Yield: 36–40 individual fish balls
75–50 walnut-size for hors d'oeuvres**

Fish (whitefish, carp, pike, or any freswater fish), filet	12 lb
Onions	4 lb
Eggs, well beaten	12
Crackers or matzos meal	2 cups
Salt	1 tbs (approx.)
Pepper	1 tsp (approx.)

Stock

Fish bones	Reserved from fish
Carrots, peeled, whole	2 lb
Onions, sliced thick	2 lb
Water	To half fill cooking pot

1. Place all items for stock in large pot and cook over low fire until fish is prepared.
2. Grind fish and onions together.
3. Add matzos meal. Add beaten eggs and seasoning. Mix well.
4. Bring stock to rolling boil then lower flame. Use no. 12 or no. 16 scoop, or shape fish balls by hand. Mixture should be slightly sticky to touch. Dip hands (or scoop) in cold water before shaping fish balls. Drop fish balls carefully into simmering stock, one at a time. Stock should cover fish balls at all times. Add hot water if needed.
5. When all fish balls are in stock, cover pot and simmer gently for 2–2½ hr, depending on size of fish balls.
6. When fish is done, allow it to cool slightly in stock, then remove fish balls gently to trays. Carrots should be removed, sliced, and reserved for garnish of individual portions.
7. If fish balls are to be served cold, refrigerate before serving.
8. Refrigerate carrot slices separately from fish.
9. Strain but do not press or mash vegetables from stock. Clear stock will jell when refrigerated and then can be served over cold fish balls.
10. Serve with white or red horseradish.
11. Walnut-size fish balls are served as hors d'oeuvres with horseradish dip.

GREEN AND GOLD SALAD

Yield: 10 servings

Lettuce, diced	2 heads
Spinach, raw, diced	1 lb
Pineapple, drained	1-lb can
Dressing	1 pt of any light dressing

1. Wash and dice lettuce.
2. Wash spinach, remove stems, and dice leaves.
3. Drain pineapple and cut into small chunks.
4. Mix pineapple with spinach and lettuce.
5. Coat with dressing; toss lightly and refrigerate until needed.

GREEN GODDESS SALAD DRESSING
Yield: approx. 1 qt

Anchovy filets	10
Spring onions	2–4
Parsley	¼ cup
Tarragon vinegar	⅓ cup
Chives	¼ cup
Mayonnaise	1½ cups
Sour cream	1½ cups heavy
Garlic, crushed (or garlic powder)	1 clove

1. Place all ingredients in blender.
2. Blend until smooth.
3. Refrigerate until serving time.

HORS D'OEUVRES, HOT

The variety of hot hors d'oeuvres (see also *Miniatures* and *Canapés* in this chapter) is as wide as the budget and preparation time will allow. In planning the hors d'oeuvre assortment, keep it in harmony with the main course of the meal, if one is to follow.

All cookbooks list a great many varieties of hors d'oeuvres. Check carefully before planning to include them in any quantity menu. While many of these are excellent for a party of 8–16, they are practically impossible for a party of 100 or more.

All hot hors d'oeuvres should be served *hot*. If they are passed on a tray, the tray should not be so loaded that they are cold before the guests can get to the last of them. They may also be served from chafing dishes or warming trays on the buffet table.

HORS D'OEUVRES, COLD

Practically all manner of solid foods, meat, fish, and vegetables can be served as cold hors d'oeuvres. A few examples are

shrimp with cocktail sauce
steak bits with Teriyaki sauce
ham bits with mustard
assorted cheeses cut into small squares or wedges
deviled eggs

Cold hors d'oeuvres are cut and set out on trays with appropriate dips. They are not decorated as canapés.

Meat and Cheese Tower   **Yield: 16 towers**

1. Stack four slices of American processed cheese alternately with four slices of any luncheon meat.
2. Insert 16 long plastic cocktail picks evenly.
3. With a sharp knife cut between picks, making 16 "towers."
4. You can use any other sliced cheese and sliced ham, salami, etc. (see Fig. 16–7.)

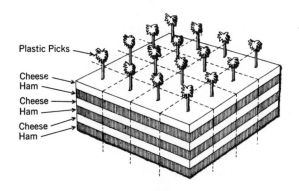

Plastic Picks

Cheese
Ham
Cheese
Ham
Cheese
Ham

Fig. 16–7. Ham and cheese tower cold hors d'oeuvre. A variety of colors can be obtained by using different types of meat and cheese.

ICE CREAM CAKE

Yield: 20 servings

1. Prepare jelly roll batter. Make two 15 × 10 × 1-in. cakes. Roll and cool.
2. Unroll on cloth covered with powdered sugar.
3. Spread thickly with softened ice cream.
4. Reroll immediately. Coat with powdered sugar; roll in waxed freezer paper and place in freezer.
5. To serve, remove from freezer immediately before serving. Slice into 1-in. thick slices and serve. Each slice may be covered with a choice of hot sweet sauce.

Various Combinations

1. Vanilla jelly roll—chocolate ice cream—chocolate sauce.
2. Vanilla jelly roll—pistachio ice cream—chocolate sauce.
3. Vanilla jelly roll—strawberry ice cream—mandarin fruit sauce.
4. Chocolate jelly roll—vanilla ice cream—mandarin fruit sauce.
5. Chocolate jelly roll—mint ice cream—mandarin fruit sauce.

KABOBS

Any assortment of compatible solid foods impaled on a long wooden or metal skewer and broiled or grilled is called a kabob.

Originally from the Near East, the shish-ka-bob was lamb pieces with various vegetables grilled over an open fire and served with accompanying rice. Shashlik is the Russian version: beef and small white onions. Hawaiian kabob consists of assorted fruit and melon. Kabobs are very popular with the teenage group and are used at barbecues and cookouts. Suggested assortments are

1. meat balls with tomato wedges and onion slices;
2. chicken livers, bacon slices, and pineapple chunks;
3. frankfurter chunks, bacon, and tomato wedges;
4. ham chunks, pineapple chunks, and thin potato slices.

LEEKS AND LETTUCE SALAD
Yield: 10 servings

Leeks, medium	2
Lettuce	2 heads
Dressing	1 pt
Bacon, crisp, crumbled	5 strips

1. Dice lettuce in somewhat smaller pieces than usual for salad.
2. Slice leeks in very thin rings. Add to lettuce.
3. Pour dressing over mixed greens; garnish with crumbled bacon. Toss lightly.
4. Refrigerate until serving time.

LIVERS, CHICKEN

With Bacon

Cut chicken livers in half. Wrap each half in half a strip of bacon. Skewer with wooden pick. Broil until bacon is crisp and liver is done. Serve immediately.

Chinese

Add a thick slice of water chestnut to liver before wrapping in bacon; proceed as above.

Hawaiian

1. Broil cut chicken livers. When half done, add a piece of fresh or canned pineapple to top of each piece of liver. Secure with wooden pick. Broil again until livers are done and pineapple is hot.
2. Proceed as with bacon above and add pineapple to top of pick when bacon is almost done. Return to broiler to finish cooking.

Fried

1. Dredge cut liver in flour, dip in well-beaten egg, and drop in seasoned bread crumbs. Deep fry until coating is golden brown. Reserve until serving time.

2. May be served with a pineapple chunk or slice of water chestnut skewered to liver.
3. To reheat, place liver on flat pan in 350°F oven until liver is hot. Serve immediately.

LIVER PATE (CHOPPED LIVER)
Yield: 36 2-oz servings

Liver, beef and/or chicken	2 lb
Onions	2 lb
Oil	½ cup
Eggs, hard-cooked	8
Chicken fat	⅓–½ cup rendered
Salt, pepper	To taste

1. Boil liver in lightly salted water until meat no longer shows red when cut. Drain and cool.
2. Dice and brown onions in oil until golden brown. Drain.
3. Cook eggs, cool, and peel.
4. When all the above are thoroughly cool, put through meat grinder two times for smooth pâté.
5. Add chicken fat, and salt and pepper. Mix thoroughly.
6. Refrigerate before serving.

Note: This pâté may be shaped into various forms for attractive buffet service. Line a mold pan with a very thin coat of mayonnaise. Press liver into mold or shape liver into design by hand. Refrigerate until serving time. Turn out mold onto a lettuce-lined serving tray. Garnish with assorted crackers and cocktail breads.

LOBSTER CANTONESE
Yield: 12 servings

Lobster meat	4 lb
Oil	½ cup
Pork, freshly ground	½ lb
Garlic, crushed	1–2 cloves
Spring onions, sliced fine	1 cup
Beef bouillon cubes	4
Water	1 qt
Cornstarch	¼ cup
Soy sauce	3 tbs
Salt	½ tsp
Sugar	½ tsp
Eggs, lightly beaten	2

1. Cut lobster meat into small chunks about 1-in. square.
2. Brown pork meat with garlic in oil. Add onions and brown.
3. Add lobster meat; cook 15 minutes more or until lobster meat is done.

4. Dissolve bouillon cubes in 1 qt water. Add cornstarch (dissolved in small amount of cold water). Add soy sauce, salt, and sugar. Bring to a boil.
5. Add lobster–pork mixture. Cook until sauce is thick and clear, stirring constantly.
6. Just before serving, stir in eggs. Remove from fire immediately as eggs start to set.
7. Serve hot with boiled or steamed rice.

LOBSTER TAILS, STUFFED
Yield: 24 servings

Lobster tails	24, ½ pound each
Water	Sufficient to cook tails
Salt	1½ tsp
Pepper	¼ tsp
Bay leaves	6
Butter or margarine	1½ cups
Lemon juice	1½ cups
Milk	1½ cups
Packaged bread stuffing	4½ cups
Cracker crumbs, coarse	4½ cups
Paprika	¾ tsp

1. Place frozen tails in covered saucepot, add 1½ gal hot water, salt, pepper, and bay leaves. Cook for 10 minutes over low heat; drain off hot water and drench with cold water.
2. Cut away undershells and remove meat, saving outside shells. Cube lobster meat.
3. Melt butter; add to stuffing mix and cracker crumbs.
4. Blend lemon juice and milk with stuffing mix.
5. Add cubed cooked lobster meat.
6. Stand shells on sides in cooking pan, allowing tails to curl around.
7. Fill each shell with 1 cup stuffing mix. Sprinkle with paprika; tie shells with heavy cord. Refrigerate until needed.
8. Bake as needed in moderate oven 350°F for 15 minutes. Remove cord to serve.

American Institute of Baking

LOUIS, CRAB OR SHRIMP
Yield: 12 complete salads

Shrimp or crab meat	2 lb
Lettuce, shredded	2–3 heads
Louis Sauce	
Horseradish	2 tbs
Chili sauce	½ cup

Green pepper, finely diced	¼ cup
Pickle or relish, finely diced	¼ cup
Scallions, finely diced	2 tbs
Lemon juice	2 tbs
Mayonnaise	1 cup
Salt	1 tsp
Pepper	¼ tsp
Worcestershire sauce	2–4 dashes

1. Mix all ingredients except crab or shrimp and lettuce.
2. Place bed of shredded lettuce on plate. Top it with portion of crab or shrimp. Cover entire salad with Louis sauce.
3. Garnish each plate with the following:

Half hard-cooked egg, or two quarters of egg	Black olives
Two or three whole white asparagus	Green olives
Two small tomato wedges— one wedge of lemon	Radish rose
	Parsley

4. Refrigerate before serving.

MANDARIN FRUIT SAUCE

Yield: approx. 1 qt

Cornstarch	6 tbs
Sugar	2 cups
Salt	¼ tsp
Orange juice	1½ cups
Lemon juice	½ cup
Water, cold	1 cup
Mandarin orange sections	1 cup (approx.)
Maraschino cherries, red, quartered	½ cup
Orange and lemon rind, thin slivers	½ cup

1. Combine cornstarch, sugar, salt, orange and lemon juice, water, and slivers of rind. Cook over low heat, stirring constantly until mixture thickens.
2. If mixture gets too thick, add some juice from mandarin orange sections.
3. Add mandarin orange sections and maraschino cherries.
4. Serve hot. May be used over baked ham, ice box cakes, ice cream, ice cream cake, and profiterole.

MEATBALLS

Meatballs are pretty much the same no matter where they are served, but the sauce makes a world of difference. Select any good, basic, meatball recipe and serve it in a multitude of ways: vary the seasoning, the types of meat used, and serve them in different sauces.

Cocktail Meatballs (Miniatures)

Make these the size of large walnuts. Increase the seasoning; add Worcestershire sauce. Roast in shallow roasting pan. Drain off cooking juices. May be refrigerated or cooled and frozen for future use. To reheat, place on cookie sheet and heat in medium oven.

Swedish Style

Use half beef and half pork meat with milk for liquid. Serve white sauce to which bouillon cube and diced dill or parsley has been added.

Italian

Season meat well with salt, pepper, and garlic. Cook in tomato sauce to which oregano and more garlic has been added. Serve with grated Parmesan cheese.

Chinese

Add 1 cup finely chopped mushrooms and 2 tbs of soy sauce to each 2 lb of meat. Brown meat balls in hot oil until almost done. Finish in Chinese sweet and sour sauce. Serve from chafing dish with rice.

Mexican

Use half beef and half pork meat. Cook meatballs in tomato sauce to which oregano, garlic, diced green peppers, and chili powder has been added. Thin tomato sauce with beef bouillon or stock.

Russian

Use half beef and half pork meat. Brown meatballs in butter or margarine. Serve with white sauce made with sour cream for the liquid, and add bouillon cube and capers (if desired).

MEAT LOAF, HAWAIIAN

1. Prepare meat loaf in usual manner. For best appearance, bake meat in loaf or pullman pans.
2. When meat is done, slice ¾ in. thick and place on serving tray, alternating slice of meat loaf with slice of canned pineapple. Retain loaf shape.
3. To serve, lift a slice of meat with pineapple on top and place on plate.

Suggested by Kraft Foods

MINIATURES

Where repeat business is concerned, it is a problem to find new and interesting hors d'oeuvres. Serving miniatures is an excellent solution. (See also *Canapés* and *Hors d'Oeuvres* in this chapter.)

Practically any well accepted dish that does not call for a sauce or gravy can be made miniature and served as an hors d'oeuvre—either hot or cold. Use any regular recipe, but make the finished item half the original size.

Miniature Chinese Egg Roll

Approximately 2 in. long and 1 in. in diameter. As hot hors d'oeuvre, serve with hot mustard dip.

Miniature Cream Puff

To serve hot, fill with any curry, Newburg, à la king dish, or cheese and crumbled bacon.

To serve cold, fill with salads, shrimp, egg, tuna, etc., and serve along with canapés.

Miniature Hamburger or Cheeseburgers on bun

Prepare meat in usual manner. Make baking powder biscuits cut with 1½-in. cutter. Bake until done. Split. Place small amount of meat on each half, or reserve tops. Broil meat until done. Place small piece of cheese over meat and return to broiler until cheese starts to melt. May be covered or left open face.

Miniature Pizzas

Prepare in usual manner, but cut dough into 1½-in. squares. Serve as hot hors d'oeuvres.

Miniature Cheese Blintzes

Prepare in usual manner but fry the skins in a 3-in. pan. Must be passed hot.

MINIATURE HORS D'OEUVRE PASTRIES

Small pastries with assorted fillings may be made in advance and refrigerated or frozen for future use.

Perfect Pastry Dough   **Yield: 100–125 1½-in. pastries**

Shortening	1 cup
Flour	4½ cups
Eggs, well-beaten	1
Water, cold	¾ cup
Sugar	½ tsp
Salt	½ tsp
Vinegar	1 tbs

1. Use pie pastry method. Cut shortening into flour. Add salt and sugar.
2. Add all liquid ingredients at once and mix thoroughly. Dough should be soft but slightly dry to touch.

3. Refrigerate, wrapped in waxed paper, for about 1 hr before rolling.
4. To fill, roll about half of dough very thin on well-floured board.
5. Place a long mound of filling along one edge of rolled dough.
6. Roll dough over filling, and around, until filling is completely covered with dough. Cut long, filled strip away from rest of rolled dough. This now resembles a small jelly roll.
7. Slice roll carefully into 1½-in. slices. If possible, loose end of jelly roll dough may be folded under to form a bottom for this small slice. Place each slice on lightly greased cookie tin.
8. If pastries are too high, press them lightly with bottom of water tumbler that has been dipped into flour.
9. Continue to roll and cut pastries. When pan is full, paint each pastry with a mixture of milk and/or well-beaten egg.
10. Bake at 400°F for 15–20 minutes, or until dough is golden brown. Baking time will vary somewhat depending on filling and actual size of finished pastries.
11. These pastries should be served hot. They can be made in advance, refrigerated or frozen for future use.
12. To reheat, place pastries on flat cookie tin, heat in 350°F oven for about 10 minutes or until pastry and filling is hot. If tops start to brown before they are thoroughly heated, cover tray lightly with a sheet of aluminum foil.

Filling

Potato and Browned Onions

Instant mashed potatoes	6 cups
Onions, large, diced	3
Salt	2 tsp
Pepper	½ tsp
Shortening	¼ cup

1. Prepare potatoes according to package instructions. Reduce water slightly.
2. Sauté onions in shortening until brown, drain, and add to mashed potatoes.
3. Add seasoning, mix, and let cool. Use as filling for miniature pastries.

Variations to Filling

1. Add 1 cup of finely diced cooked chicken to potatoes, reduce browned onions by about half. Adjust seasoning.
2. Add corned beef hash. First reduce potatoes by about ⅓ and eliminate the browned onions completely.
3. Add liver pâté. First reduce potatoes by about half. In this mixture the browned onions are optional.

Whatever filling is used for the miniature pastries, it should have the texture of very thick mashed potatoes, slightly dry to the touch.

MOCK CHAMPAGNE PUNCH
Yield: approx. 3 gal

Ginger ale	3 qt
Hawaiian fruit punch	1 gal
Lemon juice	1 qt
Sugar	2 lb
Pineapple juice	1 qt
Ice	Any amount desired

1. Mix all ingredients except ginger ale. Refrigerate.
2. Just before serving add ginger ale and ice.

MOLDED FRUIT SALADS

1. Prepare flavored gelatin as per package instructions for quantity desired.
2. Pour a thin layer on bottom of each pan.
3. When gelatin starts to set, place one piece of fruit in each 2-in. area. Keep fruit in straight lines. Refrigerate.
4. When fruit is set in bottom layer of gelatin, pour remainder of gelatin over fruit. All fruit should be completely covered. Refrigerate until serving time. Allow sufficient time for gelatin to set completely.
5. To serve, slice between rows of fruit, making uniform portions.
6. Some fruit and gelatin combinations are pear halves in lime gelatin, peach halves in lemon or cherry gelatin, pineapple slices in lime or cherry gelatin, and minted apple rings (red and green) in lemon gelatin.

Rainbow Molded Fruit Salad

1. Prepare as molded fruit salad substituting two or three different flavors and colors for total amount of gelatin.
2. Pour first color in bottom of pan and set fruit. Pour second color to half cover fruit; allow to set. Pour third color to completely cover.
3. Slice and serve as above.

MUSHROOMS STUFFED WITH RICE
Yield: 24 servings

Onions, minced	3 tbs
Butter or margarine	2 tbs
Rice, cooked	1 cup
Nutmeats, finely chopped	½ cup
Chili sauce	1 tbs
Lemon juice	1 tbs
Salt	1 tsp
Pepper	¼ tsp
Mushrooms, large, fresh	24

1. Sauté onions in butter or margarine until tender, but not brown.
2. Add remaining ingredients except mushroom caps.
3. Form into 24 small balls.
4. Remove stems from mushrooms. Wash and dry mushrooms. Place mushroom caps on rack in broiler pan, rounded side up. Brush with melted butter and broil 2 to 3 minutes.
5. Turn mushroom caps; season with salt and pepper.
6. Place ball of rice mixture in each cavity. Drizzle with melted butter and broil until golden brown.
7. Serve immediately.

Rice Council for Market Development

NEWBURG SAUCE

Yield: approx. 2½ qt

Butter	1 cup
Flour	1¼ cups
Milk or stock	1 qt
California dry sherry	1 pt
Eggs, well beaten	3

1. Melt butter, add flour. Mix thoroughly.
2. Heat milk or stock and add to flour–butter mixture. Stir thoroughly. Heat until thick. Add sherry slowly and continue to cook.
3. Add some hot sauce to beaten eggs, mix thoroughly, then add to rest of hot sauce. This will prevent eggs from separating.
4. Add salt and pepper as needed.

Crab Meat Newburg

1. Sauté crab meat in butter until hot.
2. Add half of sherry, then add balance of sherry and crab meat to base sauce.
3. Cook gently for a few minutes. When very hot, serve.

Shrimp Newburg

1. Cook shrimp in lightly salted water to which a few bay leaves have been added.
2. When shrimp is done, peel and devein and add to sauce.
3. Cook a few minutes. Serve hot.

NOODLE SQUARES FLORENTINE

Yield: 25 ½-cup servings

Medium broad noodles	1½ lb
Water	Enough to cook noodles
Salt	2½ tbs
Spinach, frozen	1 lb

Onions, diced	2 lb
Mushrooms, sliced	2 lb
Eggs	4
Oil	½ cup

1. Cook noodles according to package directions and drain. Do not rinse.
2. Cook spinach according to package instructions. Chop lightly so there are no large leaf sections.
3. Brown onions lightly in oil. Add mushrooms and cook 5 minutes more.
4. Mix all ingredients thoroughly. Add salt and pepper to taste.
5. Place mixture in well-buttered baking pan.
6. Bake at 350°F, 40–45 minutes, or until light brown on top.
7. Cut into square portions and serve.

PASTA ATIANO

Yield: 18–20 servings

Onions, large, diced	1
Celery, diced	2 stalks
Oil	¼ cup
Meat, ground	1½ lb
Mushrooms, fresh, sliced	½ lb
Tomato paste	1 cup plus 1 cup water
Tomatoes	1 no. 303 can
Eggplants, medium	1
Eggs, hard-cooked	6
Rigatoni	1 lb
Parmesan cheese, grated	½ lb
Black olives	2 cups
Salt, pepper, oregano	To taste
Garlic	1 clove (optional)

1. Brown diced onions and celery in oil. Add garlic.
2. Add ground meat. Cook until red disappears, stirring constantly.
3. Add mushrooms, tomatoes, tomato paste, and water. Simmer 45 minutes. Sauce should be rather thick.
4. Peel eggplant, slice, and fry in small amount of oil. Season with salt and pepper.
5. Boil eggs, cool, peel, and cut in wedges.
6. Cook rigatoni according to package directions. Rinse in cold water.
7. To assemble, use large deep casserole, deep roasting pan, or insert from large chafing dish. Place items in layers, in the following order:

   (a) sauce to cover bottom of pan,
   (b) rigatoni, then sauce,
   (c) eggplant, then sauce,
   (d) egg wedges, then sauce,
   (e) sprinkle with cheese, dot with olives, cover with sauce. Repeat process until all items are used up. End with cheese and olives.

8. May be refrigerated overnight for service next day.
9. To serve, bake at 350°F for ½–¾ hr, until all ingredients are hot. Serve immediately.

Vinci's North Shore

PEACH MELBA
Yield: approx. 3 cups sauce

Raspberries	1-lb can
Currant jelly	½ cup
Cornstarch	2 tbs dissolved in 2 tbs cold water
Peach halves	1 per serving
Vanilla ice cream	Quantity as needed

1. Place raspberries and jelly in pan and mash them.
2. Add cornstarch dissolved in cold water.
3. Heat until sauce bubbles and is clear.
4. To serve, place scoop of vanilla ice cream in serving dish. Top ice cream with peach halve. Spoon hot melba sauce over peach. Serve immediately.

Note: This dessert should not be set up in advance, but served immediately after being put in dessert glasses.

PEAR HELENE
Yield: 1 serving

Pear halves	1 per serving
Vanilla ice cream	Quantity as needed
Chocolate syrup or sauce	2–3 tbs

1. Place scoop of vanilla ice cream in dessert dish.
2. Place half pear (canned) on ice cream, cut side down.
3. Spoon chocolate syrup or sauce over pear.
4. Serve immediately.

Note: This dessert should not be set up in advance, but served immediately after being put into the dessert dishes.

PEAS PUREE
Yield: 20 ½-cup servings

Dried peas	3 cups
Water or vegetable stock	2 qt
Salt, pepper	To taste
Butter	¼ cup
Onions, large, finely diced	1

1. Soak peas.
2. Bring peas, diced onions, salt, pepper, and butter to a boil in 2 qt of water or vegetable stock.

3. When peas are completely cooked and fall apart, put through blender or high speed on a mixer. If peas are too thin, add 3–4 tbs of dry instant potato while mixture is still very hot. Blend thoroughly.
4. Serve as hot side dish, or as filling for tomato cup, or on artichoke bottoms.

PEAS WITH MINT

1. Add four or five fairly large sprigs of fresh mint to a 2-lb pack of frozen peas.
2. Add mint to water after peas have been added and water has boiled. Mint should not be boiled.
3. Allow it to stand in the peas until serving time.
4. Remove mint before serving.

Note: To canned peas, add approximately ¼ tsp crushed dried mint for each 20 servings when heating peas.

PERFECTION SALAD

Yield: 24 2 × 2½ × 2-in. servings

Gelatin, unflavored	¼ cup
Cold water	1 cup to dissolve gelatin
Water, boiling	1 qt
Sugar	⅔ cup
Vinegar	½ cup
Lemon juice	½ cup
Cabbage, finely shredded	1 qt
Carrots, finely shredded	1 cup
Green pepper, finely diced	½ cup
Pimiento, finely diced	½ cup
Spanish (stuffed) olives, sliced	½ cup (optional)

1. Dissolve gelatin in cold water.
2. Add vinegar, sugar, lemon juice, salt, and dissolved gelatin to the boiling water. Stir and cook until clear. Remove from heat and cool.
3. When gelatin mixture starts to set, stir in all vegetables.
4. Refrigerate until gelatin is firmly set. If vegetables start to rise to top before salad is set, stir it thoroughly before it is firmly set.
5. When gelatin is firmly set, cut into serving portions and serve from pan, or turn out on serving trays, cut into portions, and place on buffet.

PIZZAS

Dough (Four Methods)

1. Use any regular or prepared pizza dough.
2. Make baking powder biscuit dough. Roll ½-in. thick. Cut with 2-in. biscuit cutter. Bake.
3. Cut English muffins in half, sprinkle with oil, and bake lightly.
4. Make flaky pie dough. Spread on cookie sheet. Prick with fork. Bake.

Sauce

1. Pour thick tomato sauce on dough, sprinkle with oregano, salt, pepper, and garlic salt. Dot with pieces of mozzarella, Monterey Jack, or cheddar cheese. Add any of the following:

    (a) chunks or slices of sausage,
    (b) thin slices of salami,
    (c) anchovy,
    (d) browned mushrooms with onions,
    (e) tuna fish.

2. Sprinkle generously with grated parmesan cheese.
3. Return completed pizzas to oven 5–7 minutes or until cheese is melted. Serve immediately.

Note: Doughs 2 and 3 are ready to serve. Doughs 1 and 4 must be cut. The size will be determined by use. 1½- to 2-in. squares are excellent for hot hors d'oeuvres. All pizzas may be refrigerated or frozen for future use.

BAKED STUFFED PORK CHOPS
Yield: 48 servings

Pork chops	48, cut 3 per pound
Brown sugar	1½ cups packed firmly
Cinnamon	2 tbs
Salt	2 tbs
Celery salt	2 tbs
Soft bread crumbs	2 gal, ¼-in. cubes
Butter or margarine, melted	3 cups
Applesauce, canned or fresh	2½ qt

1. Blend brown sugar, cinnamon, salt, and celery salt. Add to bread crumbs.
2. Add melted butter and 1½ qt of applesauce to spiced bread crumbs.
3. Place pork chops in three ungreased steam table pans (12 × 20 × 2½ in.).
4. Place a no. 16 scoop of stuffing mix on top of each pork chop.
5. Top each portion of stuffing with 1 tbs of remaining applesauce.
6. Bake in moderate over (350°F) for 1¼ hr.

American Institute of Baking

PORK OR VEAL CHOPS A LA ENCINADA
Yield: 10 servings

Chops	20
Oil	1 cup (approx.) for frying
Onions, medium, diced	5
Bacon or ham, raw, diced	¼ lb

Salt, pepper	To taste
Bouillon cubes	4
Water	3 cups

1. Fry chops in oil. When chops are half done, stack in deep baking pan.
2. In same frying pan, brown onions. Add ham or bacon; brown.
3. Add tomatoes cut in large chunks. Reserve liquid. Cook tomatoes with brown onion mix about 5 minutes.
4. Add liquid from tomatoes, water, and bouillon cubes to make sauce. Boil for 5 minutes. Add salt and pepper as needed.
5. Pour sauce over chops in baking pan. Bake in 350°F oven until chops are fork tender (approx. 45–50 minutes). Add more liquid if needed (bouillon cube in water).
6. To serve, place chops on plate and spoon gravy over them.

POTATO PANCAKES

Yield: 25 servings, 2 each
150 miniatures

Potatoes	4½–5 lb
Onions	1 lb
Eggs	5
Flour	2 cups
Baking powder	1 tbs
Salt	1 tbs
Pepper	1 tsp
Oil	For frying

1. Peel potatoes and onions. Grind them together. Add seasoning.
2. Beat eggs thoroughly and add to potato mix. Add flour and baking powder. Mix.
3. Heat heavy-duty frying pan or griddle. Cover with oil.
4. Spoon batter onto griddle to make pancakes. Approximately 3 tbs makes one dinner size, 1 tbs (scant) makes a miniature.
5. When pancake is brown around edges, turn it over and let cook on second side until done.
6. Drain pancakes on absorbent paper. Stack in roasting pan for holding.
7. Potato pancakes can be served immediately, can be refrigerated and reheated, or frozen for future use.
8. To reheat frozen pancakes, spread on ungreased cookie tin and place in medium (350°F) oven for 8–10 minutes or until hot. Time will be determined by size of pancakes. They should always be served hot.

POTATOES AND PEPPERS

Yield: 20 4-oz servings

Green peppers	4 lb
Potatoes	2 lb
Olive oil	1 cup

Garlic, crushed	2 cloves
Tomato paste	1 cup plus 2 cups water
Onions	2 lb
Salt, pepper	To taste

1. Remove stems and seeds from peppers. Slice lengthwise, 10–12 slices per pepper. Cut potatoes as for french fried.
2. Sauté garlic in oil. Discard garlic. Sauté peppers lightly.
3. Place all other ingredients in pan with oil. Cover. Cook over low heat 35–45 minutes, or until potatoes are done. Add water if tomato paste mixture gets too dry.
4. Can be kept in warm oven or served immediately.

POTATO SALAD, HOT AND COLD

There are a great many good recipes for potato salad, and each chef has his favorite. Generally it is a cold side-dish salad served with cold sliced meats or with cold meat sandwiches.

However, in predominately German and Pennsylvania Dutch areas, hot potato salad is served with hot meats. It is a difficult item to handle for a large catered affair but can be used very successfully with smaller groups. In many parts of the country this would be a new and different way to serve potatoes.

Hot Potato Salad

1. Boil potatoes, peel, slice thickly, and keep warm.
2. Cover sliced potatoes with hot oil and vinegar dressing, highly seasoned with salt, pepper, finely diced onions, and parsley. Crumbled crisp bacon is optional.
3. Toss lightly and serve hot.

POTATOES, OVEN BROWNED

Yield: 25 servings

Potatoes	1½ no. 10 can new potatoes (75 count approx.)
Shortening	1 cup (approx.)
Paprika	2 tbs
Salt	2 tbs
Pepper	1 tsp
MSG	2 tbs (optional)

1. Potatoes should be drained until dry, and cooled.
2. Put all seasoning into shortening, melt, and cool slightly.
3. Place potatoes in shallow roasting pan and coat them thoroughly with seasoned shortening.
4. Roast at 350°F until potatoes are hot and brown crust forms on potatoes. Time will vary depending on size of potatoes.
5. Serve hot.

PROFITEROLE

Yield: 1 serving

Cream puff shell	1 large (3 in. across)
Ice cream	1 no. 8 scoop
Chocolate sauce, hot	3 tbs

1. Open cream puffs near top. Cut top off completely.
2. Fill cream puff with scoop of ice cream.
3. Replace top of cream puff.
4. Spoon hot chocolate sauce over entire cream puff.
5. Serve immediately.

Note: For excellent results, use chocolate chip or mint ice cream.

QUICHE LORRAINE

Yield: 16 servings

Dough

Pastry flour	2 cups
Butter or margarine	½ cup
Egg yolk	1
Cold water	¼ cup (approx.)

1. Cut butter into flour. Add egg yolk with water. Mix.
2. Sprinkle lightly with additional flour if needed. Do not overwork dough.
3. Roll out very thin. Line cupcake or pie tins.

Filling

Bacon, crisp	8 slices
Onions, medium, sliced, thin	2
Cheese (usually Swiss)	½ lb
Eggs, well beaten	4
Cream	2 cups
Salt	½ tsp
Cayenne Pepper	A shake on top of each Quiche

1. Fry bacon until crisp; drain and crumble.
2. Brown onions in butter.
3. Dice cheese.
4. Beat eggs; add cream and salt.
5. Heat oven to 450°F.
6. To assemble Quiche:

   (a) Line pan or cupcake tins with dough.
   (b) Sprinkle crumbled bacon on dough.
   (c) Cover with cheese.
   (d) Add browned onions.
   (e) Pour on egg mixture. Fill pans three quarters full; no higher.

(f) Bake 10 minutes at 450°F, then 20 minutes at 350°F. Check oven about every 10 minutes. Baking time will vary with size of Quiche.

Note: Everything above step 5 may be done in advance and held until needed. From step 5 down, everything must be done just prior to serving time. Quiche Lorraine should be served hot.

RELISH TRAY

In addition to the regular standby items for the relish tray, use a variety of local items to make this a most interesting, tasty, and colorful tray for any buffet. Smaller relish trays can be set on any luncheon or dinner table. Some suggested ingredients include:

Carrot sticks	Marinated cauliflower flowerlets
Celery fingers	Marinated cucumber spears
Spring onions	Pickled small whole beets
Ripe olives	Pickled baby corn
Green olives	Pickled baby carrots
Stuffed olives	Pickled green cherry tomatoes
Assorted pickles, sweet, sour, dill	Red radishes cut in various
Gherkins	designs
Marinated artichoke hearts	Red cherry tomatoes

ROSE SPARKLE PUNCH

Yield: 65 servings, for 20–25 persons

Strawberries, frozen	Four 12-oz packages
California rosé	Four ⅘-qt bottles
Lemonade concentrate, frozen	Four 6-oz cans
Sugar	1 cup
Sparkling water, chilled	2 large bottles

1. Combine thawed strawberries and one fourth of wine.
2. Cover and let stand at room temperature for 1 hr. Strain into punch bowl. Discard pulp.
3. Add frozen lemonade concentrate and sugar. Stir until completely thawed and dissolved.
4. Add remaining wine and sparkling water.
5. Add ice. Serve immediately.

Wine Institute

RICE FIESTA RELISH

Rice, cooked	1½ cups
Sauterne	⅔ cup
Cranberries, fresh, chopped fine	4 cups
Oranges, quartered, ground fine	2

Sugar	1 cup
Mincemeat, brandy flavored	1 cup
Nut meats, pecans, broken	1 cup

1. Marinate cooked rice in sauterne for about 3 hr.
2. Chop or grind cranberries and oranges. Add sugar, mincemeat, and nuts. Let stand and chill while rice marinates.
3. Combine cranberry mixture with marinated rice.

Rice Council for Market Development

RICE, FRIED CHINESE STYLE

Yield: 25 ½-cup servings

Rice	1½ lb (3½ cups)
Water	1½ qt
Oil	1 tbs
Salt	1 tsp
Eggs, whipped	8
Onions, cut	2 cups
Bean sprouts	1-lb can, drained
Meat (poultry or shrimp), cooked, diced	2 cups
Water chestnuts	One 6-oz can
Soy sauce	1 cup (approx.)

1. Prepare rice in usual manner.
2. Cut onions into thin strips, brown lightly in oil.
3. In large frying pan, fry eggs until just firm, then push them to one side of pan and add browned onions and salt. Stir.
4. Add diced meat (poultry or shrimp). Mix with eggs and onions.
5. Add rice to ingredients in frying pan. Mix well.
6. Add soy sauce a little at a time, stirring constantly. When all soy sauce is added, rice should be dark brown.
7. Hold in warm oven, uncovered. May be made ahead of time and re-heated in 350°F oven.

RICE, HUNTER STYLE

Yield: 24 ½-cup servings

Rice	1½ lb
Water	1½ qt
Salt	1 tsp
Pepper	To taste
Oil	2 tsp
Mushrooms, sliced	1 lb
Butter	¼ lb
Onions, sliced	2 lb

1. Slice onions thin. Sauté in butter until golden brown. Add mushrooms and brown lightly.
2. Cook rice in usual manner, adding the oil to boiling water.
3. When rice is done, add browned onions, mushrooms, salt, and pepper.
4. May be served immediately or held in warm oven.

Wild Rice, Hunter Style   **Yield: 24 ½-cup servings**

Substitute ¾ lb of wild rice for ¾ lb of white rice. Cook the wild and white rice separately. When both are done, mix thoroughly with onions and mushrooms as above.

Rice Carnival   **Yield: 24 ½-cup servings**

Prepare white rice in usual manner. Add 2 lb cooked carrots and peas (may be canned or frozen), 8 oz diced pimiento, 8 oz diced black olives, and salt and pepper to taste.

ROAST WITH BEER

Any roast meat, beef, lamb, veal, pork, or poultry, may be basted with any of the following: beer, champagne, ginger ale, and fruit juice (usually for poultry). Prime ribs of beef should *never* be basted with anything but the drippings from the pan, if necessary.

SALADS

Garbanzo (Chick Peas) Salad

1. Marinate garbanzo beans in spicy French dressing.
2. Add to vinaigrette (mixed vegetable) salad.
3. Drain and use on relish tray.

Kidney Bean Salad

For each 2 cups cooked or canned kidney beans add ⅓ cup French dressing, one onion sliced in thin rings, ⅓ cup each of diced celery and diced sweet pickles, and salt and pepper to taste.

Chicken Salad   **Yield: 25 ½-cup servings**

Cooked chicken, diced	2½ qt (10 cups)
Celery, finely diced	2 qt
Mayonnaise or salad dressing	5 cups
Salt	2 tsp
Pepper	½ tsp
Eggs, hard-cooked, diced	6 (optional)

1. Combine all ingredients.
2. Refrigerate before serving.
3. Serve on bed of lettuce as part of salad plate or for sandwich fillings.

Chicken Salad Hawaiian

Add one 1-lb can cubed pineapple, drained, to chicken salad.

Egg Salad

Allow 1 egg per serving plus mayonnaise, diced celery, mustard, salt, and pepper.

Egg Salad Carnival

Add finely chopped green pepper, pimiento, and black olives to egg salad. *Note:* When *carnival* items are diced, press in a strainer to remove excess liquid. Use approximately ½ cup of diced vegetables for 12 eggs.

Egg Salad with Browned Onions

Add 1 lb of onions. Dice the onions fine, sauté in butter, margarine, or oil until golden brown, drain thoroughly, and add to egg salad for 24 eggs.

Macaroni Salad

Allow 6–8 portions from 1 lb of salad-style macaroni. Prepare macaroni according to package instructions. Add

Celery, finely diced	1 qt
Mayonnaise	3–3½ cups
Vinegar	¼ cup
Mustard	2 tbs prepared
Salt, pepper	To taste
Eggs, hard-cooked, diced	6 (optional)

Macaroni Salad Carnival

Add 1 cup of combined diced green pepper, pimiento, and black olives.

Tuna Fish Salad

Allow four portions from one 6½-oz can plus mayonnaise, diced celery, lemon juice, and salt and pepper to taste. For variety, add 1 cup of either crushed potato chips, crushed corn chips, or crushed barbecue chips.

Spicy or Cocktail Tuna Fish Salad

Add 1 tsp lemon juice and 2–2½ tsp white horseradish to one can of tuna, plus mayonnaise and finely diced celery.

Vinaigrette (Mixed Vegetable) Salad   Yield: 10 4–6-oz servings

Carrots and peas, frozen	One 40-oz package
Cauliflower, medium	1 head
Green beans	One 8-oz can (not French cut)
Garbanzo	One 8-oz can drained

Cucumbers, medium	1
Tomatoes, medium, cut in chunks	3 (optional)
Italian or French dressing	1 pt

1. Cook frozen carrots and peas according to package instructions. Cool and drain.
2. Cauliflower may be used raw or cooked. Break into flowerlets.
3. Drain green beans and garbanzo beans.
4. Peel and slice cucumber thin.
5. Toss all vegetables lightly with dressing. Refrigerate before serving. Tomatoes may be added to top of salad just before serving.

Note: Mobile unit sandwiches can be made from any of the chicken, egg, meat, or fish salads. Individual portions of bean, potato, and macaroni salad may also be used for mobile unit service by putting the portion in a paper container with a tight-fitting cover.

SANDWICHES

It is generally accepted that a sandwich will be made up of two or more slices of bread or a roll, plus an appropriate filling. The sandwiches most commonly used at catered functions are tea and finger sandwiches, tea sandwich loaf, party triangles, individually wrapped mobile unit sandwiches, smorgasbord (hearty open face, not to be confused with canapés), and hot sandwiches, covered with hot gravy. Added to this are the local favorites which go by many different names: poor boy, submarine, Dagwood, and regular luncheon sandwiches.

The size and shape of a loaf of bread varies slightly from one part of the country to another so Table 16–1 can only serve as a guide. (See also Table 16–2 for proper methods of bread storage.)

Pullman or sandwich loaves to be sliced lengthwise for canapés or pinwheels have to be ordered from local bakeries, then weighed and measured to establish the exact size and number of slices from each loaf. Then the figures on cutting canapés will have to be adjusted accordingly.

Luncheon Sandwiches

When a sandwich luncheon is planned, an attractive arrangement of the cut sandwich will add considerably to the pleasing appearance of the plate.

There are a great number of different sandwich arrangements that are possible when the sandwich is cut to a specific pattern. Fig. 16–8 shows some of the different arrangements possible along with the original cutting diagrams.

Any salad, or sliced meat and cheese, or fish combination, can make a tasty sandwich. The budget will determine the type of garnish, which might

TABLE 16–1. VARIETY OF BREAD

Variety of Bread	Weight	Usable Slices	Thickness of Slice (in.)	Size of Slice (in.)
White sandwich thin	22½ oz	26	7⁄16	4 × 4
White sandwich thick	22½ oz	22	9⁄16	4 × 4
Wheat sandwich thin	22½ oz	26	7⁄16	4 × 4
Wheat sandwich thick	22½ oz	22	9⁄16	4 × 4
Rye sandwich	2 lb	28	7⁄16	4 × 4
White stub thin	22½ oz	20	7⁄16	4½ × 4½
Wheat stub thin	22½ oz	20	7⁄16	4½ × 4½
White stub thick	22½ oz	18	9⁄16	4½ × 4½
Rye stub	2 lb	20	7⁄16	4½ × 4½
Rye round top	2 lb	26	7⁄16	4½ × 4½
Raisin stub	2 lb	20	7⁄16	4½ × 4½

Dinner rolls: regular, poppy seed, sesame seed	By the dozen
Pan rolls, pic & pack, English muffins	By the dozen
Hamburger buns; plain, sesame seed, 3-in., 4-in., 5-in. double cut	By the dozen
Hot dog buns: 6-in., 8-in., New England	By the dozen
Cup cakes: assorted flavors	2 per pack
Fruit pies: all flavors	Individual pack
Layer loaf cake, slice	By the dozen
Cookies: chocolate and vanilla	4 per pack

Continental Baking Company

TABLE 16–2. PROPER METHODS FOR BREAD STORAGE

1. Buy only the amount that will be used daily.
2. Store bread at room temperature, 75 to 85°F.
3. Usual refrigerator temperature accelerates staling although freezing will retard it.
4. Keep bread storage units in dry place well above floor level.
5. Keep soft crust bread and rolls in their original moisture-proof wrappers to prevent loss of moisture.
6. Keep hard crust bread and rolls in areas that provide movement of relatively dry air to prevent crusts from becoming soggy.
7. Keep unwrapped bread where it will not be exposed to odors of other foods as it tends to absorb foreign flavors.

be a light one such as a slice of pickle and some parsley. A heavier garnish might include potato salad, cole slaw, and cranberry sauce for poultry or tartar sauce for fish plus sliced tomato on a bed of lettuce. Carrot sticks, celery fingers, radish roses, black and green olives, and gherkins can also be used. The arrangements in Fig. 16–8 leave adequate space for the garnish.

When a variety of sandwiches is to be served, all sandwiches of the same salad should be cut the same way, e.g., egg salad in squares, ham salad in strips, tuna fish salad in triangles. This will simplify serving and guarantee each guest getting exactly what was ordered.

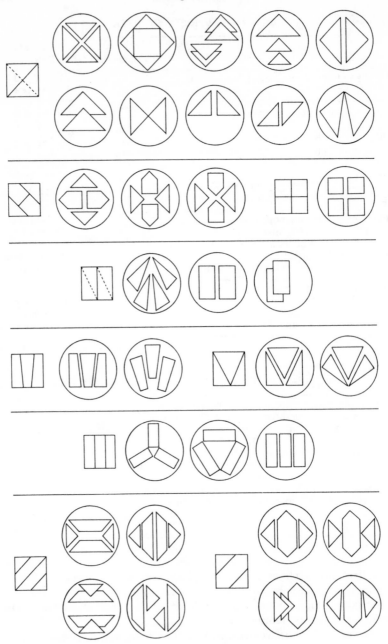

Fig. 16–8. 32 basic sandwich designs. These designs can be used for luncheon sandwiches as well as for finger and tea sandwiches. (Courtesy of American Institute of Baking.)

Tea Sandwiches

A tea sandwich is midway between a canapé and a hearty sandwich. Tea sandwiches are covered, canapés are open face. Tea sandwiches may be individually decorated or iced, or placed on a serving tray with garnish added. A hearty sandwich (two or more slices of bread plus the filling) makes three or four tea sandwiches. The method of making tea sandwiches is the same as any quantity sandwich operation.

1. Lay out half the number of slices of bread to be used.
2. Spread all with butter, margarine, or mayonnaise.
3. Spread with filling.
4. Cover with remaining slice of bread.
5. Trim crusts and cut. All the same salads should be cut into the same shapes.
6. Place on serving tray.
7. Garnish. Use parsley or radish rose; black, green, or stuffed olive; or miniature gherkins on a toothpick stuck into top layer of sandwiches.

Party Triangles

Party triangles are tea sandwiches cut only into triangles. These are secured with frilled picks and placed on the tray with points up, decorated with parsley.

Tea Sandwich Loaf

Bread, white or whole wheat, unsliced	One 2-lb loaf
Salad fillings	
Salmon salad	1 cup
Cream cheese, nut, and olive	1 cup
Egg salad	1 cup
Cheddar cheese	3–4 slices
Sliced tomato	4–5 slices

1. Remove crusts from unsliced loaf. Cut lengthwise into five slices.
2. Spread each slice with softened butter or margarine.
3. Spread bottom slice with salmon salad. Spread cream cheese, nut, and olive on next slice, egg salad on next slice, sliced cheese and sliced tomato on next slice. Top with last slice.
4. Press loaf firmly. Wrap in waxed paper and chill for 1 hr.
5. Remove paper and frost top and sides of loaf with cream cheese softened with cream or milk.
6. Garnish with chopped parsley, sliced cucumber, and fish shape cut from pimiento, or initials carved from pimiento and green pepper, or other appropriate design. Garnish serving platter with slices of tomato, parsley, and lemon wedges.
7. Slice and serve from buffet.

American Institute of Baking

Turkey Salad Sandwich Supreme   **Yield: 48 sandwiches**

Turkey meat, cooked, chopped	2 lb
Salad dressing	3½ cups
Salt	3 tsp
MSG	1 tsp
Chicken soup base	3 tsp
Pimiento, chopped	2 tbs
Celery, finely chopped	¼ cup
Pickle relish	¼ cup
Bread	96 slices

1. Mix salad dressing with other ingredients. Add chopped turkey.
2. Mix thoroughly.
3. Spread 1½ oz on 48 slices of bread. Cover with second slice of bread.
4. Cut for triangular stacking.

Commissary Cook Book

Smorgasbord Sandwiches

Smorgasbord sandwiches consist of bread, butter, and a third component. The bread is thinly sliced and buttered, and the third component may be varied indefinitely; it may consist of shellfish, fish, made-up salads, meat, pastes, sausages, eggs, cheese, or vegetables, or a combination of two or more of these ingredients. Some of the more popular smorgasbord combinations are listed below:

1. Danish salami, sliced eggs, and onion rings on brown bread spread with butter and mustard.

2. Danish ham slice, lettuce cup with carrots and peas in mayonnaise, and watercress garnish on rye bread.

3. Fresh smoked salmon with black caviar on white bread. Asparagus tip garnish.

4. Shrimp in a crowd. Buttered brown bread, covered with tartar sauce, then completely covered with tiny whole shrimp. Lemon slice garnish.

5. Rolled thinly sliced cold roast beef. Roast beef may be rolled plain or rolled around two or three whole white asparagus or a long strip of sharp cheddar sheese. Set two or three of these rolls on dark bread, with tomato wedge garnish.

6. Slice hot dogs lengthwise. Place on buttered, mustard-covered white bread. Hot dogs should cover bread completely. Place small scoop of potato salad on top of hot dogs; garnish with pickle slices.

7. Substitute cold sliced meatballs or meat loaf for hot dogs as in no. 6.

8. Spread dark bread with butter and mustard. Top with two slices of any kind of cheese. Place a small scoop of drained cole slaw in center of sandwich. Garnish with sliced hard-cooked eggs and parsley.

9. Any combination of meat and vegetables with appropriate garnish.

Smorgasbord is a hearty attractive sandwich, open face, decorated and garnished, and generally served whole. If small slices of bread are used, then two slices may be placed on the plate, and both covered. If larger slices are used, and one slice will practically cover the plate, then only one slice is used.

SPARE RIBS, CHINESE STYLE

Yield: 10 servings, 3 per person

Fresh pork spare ribs	5 lb
Soy sauce	2 cups
Garlic, fresh, crushed	2–4 cloves
Salt	2 tsp
Brown sugar	¼ cup
Sherry	¼ cup

1. Remove gristle and most of fat from meat, cut into serving portions.
2. Mix all other ingredients in large bowl or pan.
3. Place cut meat in this mixture (marinade) and allow to stand 1–2 hr. The longer the meat remains in the marinade, the stronger the seasoning will be. Turn meat occasionally.
4. Remove meat from marinade and place on broiler.
5. Broil until brown on all sides and meat is crisp and done.
6. Serve immediately.

Note: For hors d'oeuvres, cut ribs approximately 14–16 pieces to the pound. For appetizer, cut eight pieces to the pound (20 portions, 2 pieces each).

SAUERBRATEN (GERMAN SPICY POT ROAST)

Yield: 50 6-oz servings

Beef, rump or round	24 lb (3 pieces)
Salt, pepper	Sufficient to sprinkle meat
Water	2 qt (approx.)
Vinegar	2 qt (approx.)
Onions, large, thinly sliced	8
Bay leaves	10–12
Peppercorns	24
Carrots, large, sliced	4
Sugar	¾ cup
Raisins, seedless	1½ cups
Ginger snaps, crumbled	16–20

1. Sprinkle salt and pepper over meat.
2. Prepare marinade of water, vinegar, onions, bay leaves, peppercorns, and carrots.

3. Place meat in marinade. Be sure meat is covered. Allow to marinate three days. For a spicier meat, allow to marinate four days. Turn meat daily.
4. To cook, sear meat on all sides, then add vegetables and marinade. Cover and simmer for 3–4 hr or until fork tender. Add more water if necessary.
5. Melt sugar in heavy saucepan, gradually adding all liquid in which meat was cooked. Add raisins and crumbled ginger snaps. Cook about 10 minutes or until smooth and thick, stirring constantly.
6. Meat may be sliced prior to serving and replaced in gravy for holding.
7. To serve, place portion of meat on plate. Spoon some gravy over slices.

SHELLFISH MOLD EXTRAORDINAIRE

Yield: 12 ½-cup servings

Shellfish, finely chopped	3 cups (meat from 2 lobster tails and ⅔ lb shrimps)
Gelatin	2½ tbs
Water, cold	½ cup
Salt	1 tsp
Dry mustard	1 tsp
Sugar	3 tbs
Eggs	4
Cream	2 cups
Sherry	¾–1 cup

1. Soften gelatin in cold water. Reserve.
2. Mix salt, mustard, sugar, eggs, cream, and wine in top of double boiler or in heavy pot. Cook very slowly, stirring constantly, until thick and heavy as sour cream.
3. Remove from heat. Add dissolved gelatin. Reheat and stir for a minute or two until gelatin is completely cooked. *Do not boil.*
4. Add shellfish. Pour into individual molds; refrigerate until set.
5. To unmold, place each mold in shallow pan of hot water for a few seconds and then turn out on bed of crisp lettuce. Garnish with parsley or watercress. No other garnish is necessary.

SHRIMPS AND RICE ROLLS IN BACON

Yield: approx. 30 rolls

Tomato juice	½ cup
Eggs, well beaten	1
Bread crumbs, dry	½ cup
Rice, cooked	1 cup
Pepper	Dash
Parsley, chopped	1 tsp
Celery salt	½ tsp

| Shrimps, mashed | One 5-oz can |
| Bacon, cut in half | 15 slices |

1. Mix tomato juice and egg. Add crumbs, rice, pepper, parsley, celery salt, and shrimp. Mix thoroughly.
2. Roll into finger length. Wrap each roll with one half slice of bacon and fasten with toothpicks (wooden).
3. Broil, turning frequently to brown evenly.

Note: These may be made the day before and chilled.

Rice Council for Market Development

SHRIMP FRA DIAVOLO

Yield: 30 servings, 5 shrimps per serving

Shrimps	5 lb
Garlic, crushed	5 cloves
Oregano	2 tbs
Salt	1 tbs
Hot red peppers	1½ tbs
Olive oil	1 cup (approx.)
Tomato puree	1 qt
Tomatoes, canned	1 cup
Parsley, finely diced	½ cup
Brandy	½ cup (approx.)

1. Crush garlic and add oregano, salt, pepper, and oil. Simmer 5 minutes.
2. Add tomato puree and tomatoes, and boil for 25 minutes.
3. Add raw peeled shrimps. Cook 5 minutes more.
4. Add 2 tbs brandy. Place in chafing dish ready for buffet service.
5. Heat remainder of brandy. Pour gently over Shrimp Fra Diavolo in chafing dish and light it. When flame dies, sprinkle with parsley. Serve.

SOUFFLE ROTHSCHILD

Yield: 4–5 servings

Butter	3 tbs
Flour	¼ cup
Milk	1 cup
Egg yolks	4
Egg whites, stiffly beaten	4
Candied fruit	½ cup
Kirsch	4 tbs (approx.)
Sugar	½ cup

1. Make thick basic white sauce. Let cool.
2. Add egg yolks, candied fruit, kirsch, and ¼ cup sugar.
3. Beat egg whites with ¼ cup sugar until they form peaks.

4. Fold stiffly beaten egg whites into base mixture.
5. Place gently in lightly buttered soufflé dish.
6. Bake at 370°F for 35–45 minutes or until done. When knife blade inserted in soufflé comes out dry, soufflé is done.
7. Serve *immediately*.

Note: The soufflé is quite simple to make, but it should only be used for small groups.

STEAK AND KIDNEY PIE

Yield: 1 pie

Lean beef	¼ lb
Lamb kidney	¼ lb
Onions, diced	⅛ cup
Potatoes, sliced thick	¼ lb
Salt, pepper, celery seed	To taste
Beef stock	As needed
Parsley, diced	1 sprig

1. Line pie tin (4½–6 in. in diameter) with thin pastry dough. Prick with fork.
2. Cut beef into ½-in. slices. Arrange in pie tin with kidney slices, potatoes, and onions. Pie tin should be fairly full.
3. Sprinkle with diced parsley and seasoning. Add beef stock to cover.
4. Cover with pastry. Press edges securely. Brush top with well-beaten egg.
5. Bake in slow oven for 2½ hr, or until meat is fork tender. Test by inserting fork gently through pastry top and meat.
6. Serve hot.

STEW

A good hearty stew is almost as much an American tradition as Thanksgiving turkey. The various kinds of stews can be served as the main dish for lunch or dinner or .:om a buffet.

Beef goulash is chunks of beef with diced onions browned in fat and cooked in a heavy saucepan. Lots of paprika, diced green pepper, and some tomato sauce add to the flavor. It is served with buttered noodles.

Beef stew is chunks of beef cooked in natural gravy (beef stock) with carrots, potatoes, small whole onions, celery, and other vegetables.

Bouillabaisse is a fish stew using shellfish as well as lobster and local varieties of fish. The sauce is white and made with wine.

Choppino is a fish stew made with lobster and other shellfish only. These are cooked in a highly spiced tomato sauce. Onions and diced green peppers are often added to the sauce.

French stew (blanquette de veau) is veal stew in a rich white sauce. Vegetable stock or chicken stock may be used. Small white onions and mushrooms are added. Lemon juice gives this dish a slightly tart flavor. Wine is often used in preparation of the sauce.

Irish stew uses beef or lamb meat cooked in a rich white sauce made from vegetable stock. It contains small white onions and carrots cut into small chunks. Worcestershire sauce is also added.

Mulligatawny stew, originally from East India, is made from a very rich but rather thin creamed chicken soup. It is highly spiced with various herbs and curry. If the sauce is very thin it is served as soup. If the sauce is thick, the stew is served with rice.

Ragout of beef is beef chunks cooked in a thick brown gravy with potatoes, carrots, and onions. Salt, pepper, and a small amount of paprika may be used as seasoning.

STRAWBERRIES IN WINE

Yield: 6 ¾-cup servings

Fresh strawberries   7½–8 cups
Sugar   ⅓ cup
Wine   1½ cups

1. Pick and clean strawberries. Wash and drain.
2. Sprinkle with sugar. Refrigerate 2–3 hr.
3. Immediately before serving, cover with wine. Use California red, white, or champagne.

Variation

1. Substitute frozen peaches for strawberries.
2. Use California sauterne. Wine keeps peaches from turning brown.
3. Add wine before refrigerating peaches.
4. Keep covered until serving time.
5. Pineapple bits or chunks may be added to either of the above.

Wine Institute

STUFFING OR DRESSING BASIC RECIPE

Yield: 24 ¼-cup or No. 16 scoop servings

Never stuff turkey or chicken for quantity service. Poultry should be cooked separately. Stuffing (dressing) should be baked in large baking pans and scooped for individual service. The portion of poultry is placed over the scooped stuffing and the gravy is then spooned over the meat.* Double pork chops and breast of lamb should be stuffed before cooking.

---

* Individual service Rock Cornish game hens, chicken Kiev (stuffed chicken breasts and legs), etc., may be purchased already stuffed and oven ready.

Bread, day old, cubed	2 lb
Onions, diced	½ lb
Celery, thinly sliced	½ lb
Salt, pepper, sage	To taste
Chicken Stock or chicken soup	
base	As needed

1. Brown onions and celery in oil or chicken fat until golden brown.
2. Moisten bread crumbs with stock and add seasoning and browned vegetables.
3. Mix thoroughly. Spread approximately 2 in. thick in baking pan. Bake at 350°F for 1 hr or until brown on top.
4. Serve as needed.

Variations

1. Add approximately 1 lb of finely diced turkey giblets.
2. Add approximately 2 lb of cooked cubed chestnuts.
3. Eliminate onions and sage, and substitute 1-lb can of drained fruit cocktail.
4. Add 1-lb drained can of bean sprouts, 6–8 oz of diced water chestnuts, and 2 tbs soy sauce.

SWEET AND SOUR CHINESE SAUCE

Yield: 10 1-cup servings

Meat (poultry or shrimp), raw	1 qt
Vinegar	1 pt
Water	1 pt
Green peppers, large	4
Pineapple cubes	1-lb can
Sugar, mixed brown and white	2 cups
MSG	1 tsp
Tomatoes, large	3
Cornstarch	6 tbs
Catsup	6 tbs
Oil	For browning meat
Batter	
Eggs	4
Flour	1½ cups
Water	¼ cup
Salt	½ tsp

1. Cut meat or poultry into 1-in. cubes. Wash and devein, but do not cut shrimps.
2. Make batter. Dip meat (poultry or shrimp) into batter. Fry until golden brown, and set aside.

3. Cut green peppers into strips, 10–12 strips from each pepper.
4. Cut tomatoes into wedges.
5. Place all other ingredients in large pot. Mix well. Boil about 5 minutes or until cornstarch is cooked. Add green peppers.
6. Add fried meat (poultry or shrimp). Bring to a boil and cook about 5 minutes more. Add tomatoes and cook another 5 minutes. Remove from fire and serve immediately with boiled or steamed rice.

TOMATO ASPIC RING GARNISH SUPREME

Prepare tomato aspic in usual manner in individual ring molds. Prepare the following for each salad:

Large shrimps, fresh-cooked	3–4
Eggs, hard-cooked	¼
Avocados	2–3 slices (12 slices from 1 avocado)
Lettuce, shredded	¼ cup
French dressing	2–3 tbs
Lettuce leaf	Bed for salad

1. Turn out tomato aspic ring on bed of crisp lettuce.
2. Fill center of tomato ring with shredded lettuce.
3. Hook shrimps close together on one side of aspic ring.
4. Lay avocado slices around ring.
5. Place quarter of hard-cooked egg on opposite side of shrimps.
6. Spoon dressing over shrimps and lettuce.
7. Refrigerate before serving.

TONGUE WITH SWEET AND SOUR RAISIN SAUCE

Yield: 10 servings, 2–3 slices per serving

Beef tongue, pickled	One, 4–5 lb
Onions, medium	1
Garlic	1 clove
Bay leaves	2–3
Sauce	
Oil	2 tbs
Onions, finely diced	1
Flour	2 tbs
Stock from tongue	2 cups
Vinegar	½ cup
Brown sugar	½ cup
Salt	½ tsp
Red Maraschino cherries	¼ cup cut
Raisins	1 cup

1. Place tongue, onions, garlic, and bay leaves in large heavy pot and cover with water. Bring to a boil. Reduce heat, simmer 3–3½ hr, or until meat is fork tender.
2. Skin tongue and allow to cool before slicing.
3. To make sauce, melt fat, brown onions lightly therein, and add flour.
4. Add stock. Bring to a boil and reduce heat. Add vinegar, salt, cherries, and raisins. Allow to simmer 15–20 minutes.
5. Tongue should be sliced thin. Place sliced tongue (tightly stacked) in shallow roasting pan. Spoon some sauce over sliced tongue. Keep in warm oven until serving time.
6. To serve, place slices of tongue on plate and spoon sauce over slices. Each portion should have raisins and cherries.

TURKEY SANDWICH SUPREME

Yield: 25 servings

Turkey, cold roasted, sliced	1 lb 9 oz
Bread	50 slices
Eggs	10
Milk	1 pt
Cream sauce	2½ pt
California sherry	1 pt
Butter or margarine	¼ lb

1. Prepare sandwiches in usual manner using 1 oz of turkey meat for each sandwich.
2. Beat eggs with milk. Dip sandwiches in this mixture and fry to golden brown on griddle or in large skillet.
3. Make cream sauce using chicken stock as liquid. Add sherry and melted butter. Beat until smooth.
4. Pour hot sauce over each sandwich on plate. Serve with fresh fruit sections.

Wine Institute

TURKEY TETRAZZINI*

Yield: 35 servings

Turkey meat, diced	3 qt
Broad noodles	2 lb
Butter or margarine	¾ cup
Celery, finely diced	4 cups
Green pepper, diced	2 cups
Onions, finely diced	½ cup
Mushrooms, sliced	1 lb

---

* Chicken meat may be substituted for turkey.

Flour	½ cup
Milk	1¾ qt
Cheddar cheese	1 lb
Salt	2 tbs
Pepper	1 tsp
Worcestershire sauce	¼ cup (or to taste)
Sherry	½ cup
Parmesan cheese, grated	2 cups

1. Cook noodles in usual manner. Reserve.
2. Cook celery, green pepper, onions, and mushrooms in melted butter until they are slightly softened but not brown.
3. Add flour and mix thoroughly. Add milk and cook, stirring until thick.
4. Add cheddar cheese and cook until cheese is completely melted.
5. Add all other ingredients except Parmesan cheese. Heat but *do not boil.*
6. Place cooked noodles in two 9 x 13 x 2-in. pans. Pour turkey mixture over noodles. Sprinkle with Parmesan cheese. Portions may be placed in individual casseroles if desired.
7. Bake at 350°F for 20–25 minutes. Serve hot.

VEAL SCALLOPINI MARSALA

Yield: 10 4-oz servings

Veal Scallopini, cut thin	2½ lb
Flour	1 cup
Butter or margarine	½–¾ cup
Marsala wine, dry	1 cup (more if desired)
Salt, pepper	To taste
Mushrooms, sliced thin, sautéed in butter	1 lb

1. Dredge veal slices in flour to which salt and pepper have been added.
2. Sauté lightly in butter for 2 or 3 minutes to a side.
3. When all pieces are browned, return them to pan. Add the Marsala. Simmer a few minutes or until meat is fork tender. Add sliced mushrooms.
4. Place meat on plate and spoon gravy over it. Serve hot.

Note: If the veal is fried in advance of serving time, it can be stacked in a shallow roasting pan and held. Just before serving time, add some more wine and mushrooms, bring to a boil; then lower heat and simmer gently until meat is done. Serve with sauce spooned over the meat.

Variation

French style: Add 1 lb of small white onions (1 can drained) when the mushrooms are added.

VICHYSSOISE

Yield: 20 ½-cup servings

Potatoes, raw	7 cups (approx. 2½ lb)
Leeks, large	3
Chicken stock	1½ qt
Celery seeds	1 tsp
Salt	1 tsp
Pepper, white	½ tsp
Cream	1 qt

1. Dice potatoes, slice leeks, and boil with seasoning in chicken stock until potatoes crumble and leeks are very soft.
2. Put all through blender or high-speed mixer until extremely smoothe.
3. To serve cold, refrigerate. Mix cream in just before serving.
4. To serve hot, return blended soup to stove. When very hot, but just under boiling, add cream a little at a time. Serve immediately.
5. Garnish with some thinly sliced leeks or finely diced parsley.

VIENNESE STUFFED CABBAGE IN SWEET AND SOUR RAISIN SAUCE

Yield: 100 dinner-size servings
200 miniatures

Leaves

Cabbage	12–14 heads
Vinegar	1 pt
Salt	2 tbs
Water	Sufficient to blanch cabbage

Filling

Ground beef	9 lb
Rice, raw	3½–4 cups
White bread	20 slices soaked in water
Eggs	9
Salt, pepper	To taste

Sauce

Tomato puree	Two no. 2½ cans, plus equal amount of water
Whole tomatoes	Two no. 2½ cans
Brown sugar	1 lb
White sugar	1 lb
Lemon juice	¼ cup or more to taste
Salt	1 tbs
Pepper	1 tsp
Raisins, seedless	1 lb

1. Blanch cabbage in water, vinegar, and salt. When leaves are soft enough to roll without breaking, remove to work pan.
2. Slice spines off. Cut leaves in sizes as needed (approximately 5-in. diameter of flat cabbage leaf for cocktail size, and approximately 8-in. diameter for dinner size).
3. Dice spines and odds and ends of cabbage leaves and lay in deep roasting pan.
4. Mix all filling ingredients.
5. Place 3 tbs of meat for dinner size in center of cabbage. Use 1 tbs of meat mix for miniatures or cocktail size. Fold as blintzes (see Fig. 16–1) but in step no. 4 bring last edge well over other and wrap it completely around cabbage roll if possible.
6. Place cabbage rolls in roasting pan, on top of bed of diced spines and end pieces. Place rolls close together and half cover with sauce.
7. Place another layer of cabbage rolls on top and again cover with sauce. Continue until all meat and cabbage leaves are used. If cooking this in a deep roasting pan in oven, do not stack cabbage rolls more than three deep. Sauce should just about cover top layer. If cooking in a deep pot on top of stove, cabbage rolls should not be stacked more than five deep. Sauce should just about cover top layer. Great care must be exercised in removing cooked cabbage rolls from pot or pan or they will break and fall apart.
8. Reserve some sauce for reheating or to be added during last half hour of cooking if necessary.
9. Cover pan tightly. If no cover is available, make a cover from heavy-duty aluminum foil.
10. Place pan in oven at 350°F. Allow to cook from 1–2½ hr, depending on the size of rolls and number in pan. After 1 hr, remove one cabbage roll from pan and test if done. If cooking on top of stove, place pot over a medium flame. Simmer for 1½–2½ hr. After 1 hr test if done.
11. Finished cabbage rolls may be left in same pan for reheating or may be served immediately. The rolls may be cooled and placed in smaller pans to be refrigerated or frozen for future use.

Variation

Scandinavian rolled cabbage: Prepare as above but use equal parts of meat and rice. Prepare a rich brown sauce instead of tomato sauce. Cook as above.

Glossary

À la King: Served in cream sauce made with mushrooms and pimiento or green pepper. Well seasoned.

À la Newburg: Served in a rich cream sauce made with eggs, cream, and wine.

Amandine: With almonds.

Antipasto: (Italian) An appetizer, which includes prosciutto ham, garbanzo beans, sliced onions, pimiento, marinated artichoke hearts, olives, and deviled eggs.

Aubergine: (French) Eggplant.

Au Gratin: (French) With grated cheese.

Baklava: (Turkish) Paper-thin dough in many layers with chopped nuts between layers, soaked in honey.

Bar-le-Duc: (French) With currant jelly.

Bearnaise: (French) Sauce made with shallots, wine, eggs, and butter.

Béchamel: (French) Thick white sauce made with chicken stock.

Bigarade: (French) Sauce of roast duck drippings made with orange juice.

Blanquette de Veau: (French) Veal stew in rich white sauce.

Blintzes: Crépes, egg pancakes filled with cheese, etc., fried or baked.

Bouillabaisse: (French) Fresh fish chowder made with wine, cream, and tomato sauce.

Bourguignone: (French) Dark rich sauce for beef made with onions, celery, and red wine.

Busboy: Assistant to waiter. May pass bread and rolls, pour coffee, and assist in clearing tables.

Busbox: Large metal or heavy-duty plastic box used to carry dirty dishes from dining room to kitchen.

Café Espresso: (Italian) Black coffee served with lemon or cognac.

Canapé: (French) Bite-size bits of savory food served on bread, decorated, and served cold.

Chafing Dish: Five-piece unit (stand, heating unit, water pan, food pan, and cover) for keeping food hot on buffet.

Chaud-Froid: (French) A sauce for coating food to be decorated for fancy buffet work. Sauce is made hot but served cold.

Chicken Cacciatore: (Italian) Chicken sautéed with onions, peppers, and tomatoes. Highly seasoned.

Chicken Tetrazzini: (Italian) Chicken boiled, boned, and served in thick white sauce made with wine and Parmesan cheese.

Chop Suey: (Chinese) Veal, chicken, pork, beef, or shrimp sautéed with celery, onions, and bean sprouts, seasoned with soy sauce and served with rice.

Chow Mein: (Chinese) Basically the same as chop suey; meat and vegetables served with crisp noodles.

Commissary: Department supplying equipment and provisions. In mobile unit catering, the place where drivers pick up all supplies. Location caterer often refers to base of operations containing kitchen, store rooms, offices, etc., as "the commissary."

Cover: The complete place setting or the price of an entire meal.

Coq au Vin: (French) Chicken cooked in wine sauce.

Chioppino: (Italian) Shellfish meat cooked in highly seasoned tomato sauce. Fish stew.

Crêpes Suzette: (French) Dessert pancakes usually served with flaming sauce.

En Brochette: (French) On skewers, kabobs.

Escallopes: (French) Thin slices of meat, usually veal.

Escargots: (French) Snails.

Fettucini: (Italian) Narrow egg noodles.

Florentine: With spinach.

Garbanzos: Chick peas.

Gefilte Fish: (Jewish) Ground fish meat with onions, boiled in stock, and served as appetizer with ground horseradish.

Glâcé: (French) Glazed, usually with a gelatin or *chaud-froid.*

Hassenpfeffer: (German) Rabbit stew in thick sauce.

Hollandaise: Sauce made of butter, eggs, and lemon juice.

Hunter: With browned onions and mushrooms in brown sauce.

Hors d'Oeuvres: (French) Bite size bits of savory food served hot or cold. In American catering very little differentiation is made between canapés and hors d'oeuvres. Canapés should have a bread base, hors d'oeuvres need not.

Indienne: Any curry dish usually served with rice.

Jardiniere: (French) Served with cooked vegetables on the side.

Jeroboam: Double magnum of wine, usually champagne.

Julienne: (French) Cut into thin strips.

Kartoffel Kloesse: (German) Potato dumplings.

Königsberger Klops: (Norwegian) Meat balls in highly seasoned sauce.

Kosher: (Jewish) Any food that is traditionally clean according to Jewish religious standards, and therefore fit for Jewish consumption.

Lasagne: (Italian) Layers of wide noodles alternating with cheese and meat cooked in a rich tomato sauce, then baked.

Lyonnaise: (French) With onions.

Maitre d'Hotel Sauce: (French) Sauce made of butter, parsley, and lemon.

Magnum: Double size wine bottle, usually 52 fluid oz, used mostly for sparkling wines or champagne.

Marinate: To soak in a mixture of oil, vinegar, salt, pepper, garlic, and sliced onions.

Mornay Sauce: Rich cream sauce made with a white cheese.

Mousseline: Hollandaise sauce to which whipped cream or beaten egg whites have been added.

Pilaf: Rice sautéed in butter then cooked in meat stock. Might also refer to Oriental stew dishes with meat, vegetables, and rice. Any stew-type dish prepared with rice.

Prosciutto: Smoky Italian ham, sliced paper thin for an antipasto salad.

Pullman Loaf: Loaf of bread, 1¾–2 lb without domed top. Average 28 (½-in.) slices or 36 (⅜-in.) slices. Cut lengthwise for canapés, averages 6 or 7 slices.

Quiche Lorraine: (French) Rich cheese and bacon pie served hot.

Russe: (Russian) Served with sour cream. Same as *à la russe.*

Saltimbocco: (Italian) Veal bits with ham and cheese, sautéed in seasoned butter and wine.

Sandwich: Various items of food presented between two slices of bread. The variations are legion.

Scallopini: (Italian) Thin slices of veal with mushrooms and seasoning, cooked in butter and sherry.

Schnitzel Holstein: (German) Veal cutlet served with fried egg.

Shashlik: (Russian) Various food items, meat, and vegetables, served en brochette; flame is optional.

Shish-kebob: (Armenian) Lamb, onions, green peppers, and tomatoes broiled on skewers.

Smorgasbord: (Swedish) Also *Smorrebrod.* A large open-face decorated meal-size sandwich. A buffet consisting of a variety of hot and cold dishes. A buffet consisting of fish dishes.

Sou-chef: (French) Assistant chef. Should be able to carve meat at buffet table.

Spumoni: (Italian) Ice cream.

Sukiyaki: (Japanese) Meat sliced paper thin or shrimp with onions, spinach, and bean sprouts sautéed quickly on a brazier at the table, seasoned with soy sauce.

Tournedos: (French) Fillets of beef wrapped in strips of bacon, grilled.

Truffles: Tubers similar to mushrooms, usually black, used for garnish and decoration on white *chaud-froid.*

Velouté: (French) Cream sauce made of chicken or veal stock, thickened with butter and flour.

Veronique: (French) Served with grapes.

Vichyssoise: (French) Potato and leek soup made with butter, chicken stock, and cream. May be served hot or cold.

Vinaigrette: (French) Salad dressing of vinegar, oil, and spices. (Russian) Salad of mixed vegetables with French dressing.

Wiener Schnitzel: (German) Breaded veal cutlet served with lemon and anchovy garnish.

Yorkshire Pudding: (English) Popovers made in pan drippings from, and served with, roast beef.

Zabaglione: (Italian) Rich custard made with eggs and wine.

Schools for Food Service and Catering

Formal training in food service is necessary background for the good caterer. The following list covers schools with courses in the many different phases of the food industry.

The capital letters appearing on a separate line after the name and address of the school indicate the type of courses and degrees offered by the various schools and are keyed as follows:

A   General food services
B   Catering
C   Degree
D   Diploma
E   Certificate
F   Short courses

For specific information concerning any particular school and its courses, requirements for enrollments, etc., inquire from the director of the school or from the board of education of the city in which the school is located.

For information about foreign schools, write to the Washington, D.C., Office of the Consulate for the country in which the school is located.

ALABAMA

Ala. Polytech. Inst.
Auburn
ABC
Glenn Voc. Trade School
Rt. 1, Box 474
Glenn
AEF
Florence State College
Florence
AC
Jacksonville State College
Jacksonville
ABC

Alabama College
Montevalo
AC
Alabama Agricultural and Mechanical College
Normal
ABC
Tuskegee Inst.
Tuskegee
ACD
University of Alabama
University
ABC

269

ARIZONA

Phoenix Union High School, Voc. Tech.
Div.
512 E. Van Buren St.
Phoenix
AEF
Phoenix Indian School
Phoenix
A
University of Arizona, College of Agriculture
Tucson
AB

ARKANSAS

Arkansas Voc. Tech. School
Pine Bluff
A

CALIFORNIA

Long Beach City College
1305 E. Pacific Coast H'way
Longbeach
ACF
Los Angeles Trade-Tech. College
400 W. Washington Blvd.
Los Angeles
AEF
Oakland Junior College, Laney Trade-Tech. Div.
1001 3rd Ave.
Oakland
ACEF
City College of San Francisco
Ocean and Phelan Aves.
San Francisco
ACEF
John A. O'Connell Voc. & Tech. Inst.
San Francisco
AD
Contra Costa College
2801 Castro Rd.
San Pablo
ACE

COLORADO

Emily Griffith Opportunity School
12th and Welton Sts.
Denver
AEF
University of Denver, School of Hotel and Restaurant Management
Denver
ABCEF

CONNECTICUT

E. C. Goodwin Tech. School
161 S. Main St.
New Britain
AD
Culinary Institute of America
393 Prospect St.
New Haven
ADEF
J. M. Wright Tech. School
Woodside Park
Stanford
AD
University of Connecticut
Storrs
AC

DELAWARE

William C. Jason Comprehensive High School
Georgetown
AD
Howard High School
13th and Poplar Sts.
Wilmington
AD
H. Fletcher Brown Voc. High School
14th and Market
Wilmington
ADEF

DISTRICT OF COLUMBIA

Anna Burdick Voc. High School
1300 Allison St., N.W.
Washington, D.C.
ABDE
John A. Chamberlain Voc. High School
14th and Potomac Ave., S.E.
Washington, D.C.
ADE

FLORIDA

Lindsey Hopkins Education Center
1410 Northeast 2nd Ave.
Miami
AEF
Northwestern Senior High School
1316 Northwest 63rd St.
Miami
A
Florida State University
Tallahassee
AC

GEORGIA

University of Georgia, School of Home Economics
Athens
AC
Carver Voc. High School
1275 Capitol Ave., S.W.
Atlanta
A
Smith-Hughes Voc. Evening School
Atlanta
AE
Distributive Education Services
Atlanta
Columbus
Macon
Savannah
AEF
Georgia State College for Women
Milledgeville
AC

HAWAII

Hawaii Tech. School, Dept. of Culinary Arts and Catering Management
Hilo
AB
Kapiolani Tech. School (Hotel and Restaurant Dept.)
2013 Kapiolani Blvd.
Honolulu
A

ILLINOIS

University of Chicago
Chicago
AC
Washburne Trade School
3233 W. 31st St.
Chicago
ABEF
University of Illinois
Urbana
ABC

INDIANA

Indiana University
Bloomington
AC
Purdue University
Lafayette
AC

IOWA

Iowa State University of Science and Technology
Ames
ABC
Des Moines Tech. High School
Des Moines
A

KANSAS

Kansas State University of Agriculture
Manhattan
AC

KENTUCKY

Berea College
Berea
AC
Central High School
12th and Chestnut
Louisville
A

LOUISIANA

Capitol Area Voc. School
1500 S. 13th St.
Baton Rouge
AD
Delgrado Trade and Tech. Inst.
615 City Park Ave.
New Orleans
ADF
Orleans Area Voc.–Tech. School
P.O. Box 8202
New Orleans
AD

MAINE

University of Maine
Orono
AC
Maine Voc.–Tech. Inst.
South Portland
A

MARYLAND

George Washington Carver Voc. Tech. High School
Presstman and Bentalou Sts.
Baltimore

Mergenthaler Voc. Tech. High School
Hillen Rd. and 35th St.
Baltimore
AD

University of Maryland
College Park
AC

MASSACHUSETTS

University of Massachusetts
Amherst
AC

Endicott Junior College
Beverly
AC

Boston Trade High School Annex
690 Washington St., Dorchester
Boston
AD

Boston Trade High School for Girls
56 The Fenway
Boston
ADE

Boston University, Evening Extension
Div.
685 Commonwealth Ave.
Boston
AEF

Simmons College
300 The Fenway
Boston
AC

Massachusetts Dept. of Education
Chicopee
AF

Henry O. Peabody School
Peabody Rd.
Norwood
ABDEF

Springfield Trade High School
Springfield
AD

University of Massachusetts
Stockbridge
ADF

Regis College for Women
Weston
AC

David Hale Fanning Trade High School
Chatham and High Sts.
Worcester
AD

MICHIGAN

Albion College
Albion
A

Chadsey High School
5335 Martin St.
Detroit
ADF

Wayne State University
Detroit
ACF

Wilbur Wright Cooperative High School
4333 12th St.
Detroit
A

American Hotel Inst., Michigan State
University
East Lansing
AE

Western Michigan University
Kalamazoo
A

Lansing Public Schools
419 N. Capitol Ave.
Lansing
AF

MINNESOTA

Duluth Area Voc. Tech. School
East London Rd.
Duluth
ABEF

Minneapolis Voc. High School
3rd Ave. S. and 11th St.
Minneapolis
ABDEF

Girls Voc. High School
97 East Central St.
St. Paul
ABD

MISSOURI

Hadley Tech. High School
3405 Bell Ave.
St. Louis
AD

MONTANA

Montana State College
Bozeman
AC

Montana State University
Missoula
AC

NEBRASKA

University of Nebraska
Lincoln
AC

Omaha Tech. High School
3201 Cumming St.
Omaha
AEF

NEW HAMPSHIRE
Davis Voc. School
Dover
AD
University of New Hampshire
Durham
AC

NEW JERSEY
Thomas A. Edison Voc. and Tech. High
School
Summer St.
Elizabeth
ABD
Bergen County Voc. and Tech High
School
200 Hackensack Ave.
Hackensack
ADE
Camden County Voc. School
Browning Rd.
Merchantville
AD
Essex County Voc. and Tech High
School
300 N. 13th St.
Newark (for girls)
AD
Sussex Ave. at First St.
Newark (for boys)
AD
300 N. 13th St.
Newark (adult)
ADF
Fairleigh Dickinson University
Rutherford
AC
Middlesex County Voc. and Tech. High
School
Convery Blvd.
Woodbridge
ADE

NEW MEXICO
Eastern New Mexico University
Portales
AC

NEW YORK
Jane Addams Voc. High School
900 Tinton Ave.
Bronx
AD
Brooklyn College, Div. of Voc. Studies
Bedford Ave. and Ave. H
Brooklyn
ABD
Clara Barton Voc. High School
901 Classon Ave.
Brooklyn
AD
New York City Community College
300 Pearl St.
Brooklyn
ABCEF
Pratt Institute
215 Ryerson St.
Brooklyn
AC
Sarah J. Hale Voc. High School
345 Dean St.
Brooklyn
AD
Emerson Voc. High School
1405 Sycamore St.
Buffalo
A
Erie County Tech. Institute
1685 Elmwood Ave.
Buffalo
AC
Fosdick-Masten Voc. High School
Masten and North Sts.
Buffalo
State University Agricultural and Tech.
Inst.
Canton
AC
Cobleskill
ABC
Delhi
ABC
Morrisville
ABC
Cornell University, School of Hotel
Administration
Ithaca
ACF
Edison Voc. and Tech. High School
Mt. Vernon
ABD
Rockland County Voc. Education
New City
ABD

New Rochelle High School
  New Rochelle
  AD
Central Commercial High School
  214 E. 42nd St.
  New York City
  AEF
Food Trades Voc. High School
  17 Lexington Ave.
  New York City
  ABDEF
Hunter College
  695 Park Ave.
  New York City
  AF
McKee Voc. and Tech. High School
  290 St. Mark's Place, St. George
  Staten Island
  AD
Mabel D. Bacon Voc. High School
  22nd St. and Lexington Ave.
  New York City
  AD
New York Institute of Dietetics
  154 West 14th St.
  New York City
  ABEF
Paul Smith's College of Arts and Science
  Paul Smiths
  AC
Rochester Institute of Technology
  65 Plymouth Ave. S.
  Rochester
  ABC
Syracuse Central Tech. High School
  717 S. Warren St.
  Syracuse
  AD
Syracuse University
  Syracuse
  ABC
Westchester Community College
  75 Grasslands Rd.
  Valhalla
  AC
High School of Commerce
  North Broadway
  Yonkers
  ABD

NORTH CAROLINA
West Charlotte High School
  Charlotte
  AE
Williston Industrial High School
  Wilmington
  AE

NORTH DAKOTA
North Dakota Agricultural College
  Fargo
  AC
University of North Dakota
  Grand Forks
  AC

OHIO
Ohio University
  Athens
  AC
Timkin Voc. High School
  521 Tuscarawas St. West
  Canton
  AD
Central High School
  3520 Central Parkway
  Cincinnati
  AD
University of Cincinnati
  Cincinnati
  AD
Jane Addams Voc. High School
  4940 Carnegie Ave.
  Cleveland
  ADF
Western Reserve University
  2023 Adelbert Rd.
  Cleveland
  AC
Ohio State University
  Columbus
  AC
Norwood Tech. High School
  2023 Elm Ave.
  Norwood
  ADE
Whitney Voc. High School
  Washington St. at 17th
  Toledo
  ADEF

OKLAHOMA
University of Oklahoma
  Norman
  AC
Oklahoma State Tech.
  Okmulgee
  A
Oklahoma State University, School of Hotel and Restaurant Administration
  Stillwater
  · ACEF

OREGON

Oregon State College
Corvallis
AC

PENNSYLVANIA

Bucks County Area Tech. School
Wistar Rd.
Fairless Hills
AD
Central-Dauphin High School
4600 Locust Lane
Harrisburg
AD
Dobbins Tech. High School
Lehigh Ave. at 22nd
Philadelphia
ADEF
Drexel Institute of Technology
32nd and Chestnut Sts.
Philadelphia
AC
Edward Bok Voc.–Tech. School
8th and Mifflin Sts.
Philadelphia
ADEF
Temple University, Div. of Voc. Teacher
Education
Philadelphia
AF
Arsenal Girls' Voc. High School
40th and Butler
Pittsburgh
AD
Irwin Ave. Voc. School
1740 Brighton Rd.
Pittsburgh
ADE
Margaret Morrison Carnegie College,
Women's Div.
Schenley Park
Pittsburgh
A
University of Pittsburgh, Div. of Voc.
Teacher Education
Pittsburgh
A
Pennsylvania State University
University Park
AC

RHODE ISLAND

University of Rhode Island
Kingston
AC

SOUTH CAROLINA

South Carolina Area Trade School
Denmark
AD
South Carolina State College
Orangeburg
AC

SOUTH DAKOTA

South Dakota State College
Brookings
AC

TENNESSEE

Howard School
2500 Market St.
Chattanooga
AF
Kirkman Tech. High School
215 Chestnut St.
Chattanooga
AE
Austin High School
Knoxville
AE
Fulton High School
2509 N. Broadway, N.E.
Knoxville
AD

TEXAS

University of Texas
Austin
AC
Distributive Education Dept., Div. of
Extension
Austin
AF
North Texas State College
Denton
AC
Central High School
Galveston
A
University of Houston
Houston
AC
Washington High School
Houston
A
Jack Yates High School
Houston
A

Texas Tech. College
Lubbock
AC
Prairie View Agricultural and Mechanical College
Prairie View
AEF

UTAH

Utah State University
Logan
ACF
University of Utah
Salt Lake City
AC

VERMONT

Burlington High School
Burlington
AD
Springfield High School
Springfield
AD

VIRGINIA

Virginia Polytech. Inst.
Blacksburg
AC
Woodrow Wilson Rehabilitation Center
Fisherville
AF
Hampton Inst., Senior College
Hampton
AC
Madison College
Harrisonburg
AC
Virginia State College (Trade)
Norfolk
AE
Virginia State College, Dept. of Commercial Foods
Petersburg
AE
I. C. Norcom High School (Trade)
Portsmouth
AE
Radford College, Women's Div. Virginia Polytech. Inst.
Radford
A

Maggie L. Walker High School
Richmond
AE

WASHINGTON

Bellingham Tech. School
3028 Lindberg Ave.
Bellingham
AEF
Edison Tech. School
1712 Harvard Ave.
Seattle
AE
University of Washington
Seattle
AC
Spokane Tech. and Voc. School
3403 Mission Ave.
Spokane
AE
Tacoma Voc.–Tech. School
1101 S. Yakima Ave.
Tacoma
ADEF
Clark College
1925 Fort Vancouver Way
Vancouver
AC

WEST VIRGINIA

Stratton Voc. School
Beckley
AD

WISCONSIN

Green Bay School of Voc. and Adult Education
200 S. Broadway
Green Bay
ADEF
Madison Voc. and Adult School
211 N. Carroll St.
Madison
AD
University of Wisconsin
Madison
AC
Stout State College
Menomonie
AC
Milwaukee Inst. of Technology
Milwaukee
ACEF

PUERTO RICO
Hotel School of Puerto Rico
San Juan
AE

CANADA
Provincial Inst.
13th Ave. and 10th St., N.W.
Calgary, Alta.
AEF
Vancouver Voc. Inst.
250 W. Pender St.

Vancouver, B.C.
AEF
St. John Voc. School
Douglas Ave.
St. John, N.B.
A
Ryerson Inst. of Technology
50 Gould St.
Toronto, Ont.
A
Commercial Trades School
Montreal, P.Q.
AEF

Where to Get Information and Quantity Recipes*

American Can Co.
Home Economics and Consumer Service
100 Park Ave.
New York, N. Y. 10017

Booklet—*Purchase and Use of Canned Foods*—a guide for institutional buyers and meal planners with information on how to use, how to store, number of servings per can, number of cans required per 100 servings, and cost per serving. †

Angelica Uniform Co.
700 Rosedale Ave.
St. Louis, Mo. 63112

Uniform catalog.

American Institute of Baking
Consumer Service Dept.
400 E. Ontario St.
Chicago, Ill. 60611

Two excellent guide booklets: *Modern Sandwich Methods* and *Cake Cutting Guide.*

American Spice Trade Assoc.
Institutional Dept.
Empire State Building
New York, N. Y. 10001

Spice information, recipes, and chart.

Armour Food Service Co.
Food Service Dietitian
401 N. Wabash Ave.
Chicago, Ill. 60611

Quantity recipe cards.

Canned Salmon Institute
911 Republic Building
Seattle, Wash.

Quantity recipes using salmon.

Cres-Cor Metal Products
12711 Taft Ave.
Cleveland, Ohio 44108

Hand-lift insulated cabinets and food handling equipment.

---

*When requesting information from the companies listed, please write on letterhead or business stationery.

† Although this book is no longer available from American Can Co., interested readers may be able to borrow it from food-service school libraries.

278

Durham Manufacturing
Public Seating Dept. 800
W. Willard St.
Muncie, Ind.

Folding metal tables, chairs, and institutional seating.

Hodges and Irvine
8124 Charlevoix
Detroit, Mich. 48214

Information on caterer's function and appointment books.

The Hunt–Wesson People
Box 2387
Fullerton, Calif.

Quantity tested recipes.

Idle Wild Farm
Pomfret Center, Conn.

Information and recipes for Rock Cornish game hens.

Institutions
1801 Prairie Ave.
Chicago, Ill. 60616

This is the magazine of mass feeding. Quantity catering recipes.

Kaiser Institutional Foil
Room 841
Kaiser Center
Oakland, Calif. 94604

Quantity recipes and color pictures for institutional, restaurant, and caterer's operations.

Kitchen Bouquet
Dept. CGC
West Chester, Penna.

Quantity recipe cards.

McIlhenny Co.
Dept. 12-A
Avery Island, La. 70513

Quantity recipes using tabasco sauce.

National Artcrafts, Inc.
910 Broad Hollow Rd.
Farmingdale, N. Y. 11735

1700 W. Pico Blvd.
Los Angeles, Calif. 90015

3000 W. Fort St.
Detroit, Mich. 48216

Social printers. Invitations and announcements for weddings and all social occasions. Also printed matches, napkins, etc.

Poultry and Egg National Board
Div. of Home Economics
8 S. Michigan Ave.
Chicago, Ill. 60603

Quantity recipes for broiler–fryers. Charts and instructions on how to carve turkey.

Rice Council
P. O. Box 22802
Houston, Tex. 77027

Institutionally tested rice recipes and "profitable portions."

The Rumrill Co., Inc.
Public Relations Div.
300 E. 42nd St.
New York, N.Y. 10017

Lea and Perrins Worcestershire Sauce cook book.

Shane Uniform Company
Evansville, Ind. 47707

Uniform catalog.

Superintendent of Documents
Government Printing Office
Washington, D. C. 20402

Booklets and pamphlets for food preparation, sanitation, good business practices, etc.

Swift and Co.
Box 2021
Chicago, Ill. 60609

Quantity recipes.

Vend Magazine
  188 W. Randolph
  Chicago, Ill. 60601

Magazine for *Automatic Vending Coin Commissary Cook Book.*

Wilton Enterprises
  833 W. 115th
  Chicago, Ill.

Catalog of bakers' supplies, many of which are useful for caterers.

Wine Advisory Board
  Wine Institute
  717 Market St.
  San Francisco, Calif.

Quantity recipes using wine. Free wine study course.

Caterer's Reference Library

Editors of Sunset Books. *Sunset Barbecue Cook Book,* revised ed. Menlo Park, Calif.: Lane, 1966.

Chamberlain, S. *Bouquet de France,* revised ed. New York: Gourmet Distributing Corp., 1966.

Coin Commissary Cook Book. Chicago: *Vend* Magazine, 1964.

Lucas, D. *Cordon Bleu Cook Book.* Boston: Little Brown, 1947.

Editors of Sunset Books. *Dinner Party Cook Book.* Menlo Park, Calif.: Lane, 1967.

Wise Encyclopedia of Catering. Union City, N.J.: Wise, 1955.

Vanderbilt, A. *New Complete Book of Etiquette.* New York: Doubleday, 1963.

Fowler, F. S. and West, B. B. *Food for Fifty,* 4th ed. New York: Wiley, 1961.

Taglienti, M. L. *Italian Cookbook.* New York: Random House, 1955.

Grossinger, J. *Art of Jewish Cooking.* New York: Random House, 1958.

Waldo, M. *Complete Book of Oriental Cooking.* New York: McKay, 1960.

Waldner, G. K. *65 Quality Menus for Quantity Service.* New York: Ahrens, 1965.

Recipes for Quantity Service. Washington, D.C.: Superintendent of Documents, Government Printing Office, 1958.

Index

282